IMAGES
of America

PAWNEE COUNTY

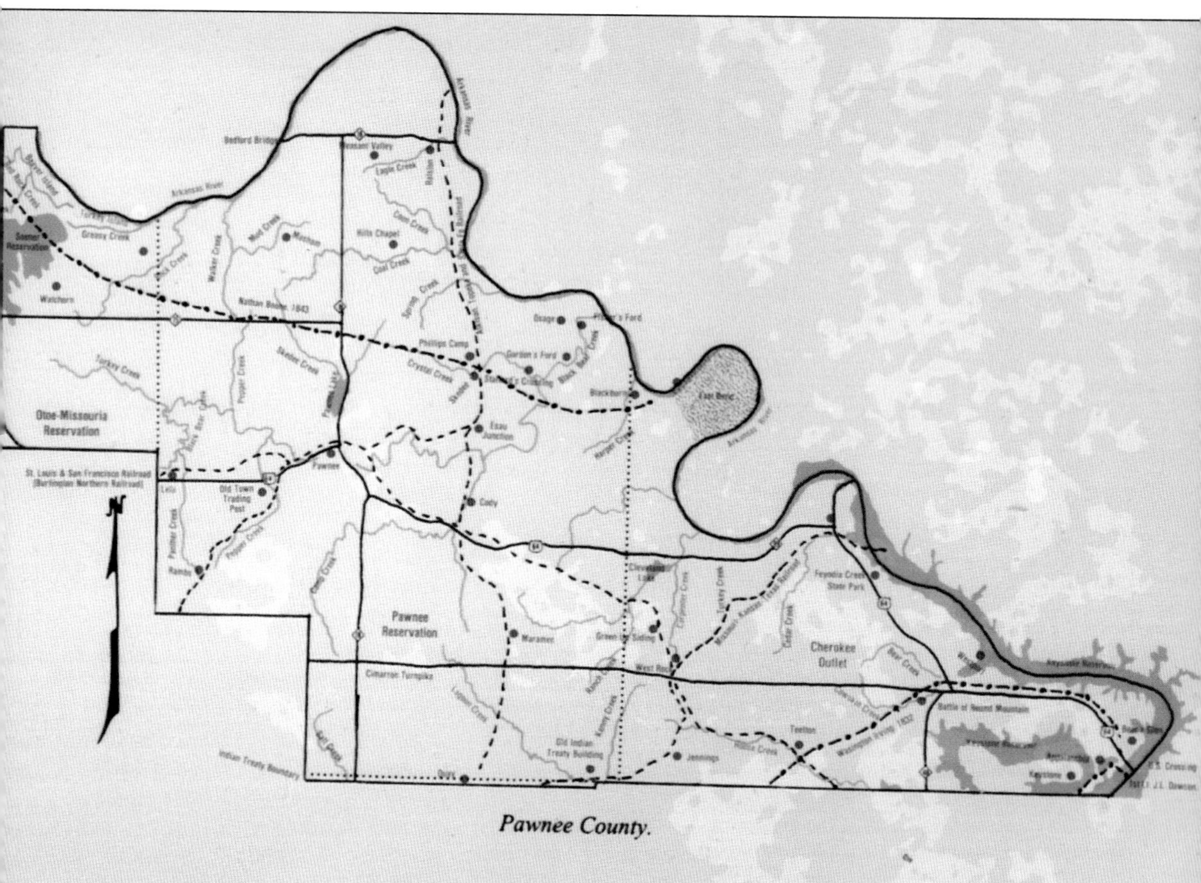

This map of Pawnee County shows important locations such as US Crossing, a natural ford across the Arkansas River, on the lower right. The southern boundary of Pawnee County was supposed to be the Indian Treaty Boundary with the Creek Nation; however, the surveyors made an error of about half a mile. That resulted in the jog of the southern border. (Author's collection.)

On the Cover: Retailers Day in Pawnee always drew huge crowds of people from the surrounding area. This is a horse auction on the west side of the courthouse square in the middle of Sixth Street. Note that an improvised arena has been formed by a rope being held by the men on the front row of the circle. The auctioneer is standing inside the ring with his hand raised, encouraging bidders. His assistant is leading a horse around the inside of the circle to be viewed by potential buyers. (Courtesy of the Pawnee County Historical Society.)

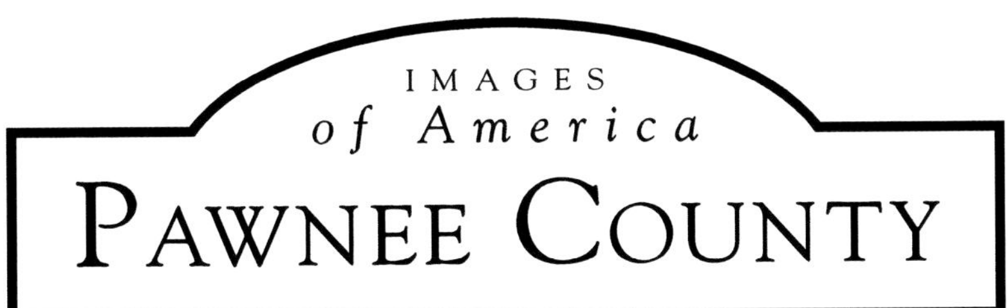

Clyda Reeves-Franks

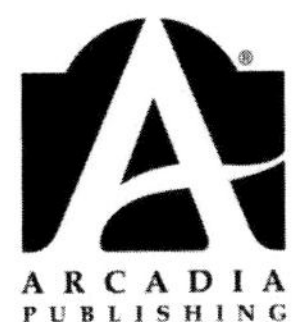

ISBN 978-1-4671-1471-4

Published by Arcadia Publishing
Charleston, South Carolina

Printed in the United States of America

Library of Congress Control Number: 2015935816

For all general information, please contact Arcadia Publishing:
Telephone 843-853-2070
Fax 843-853-0044
E-mail sales@arcadiapublishing.com
For customer service and orders:
Toll-Free 1-888-313-2665

Visit us on the Internet at www.arcadiapublishing.com

Contents

Acknowledgments

Pawnee County is my home territory. Born and reared in Cleveland, Oklahoma, I graduated from Cleveland High School in 1964, went off to seek my fortune in Tulsa and moved back to Cleveland to rear my own two sons in a small-town environment. After working several years as the editor of the *Cleveland American* newspaper, I migrated to a job in Pawnee.

The people of First National Bank gave me a portrait of the "other" side of the county. While Cleveland is a lakeside community, more closely affiliated with the city of Tulsa, Pawnee is more of a rural setting. While there are many differences in lifestyle, the people of Pawnee County are primarily family-oriented, warm, friendly, and proud of their heritage and home. This book is for them.

The Pawnee County Historical Society was immensely helpful in this endeavor, especially its archivist/researcher Gladys Kitchen. She provided a wealth of background material, photographs, and moral support. Ronnie and Erin Brown, who are the manager and curator of collections at the Pawnee Bill Ranch, offered their expertise and assistance whenever called upon. Evelyn "Zeke" Cheek of the Cleveland Tag Office cleared her office walls of vintage photographs for use in the book. Many other individuals were instrumental in putting this collection of photographs together, and I am grateful for their help. Most of all, I owe a big thank-you to my personal historian, mentor, and friend—my husband, Dr. Kenny A. Franks.

INTRODUCTION

Pawnee County straddles the boundary between lush eastern Oklahoma and arid western Oklahoma, an area of transition between the hilly, forested East, and the flatter grasslands of the West. Thus it is a boundary between two distinctive zones of vegetation. Likewise, it is a border zone between forest and prairie animal life. These geographical circumstances played a major role in the history of the region and its pattern of settlement. It represents a microcosm of the state's culture and heritage.

Pawnee County's history begins with the arrival of the Clovis people, among the earliest to settle in North America around 12,500 years ago; these were followed by the Folsom Bison Hunters, who lived off the huge prehistoric bison herds that roamed the region. About 2,000 years ago, these primitive people gave way to more permanent cultures that built huge mounds and developed an extensive trade network up and down the Arkansas River.

Occupying the area between the Osage Hills on the east and the Osage Plains on the west, the area quickly became a major hunting area for early tribes. Archaeological excavations around Pawnee Lake revealed 900-year-old campsites. Among these early tribes were the Wichitas, who were forced southward with the arrival of the Osages.

Then came the Cherokees, who first crossed the Mississippi River into Oklahoma in the late 1770s and established themselves as the Western Cherokees. By 1805, the Cherokees and Osages were contesting the hunting land along the Arkansas River. War broke out in 1817, and the Osages were defeated at the Battle of the Strawberry Moon. In 1825, the Osages ceded what later became Pawnee County and their other land along the Arkansas River, and in 1835 the Cherokee Nation East agreed to join their brethren in the west. The Treaty of New Echota also guaranteed the Cherokees a perpetual outlet to the buffalo grounds to the west. Known as the Cherokee Outlet, it included the area of Pawnee County.

In 1832, an American expedition of mounted rangers marched through Pawnee County to contact the Plains tribes. Accompanying the troops were four civilians—Washington Irving, Henry Ellsworth, Albert-Alexandre de Pourtales, and Charles Latrobe. Irving's colorful book, *A Tour on the Prairies*, published in 1835, was the first original account of Pawnee County to appear in print. Bear's Glen in eastern Pawnee County was named by Irving.

In 1831, the Reverend Isaac McCoy was appointed to survey the Cherokee-Creek boundary, and 1st Lt. James L. Dawson commanded the military escort that accompanied McCoy. Dawson marked a crude road along the Osage Trace to a natural ford over the Arkansas River near Keystone in Pawnee County. Dawson named the ford US Ford, and it became a major crossing point on the river.

In 1843, Capt. Nathan Boone led an expedition through Pawnee County along the divide between Harper and Black Bear Creeks. He described the country as "broken timber post oak and blackjack openings, and prairie, the soil sandy." Boone continued on, passing near Skedee and Watchorn.

During the Civil War, the Cherokees sided with the Confederacy. The only military action in Pawnee County was the withdrawal of the pro-Northern Creek under Opothleyahola, who fled the Southern troops for safety in Kansas. Most historians believe the Battle of Round Mountain, fought on November 19, 1861, took place between the Cimarron River and the southern border of Pawnee County. It was a running fight that spread over several miles. During the fighting, Opothleyahola's followers forded the Arkansas River at US Crossing into Pawnee County and fled westward to Hell Roaring Creek and then north toward Kansas. The Battle of Round Mountain was the first Civil War battle in Oklahoma.

When the South, along with the Cherokees, was defeated by the Union in the Civil War, the federal government demanded a new treaty with the Indians. The Cherokee Reconstruction Treaty of 1866 demanded that the Cherokees agree to the settlement of other tribes on land ceded by the Indians. In 1874, the Pawnee surrendered their homelands in Nebraska for another reservation in Pawnee County. Their new home was near the junction of Black Bear Creek and the Arkansas River in central Pawnee County west of present highway OK 99. An agency was opened on the east side of Black Bear Creek at the present-day town of Pawnee.

In 1891, the Pawnees were forced to accept individual allotments. Every tribal member over the age of 18 received 160 acres anywhere within the reservation. Those under 18 were granted 160-acre allotments chosen by their parents. Surplus land was sold to the government for $1.25 an acre and opened to homesteaders with the opening of the Cherokee Outlet in 1893.

The Cherokees retained ownership of that part of Pawnee County east of OK 99, which remained a part of the Cherokee Outlet. The outlet was eventually leased to the Cherokee Strip Live Stock Association in 1883 and used to graze cattle before shipping them to market in Kansas. The lease agreement continued in force until 1892, when the government refused to allow it to be renewed. The Cherokee Strip Live Stock Association offered to purchase the outlet for $3 an acre, but the government refused to allow the Cherokees to sell. The government eventually purchased the outlet for $1.25 an acre and opened it to homesteaders in 1893.

The Otoes originated along the western Great Lakes and migrated south to the junction of Kansas, Nebraska, and Iowa. In 1855, they were concentrated on a reservation along the Kansas-Nebraska border and in 1881 moved to a new reservation in the Cherokee Outlet. The reservation was partially in far western Pawnee County, west of Township 2 East. With the passage of the Dawes Act of 1887, the policy of the government was to force allotment of tribal lands and open any land that remained to homesteaders. In 1891, a special allotting agent was appointed to the Otoes and in 1894 their reservation was divided into individual allotments. With the allotment of Indian land and the opening of the area to homesteaders came the transformation of the region from public land to private property. Oklahoma Territory had been created in 1890, and once the Indian title to what became Pawnee County had been extinguished, the region was added to Oklahoma Territory as Q County. Later, the county name was changed to Pawnee.

The vibrant agriculture and cattle economy in early Pawnee County soon made the region an economic center of Oklahoma Territory, especially with the arrival of the railroads. After 1904, with the discovery of the Cleveland Oil Field came the rush for oil. With the discovery came a hoard of fortune-seekers, including J. Paul Getty, who once was proclaimed the "richest man in the world." Thousands of wells produced millions of dollars in black gold. Along with the thousands of oilmen who hurried to the region came the camp followers—gamblers, conmen, prostitutes, bootleggers, and other ne'er-do-wells. Among them was Sally Rand, a famous striptease dancer who used to perform on the tops of oil-field toolsheds for the silver dollars that the oilmen tossed to her. It was a boomtown atmosphere that rivaled anything in the Wild West.

One

Native Americans

The Wichita and the Osage tribes migrated to the area almost 900 years ago; however, it was the Osages who dominated the region until 1785, when the Chickamauga Cherokees moved into the Osage hunting grounds. War between the Cherokees and Osages lasted until 1822, when the Osages ceded their land along the Arkansas River, and in 1828 it became part of the Cherokee Nation West. Seven years later, the Cherokee Nation East was removed westward, and the two branches united as the Cherokee Nation.

In 1874, the Pawnees accepted a new reservation near the junction of Black Bear Creek and the Arkansas River in central Pawnee County. Their agency was located east of Black Bear Creek east of the town of Pawnee. In 1891, the federal government forced individual allotments on the Pawnees, and every tribal member received 160 acres of land. The Curtis Act in 1898 abolished Pawnee tribal government.

In 1934, the Federal Indian Reorganization Act allowed the Pawnees to form a tribal business council. Although the tribe had a government, it had no land. It was not until 1957 that the tribe was allowed to use the Pawnee Reserve that surrounded the old agency grounds. Finally, in 1968, ownership of the Pawnee Reserve was transferred to the tribe.

The Cherokees retained ownership of that part of Pawnee County east of OK 99, which was organized as part of the Cherokee Outlet and intended to provide the Cherokees access to the buffalo lands west of their new home in Oklahoma. Very few Cherokees made their permanent homes in the outlet, and with the passage of the Five Civilized Tribes Act in 1905, which divided the Cherokee Nation into individual allotments, only 71 Cherokees were granted allotments in the outlet.

Originally, the Otoes lived along the western shore of Lake Michigan. They were removed in 1891 to a new reservation in western Pawnee County. In 1894, each Otoe received an allotment of 280 acres. In 1916, a five-member tribal council committee was created to govern the tribe. It was updated in 1949.

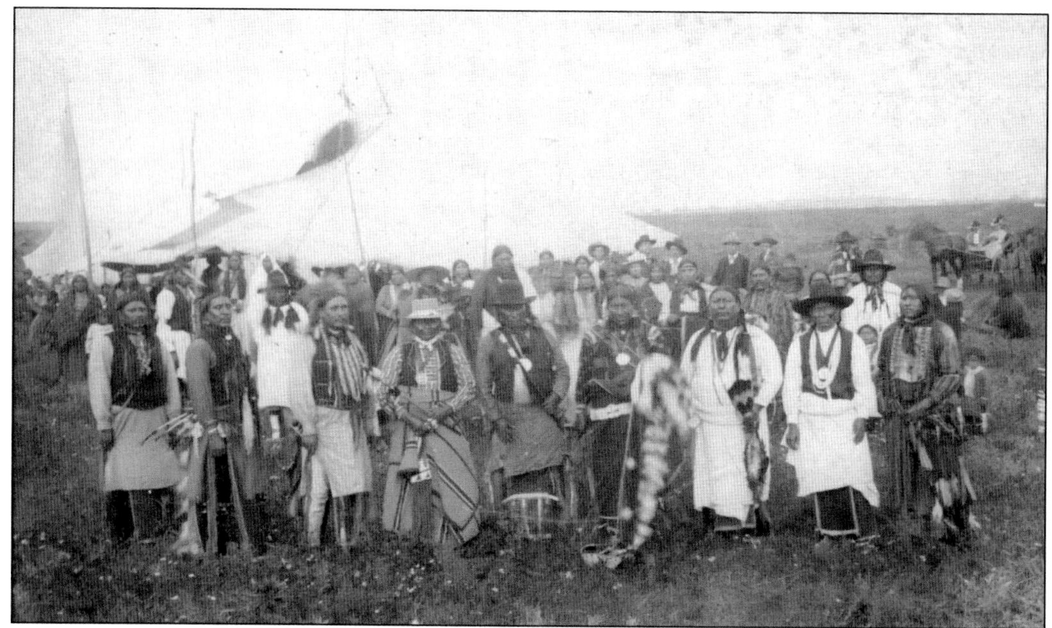

A group of Pawnees is gathering on Lone Chief allotment north of the town of Pawnee. Note the buggies with non-Indians in the upper right of the photograph. Lone Chief was a member of the Shady Lane clan of the Skidi band. His wife was also a Skidi but a member of the Pumpkin Vine clan. Generally, Pawnees did not marry outside of their clan. (Courtesy of the Pawnee County Historical Society.)

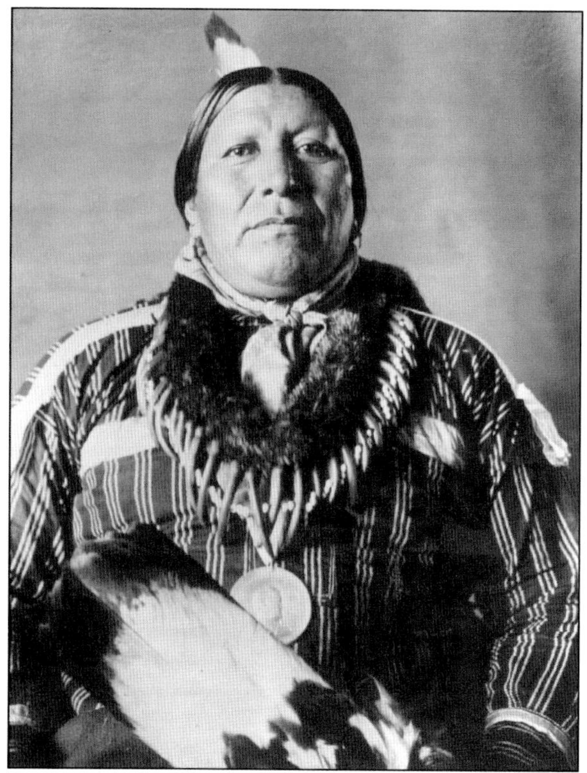

Roam Chief, or Koot-tat-we-coots-oo-pah, which means Red Hawk, is wearing a traditional Pawnee bear-claw necklace. Attached is a peace medal from Pres. Ulysses S. Grant. Roam Chief was a member of the Chaui band of Pawnees, and his wife, Eva, was a member of the Pitachauert band. They lived in a large two-story Colonial-style home south of Pawnee. Beside the house, however, he built a traditional earth lodge where he often entertained his friends. (Courtesy of the Field Museum of Natural History.)

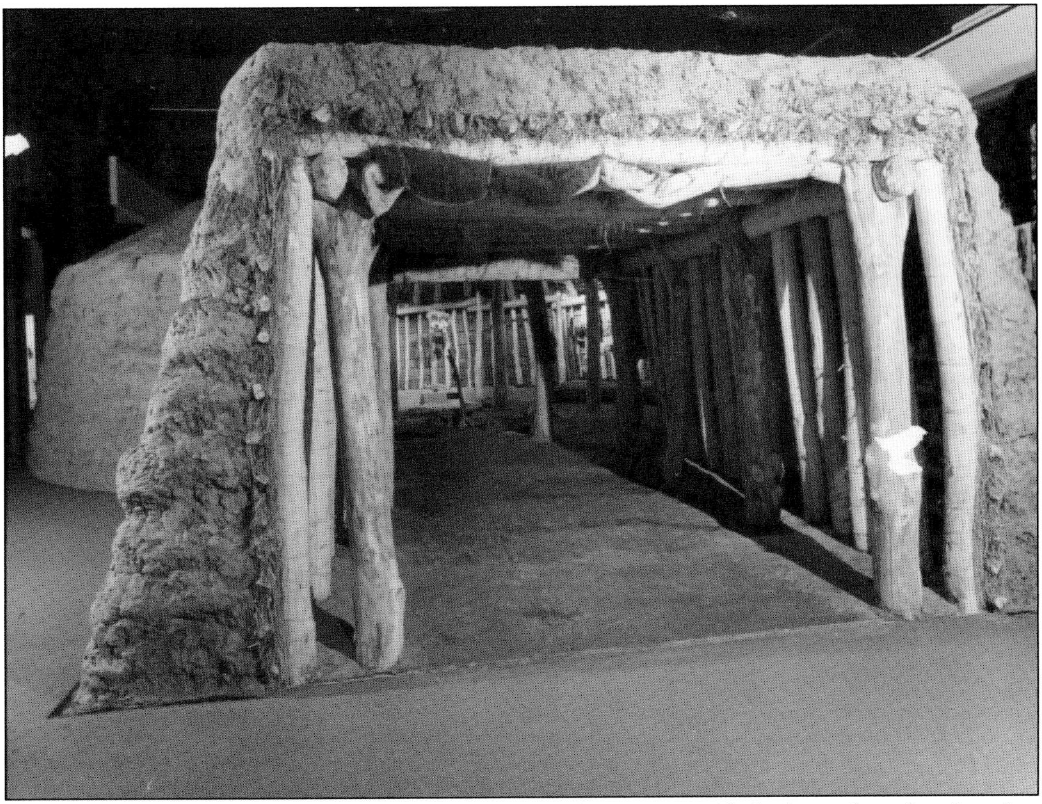

The construction of a Pawnee earth lodge started with two rows of forked upright poles placed in the ground. Crossbeams were placed in the forks. The crossbeams supported rafters that created a roof. Grass and willow branches were woven between the rafters, and between the poles the entire structure was covered with dirt. The entrance was a covered walkway that always faced east. (Courtesy of the Field Museum of Natural History.)

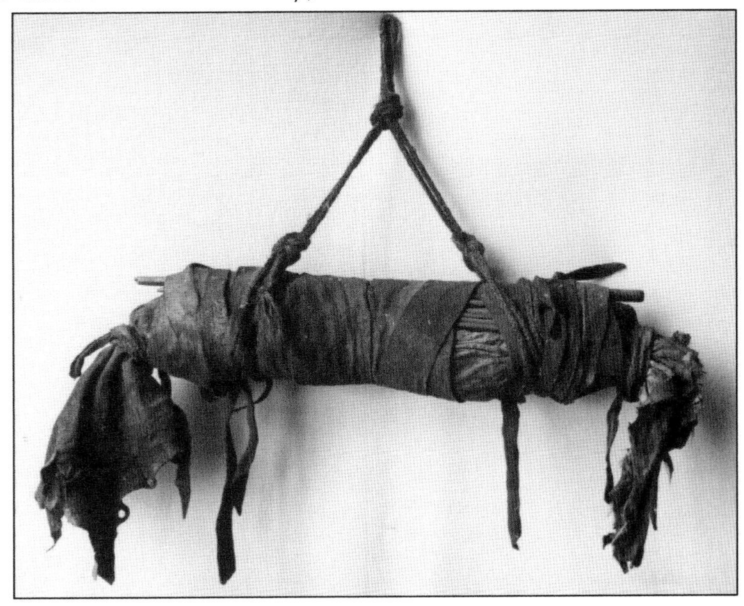

A sacred bundle of the Pawnees is depicted here. On the west side of the earth lodge interior was the Wiharu, a place for the garden of the Eastern Star. The Wiharu was the first to catch the sunlight at daybreak. Above the Wiharu was a buffalo skull and above the skull was a special place for the family's sacred bundle. (Courtesy of the Field Museum of Natural History.)

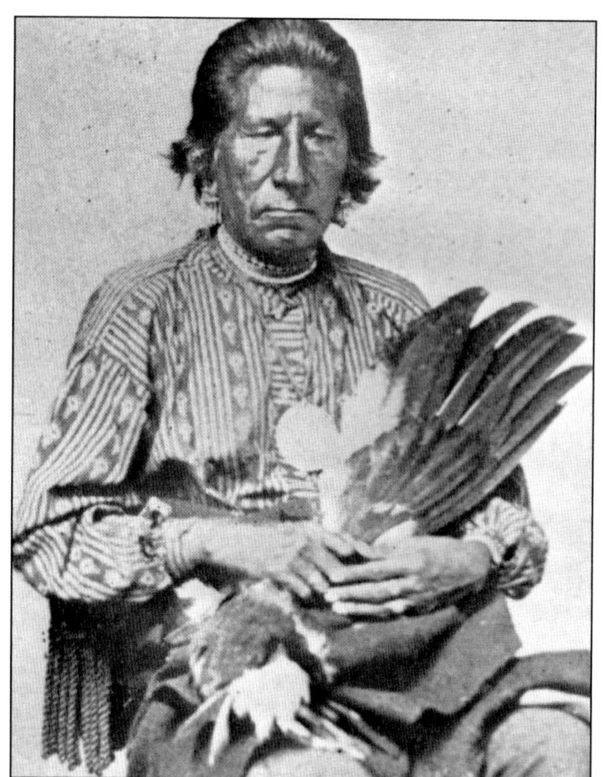

Ter-ra-re-caw-wah and his followers in the Pitahauerat band of Pawnees staunchly opposed the surrender of the Pawnee homeland in Nebraska in exchange for a new home in Pawnee County. However, in 1874 a grasshopper plague swept the Pawnee Reservation in Nebraska, destroying much of their crops and convincing many in the tribe to move south. (Courtesy of the Pawnee County Historical Society.)

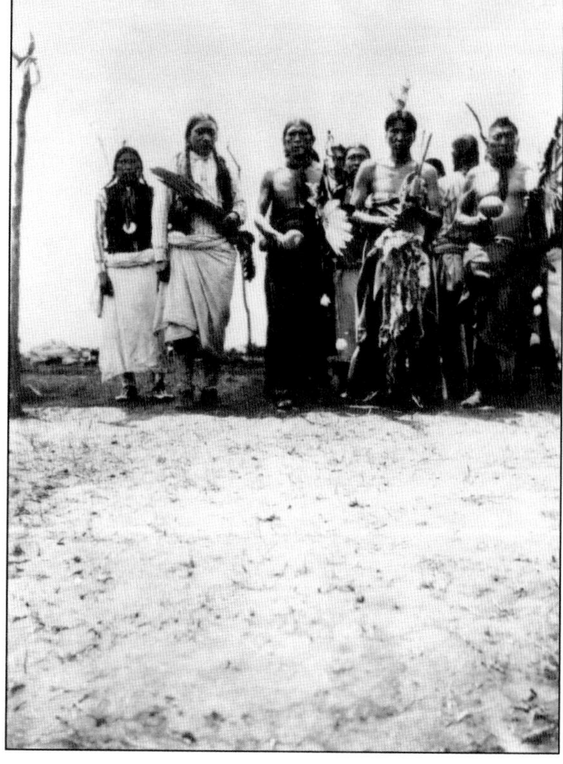

Members of the Chaui band of Pawnees are preparing for their calumet ceremony. Tom Morgan is standing behind the fourth man from the left. On the right holding a gourd is Tom Yellowhorse. The third man from the left is John Rou-Walk. The calumet is a sacred pipe with a feathered shaft. The ceremony was used to adopt outsiders into the tribe and promote social unity within tribes. (Courtesy of the Field Museum of Natural History.)

Two members of the Skidi band are seen waiting for the start of the Pawnee sacred bundle ceremony. The man on the right is holding a pipe, and the man on the left is holding a four-feather fan. The four feathers represent the four bands of the Pawnees—the Skidi, Chauis, the Kitkahahkis, and the Pitahawirata. Originally, the Skidi settled along the Republican River and then the Loup River in central Nebraska; the Chauis and Pitahawirate bands made their home along the Platte River in southern Nebraska and the Arkansas River in southern Kansas; the Kitkahahkis also lived along the Republican River in central Nebraska. (Courtesy of the Field Museum of Natural History.)

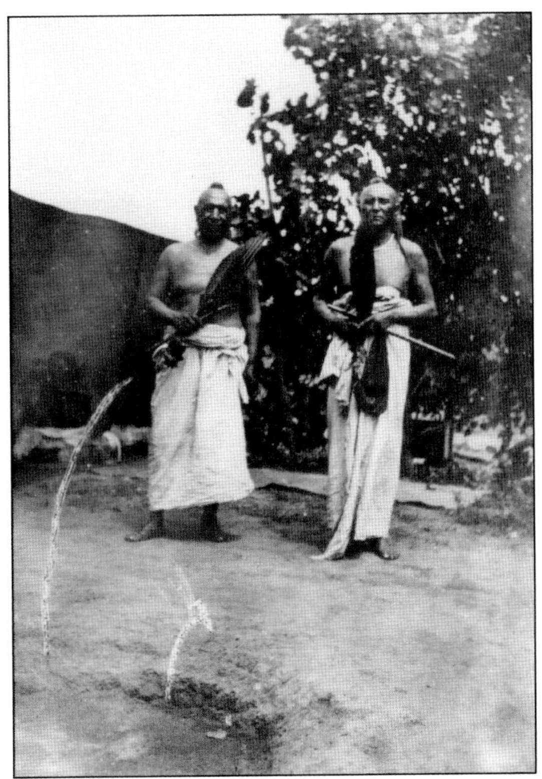

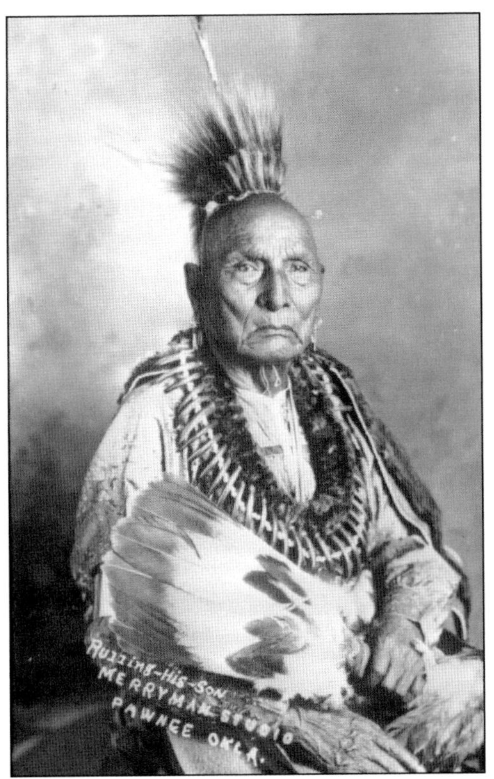

Ruling-His-Son or Fox Chief, also known as Ke-wuck-oo-lel-la-shar, is seen here wearing a traditional scalp lock and bear-claw necklace. Ke-wuck-oo-lel-la-shar was a member of the Pawnee Scouts, a battalion of Pawnee warriors raised by Frank North to end the depredations of the Cheyennes on the northern plains. (Courtesy of the Pawnee County Historical Society.)

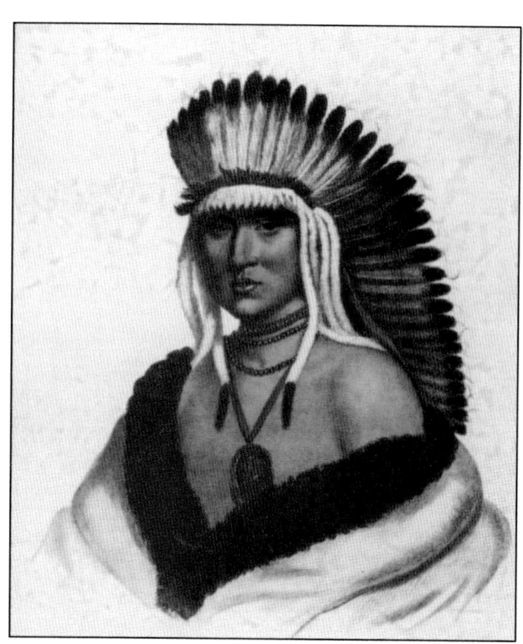

Pawnee chief Pet-al-esh-ar-oo is credited with ending the Skidi practice of human sacrifice in the early 18th century. It was one of the most unsettling aspects of early Pawnee culture, but the Skidi considered the human sacrifice a religious ceremony necessary to ensure a bountiful harvest and successful buffalo hunt. (Courtesy of the Pawnee County Historical Society.)

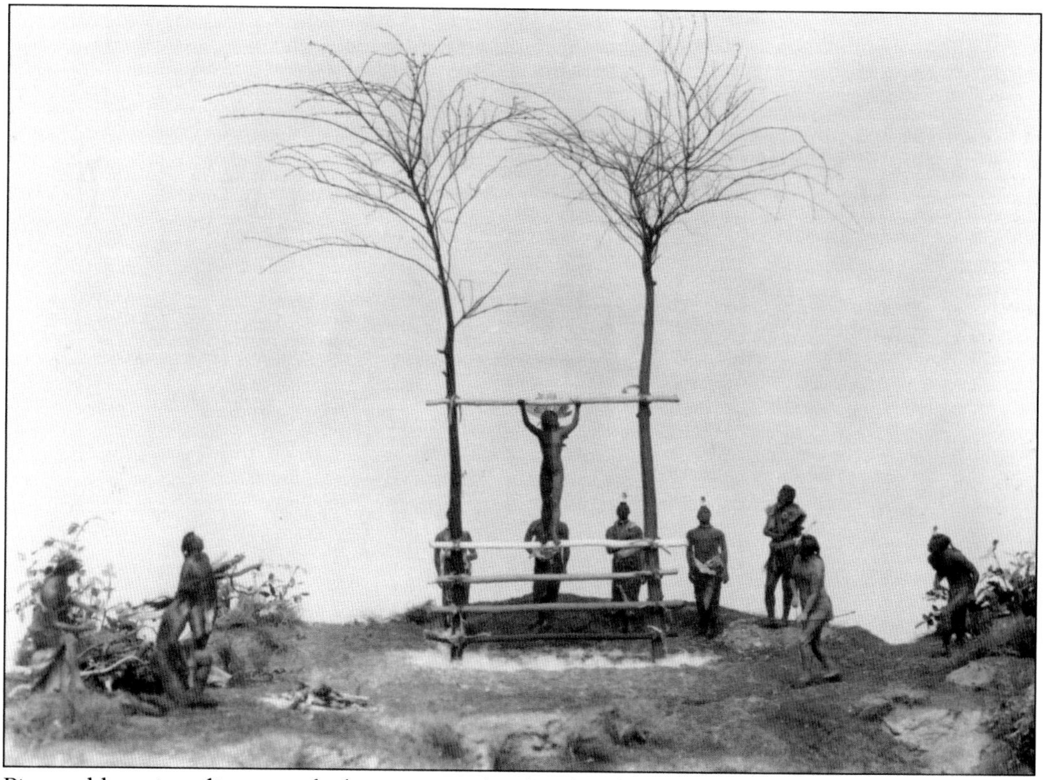

Pictured here is a diorama of a human sacrifice by the Skidi. The victim was a young woman, usually a Caddo or Wichita who had been captured. She was tied between two trees and then every adult male in the village shot her with an arrow. The arrow was a phallic symbol indicative of fertilization. Her blood then was allowed to flow onto the ground and fertilize the field to ensure a bountiful crop. (Courtesy of the Field Museum of Natural History.)

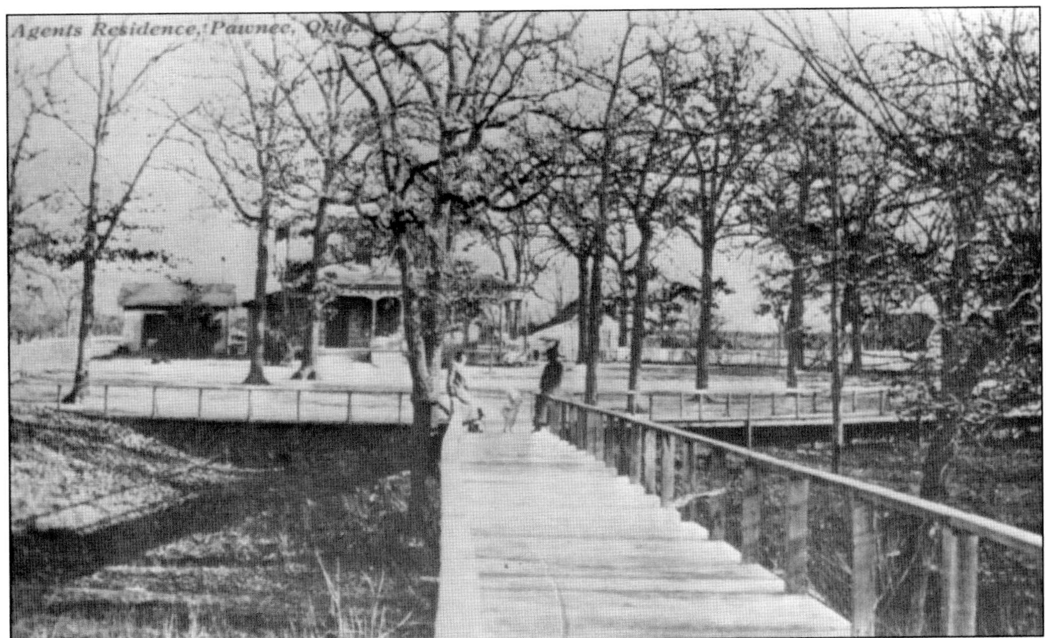

The Pawnee Agency and School were to the east of Pawnee, separated from the town by Black Bear Creek. Seen here is the wooden bridge over the creek that connected the agency with the town of Pawnee. The structure in the background is the Pawnee agent's residence. (Courtesy of the Pawnee County Historical Society.)

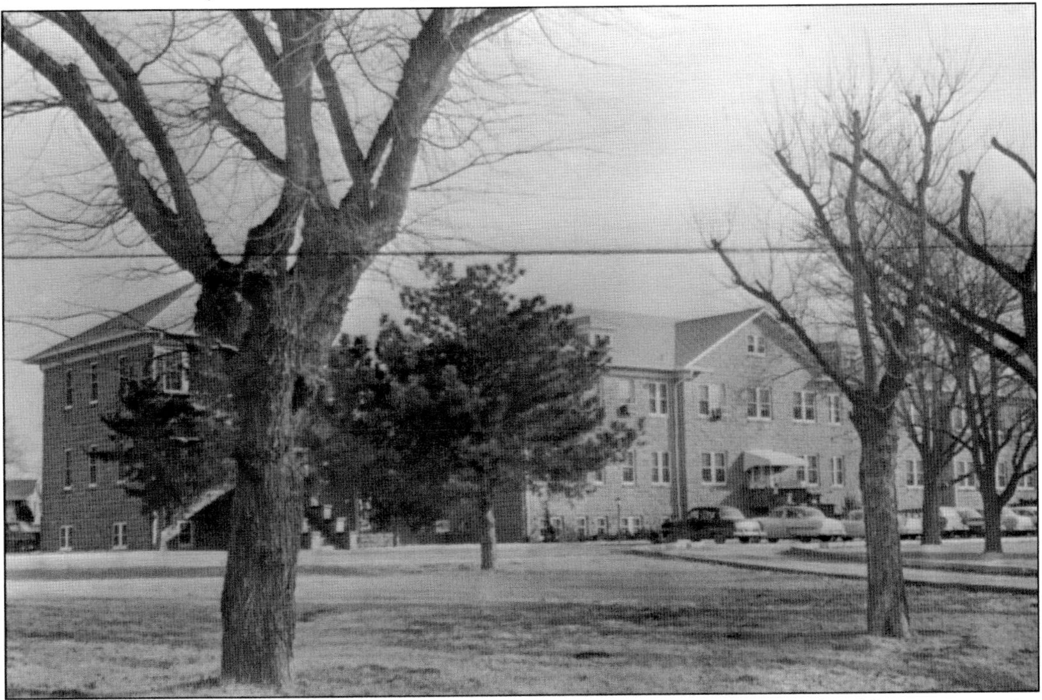

The 50-bed Indian Hospital, pictured here, was maintained by the public-health service at the Pawnee Agency. While this is a photograph from the 1950s, a new clinic now operates with the most modern medical equipment available. (Author's collection.)

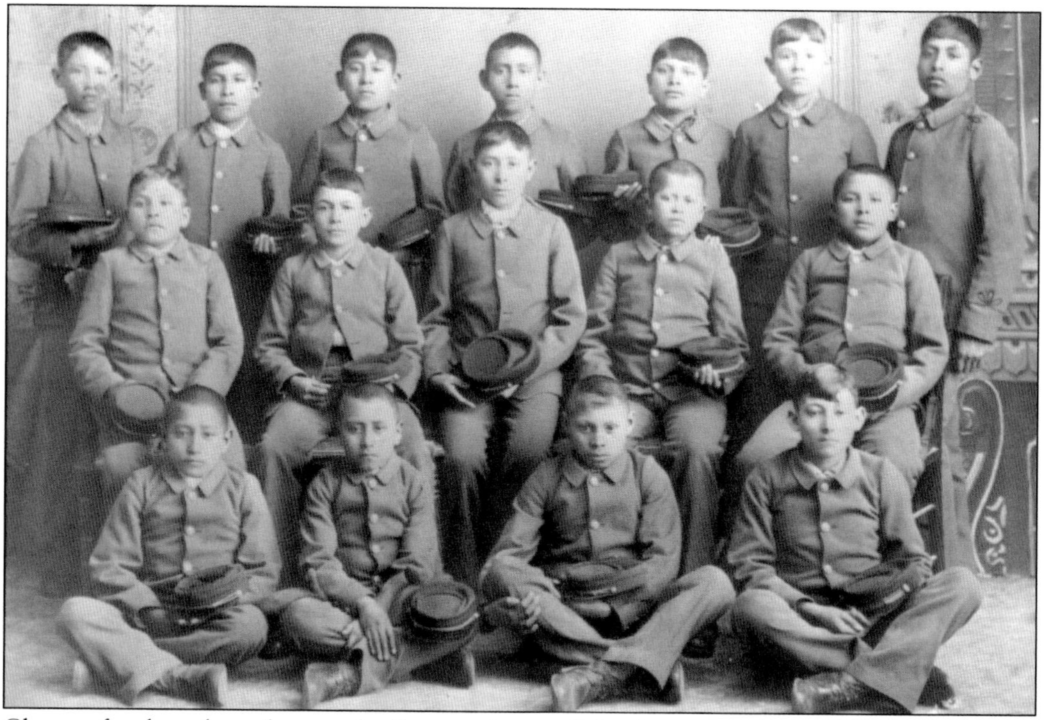

Classes of early male students at the Pawnee Agency School were organized along military lines. The students wore wool pants with a stripe down the outside of the leg, a high-neck tunic, black socks, black shoes, and small caps. They marched to class from their dormitories. (Courtesy of the Pawnee County Historical Society.)

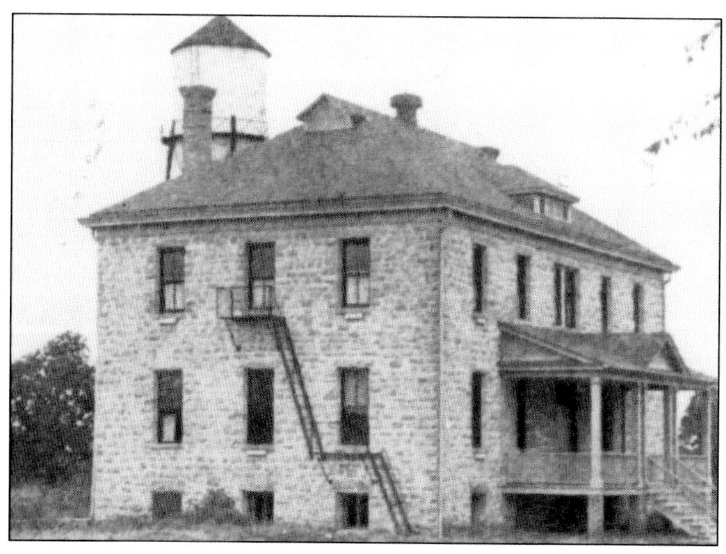

This is the boys' dormitory at the Pawnee Agency School. Speaking Pawnee was prohibited at the school, and rule-breakers could have their mouths washed out with soap. Students also could be whipped for playing traditional Pawnee games. When the students were treated to a movie on Saturday, the boys would line up in formation and march to the local movie theater. (Courtesy of the Pawnee County Historical Society.)

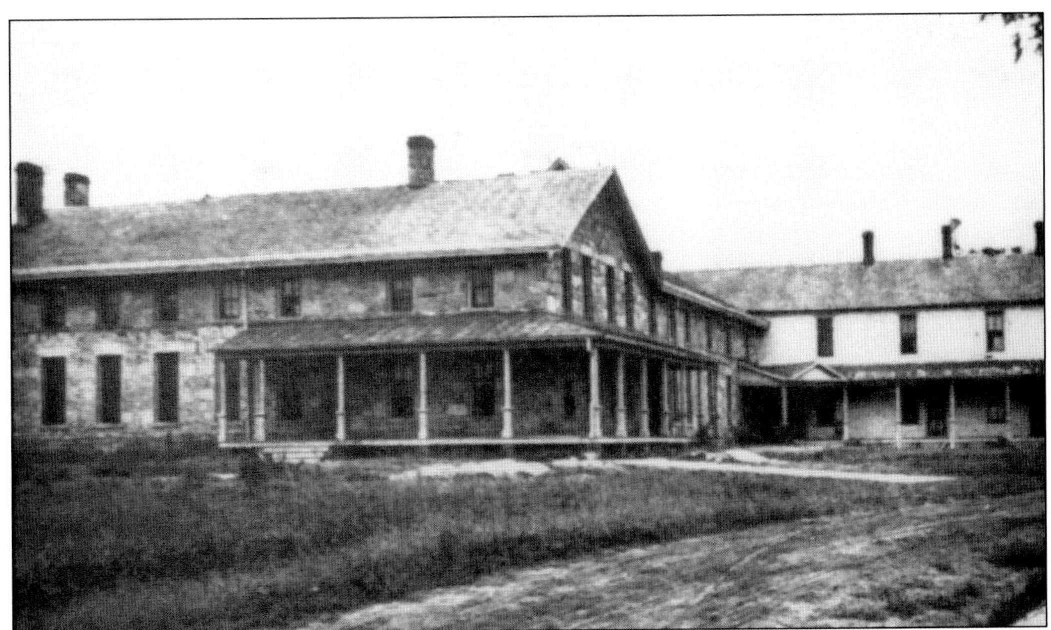

The administrative building is on the left and the female dormitory on the right at the Pawnee Agency School. All classes were taught in English, and new students were assigned to older students who would help them learn the new language. This resulted in the loss of tribal tradition and the Pawnee language. (Courtesy of the Pawnee County Historical Society.)

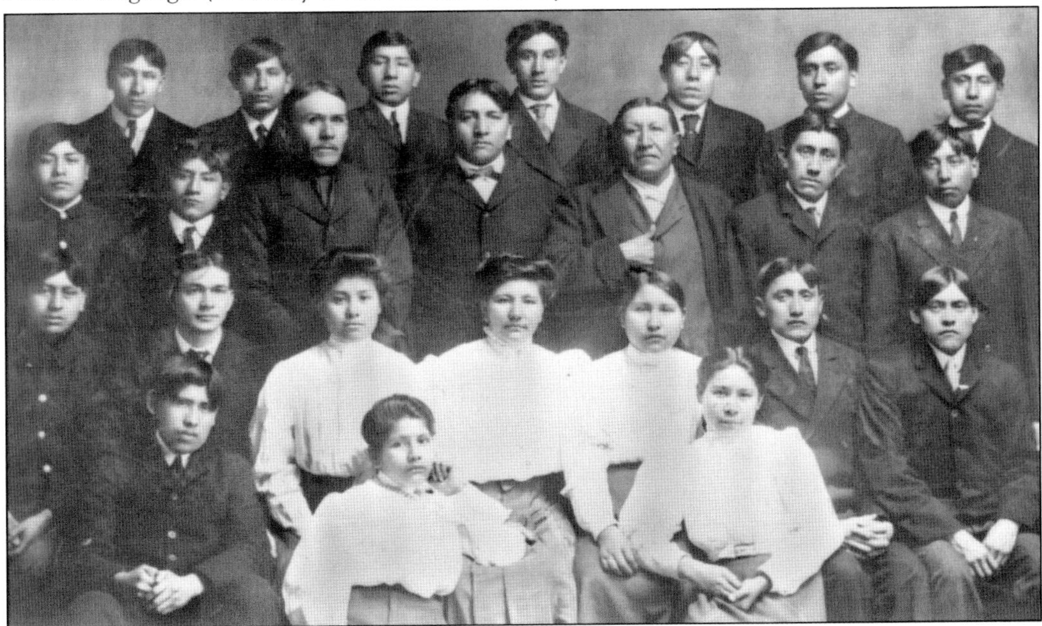

Pictured here in 1904 are the upperclassmen at the Pawnee Indian School. From left to right are (first row) Sam Ashorne, Cecilia Mattock, and unidentified; (second row) unidentified, William Pappan, Blanche Bill, Etta Mattock, Flora Eagle Chief, and two unidentified students; (third row) two unidentified students, Rush Roberts, Stacy Mattock, Eagle Chief, unidentified, and Harry Cummings; (fourth row) three unidentified students, Jim Blaine, St. Elmo Jim, Walter Hurst, and Edgar Moore. (Courtesy of the Pawnee County Historical Society.)

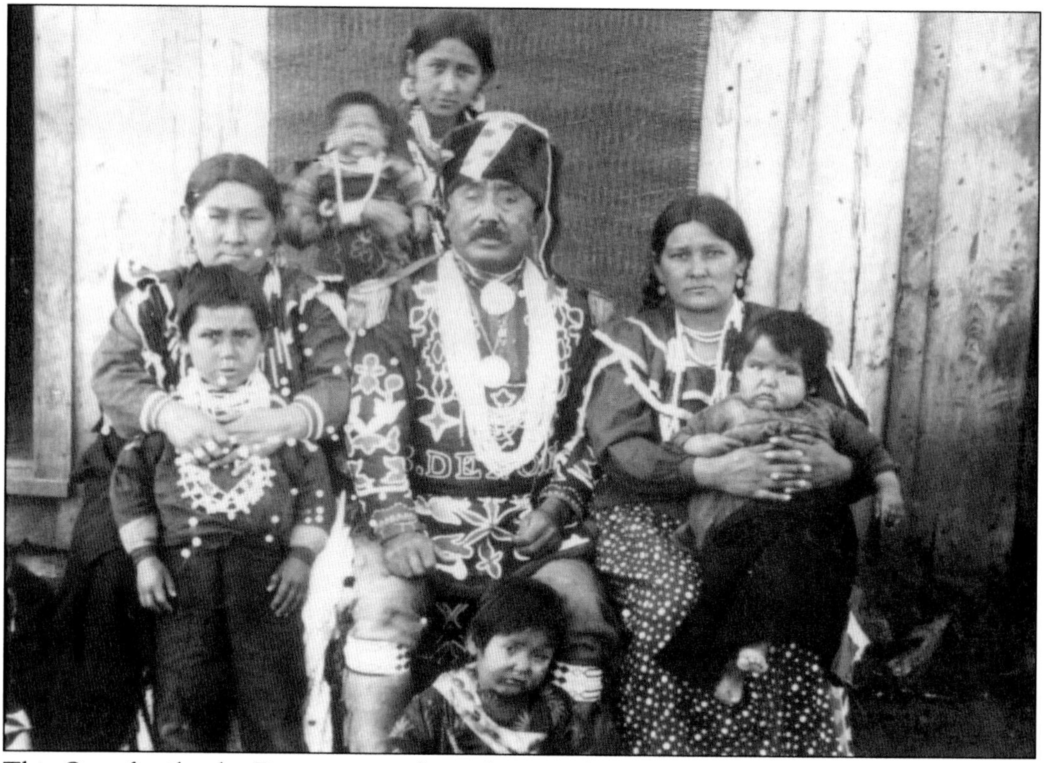

This Otoe family, the Deroins, pose for a photograph. The man is wearing traditional Otoe headgear and leggings and has the family name in beadwork across the bottom of his shirt. The young boy on the left is about the age that Otoe culture dictated he be given miniature weapons and taught to hunt small game. (Courtesy of the Oklahoma History Center.)

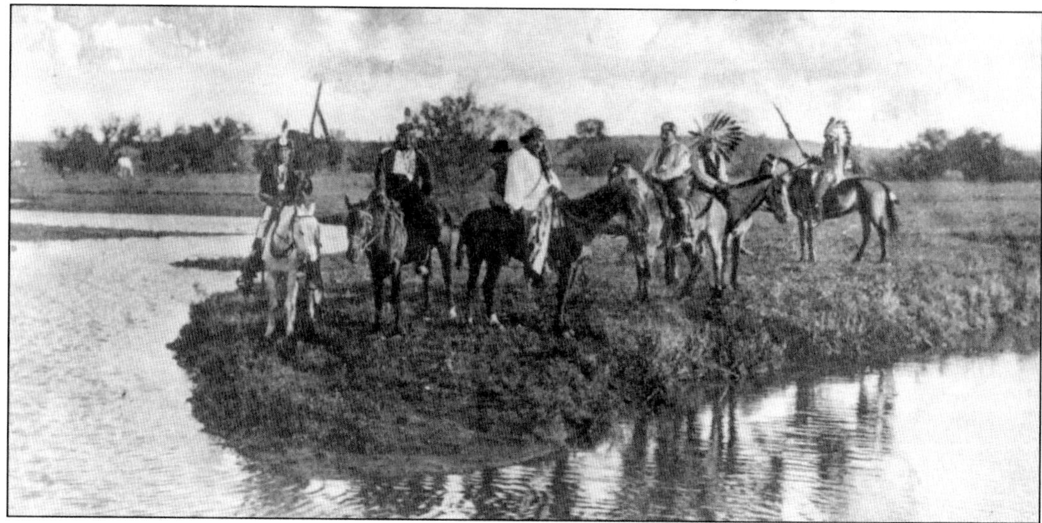

These Otoe warriors on horseback are holding lances. The 12-foot-long lances were used to kill buffalo as the warriors rode alongside the shaggy beast and thrust the lance into its side, hoping to penetrate either the heart or lungs. The Otoes joined with the Pawnees for one of their last successful buffalo hunts, along the Elkhorn River in Nebraska in 1859. (Courtesy of the Oklahoma History Center.)

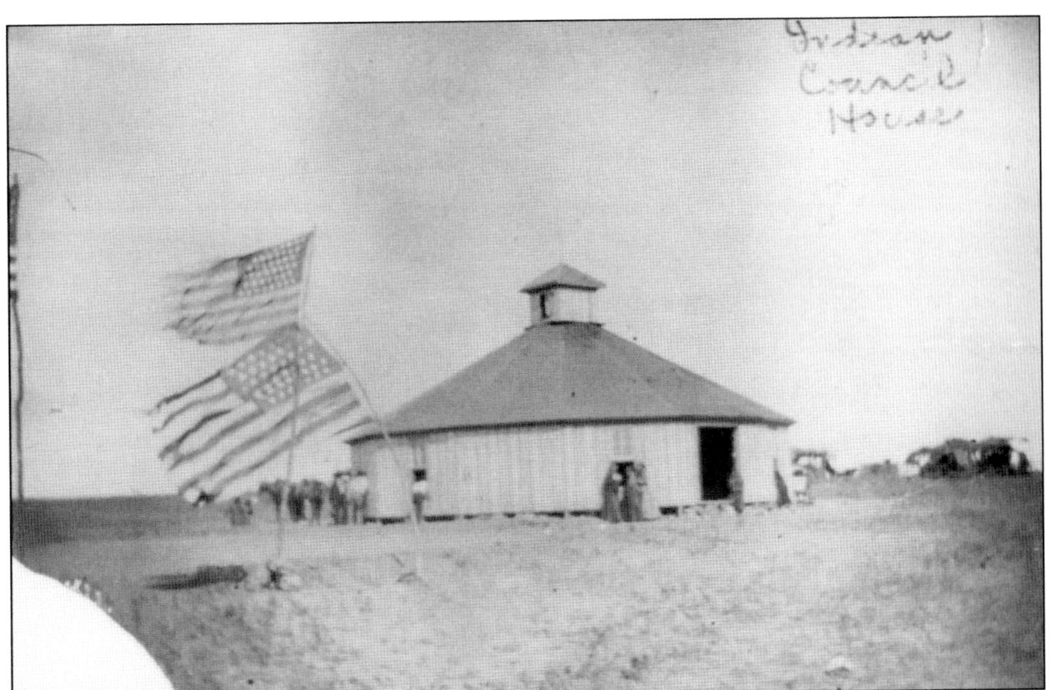

Otoe tribal members are gathered around the council house. Note the 45-star American flag in the left foreground. Some are looking through the windows to observe what is happening inside. Others are camped on the right in the background. (Courtesy of the Cherokee Strip Museum.)

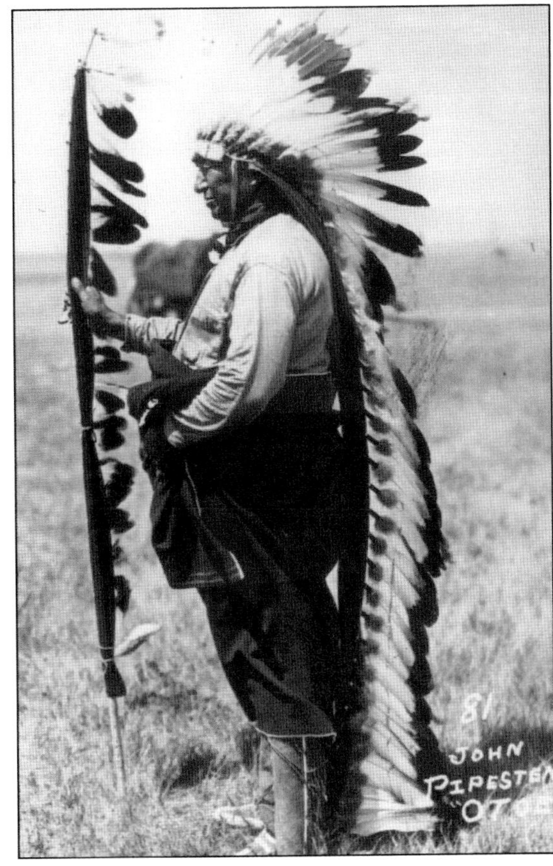

John Pipestem is dressed in his ceremonial clothes of a full-length feather headdress and holding a staff decorated with feathers. Normally in the summer, the male Otoes dressed in breechcloths and moccasins. In cooler weather, they wore loose-fitting fringed deerskin shirts, to protect the upper trunk, and leggings. In bitter cold, they wore buffalo robes. (Courtesy of the Oklahoma History Center.)

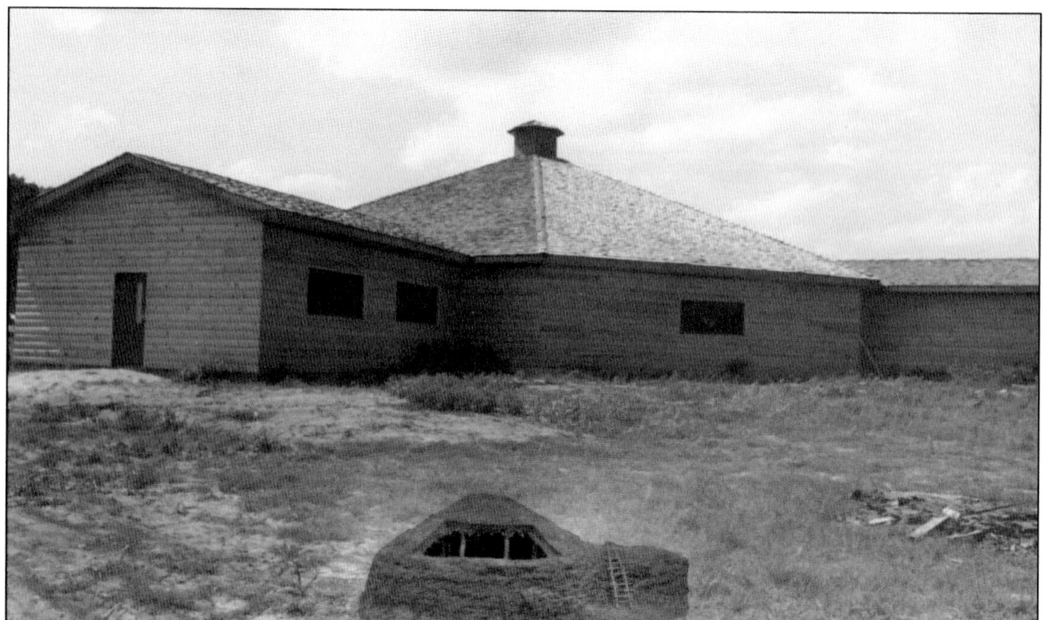

The Pawnee Tribal Roundhouse was constructed on the Pawnee Reserve during the administration of Pawnee chief Tom Morgan. It is used for tribal meetings, feasts, dancing, and other gatherings. In the foreground is a model of a traditional Pawnee earth lodge. (Courtesy of the Pawnee County Historical Society.)

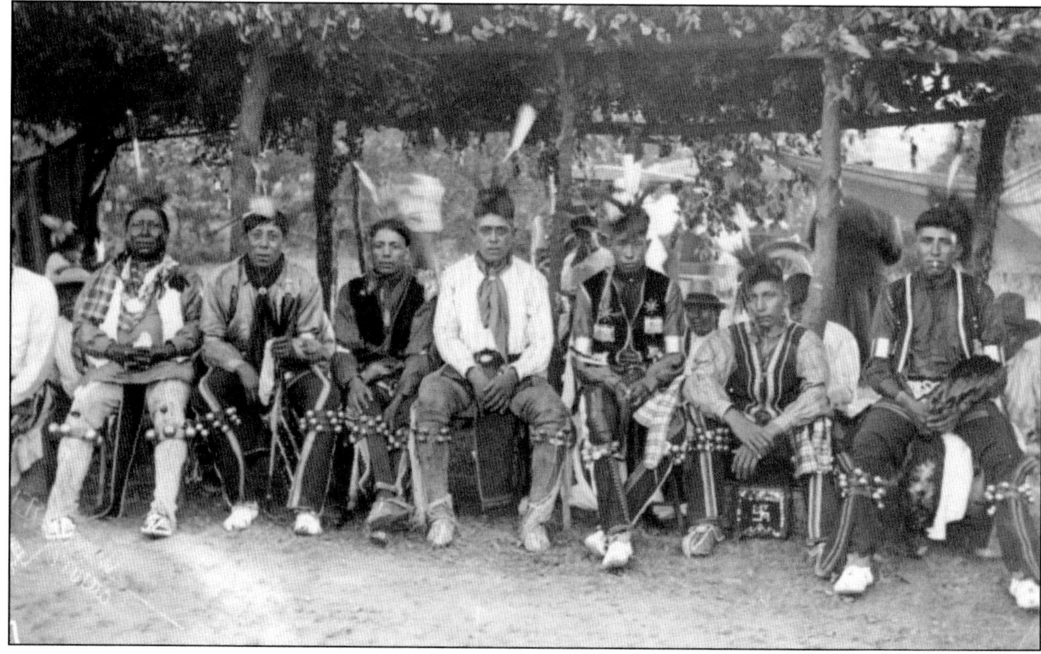

A group of Pawnee dancers in traditional dress is sitting beneath a brush arbor at the Pawnee Agency. A brush arbor was nothing but a temporary framework of poles covered with branches to provide shade during the summer for tribal ceremonies. Note the reversed swastika on the man second from the left. The reversed swastika was a good-luck symbol for many Native Americans. (Author's collection.)

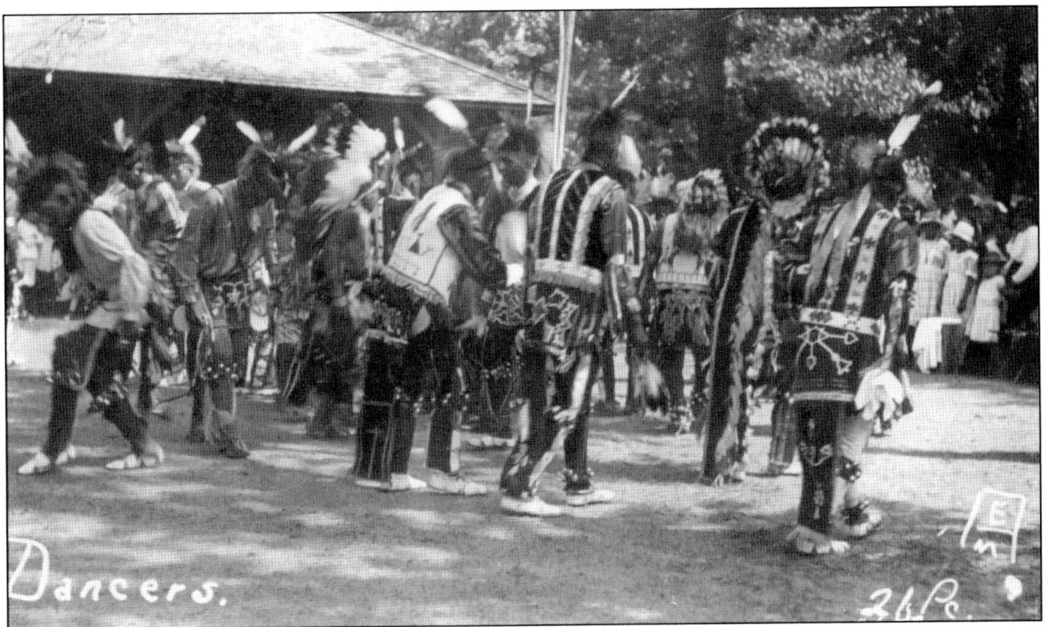

Pawnee dancers are performing a traditional all-male dance. Note the roaches, beaded moccasins, and colorful dress on the dancers. (Courtesy of the Pawnee County Historical Society.)

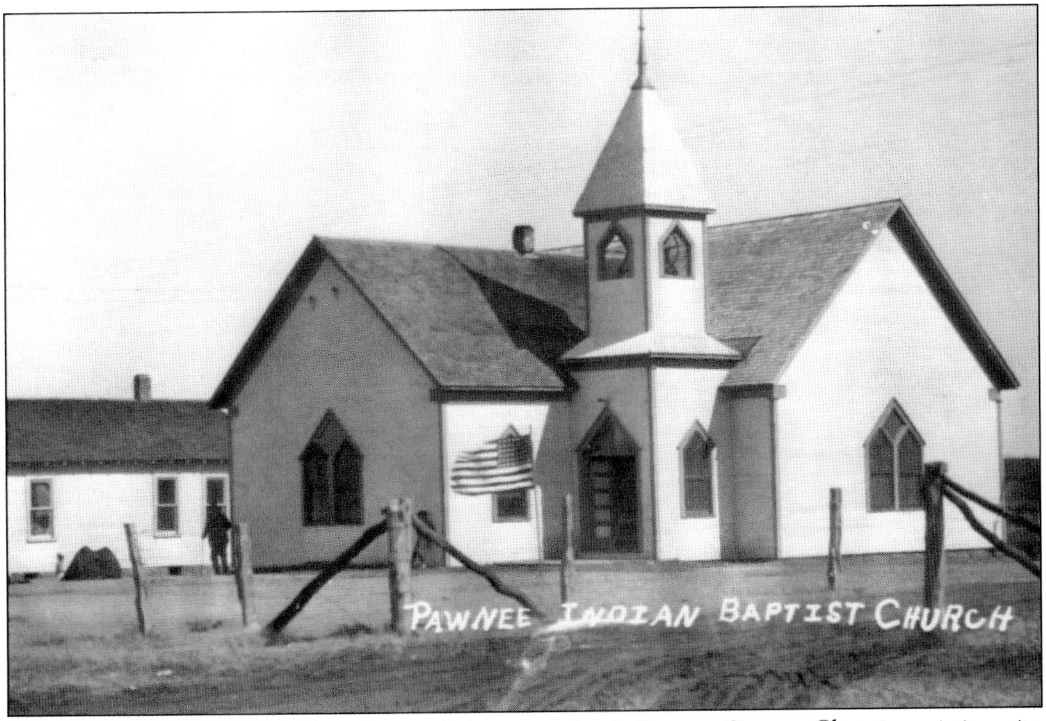

The Pawnee Indian Baptist Church is on their reservation in Pawnee County. Christian missionaries converted many of the Pawnees after the tribe settled into their new homeland. The missionaries also opposed traditional religious dances. The last of the Pawnee doctor dances was in 1927. (Courtesy of the Pawnee County Historical Society.)

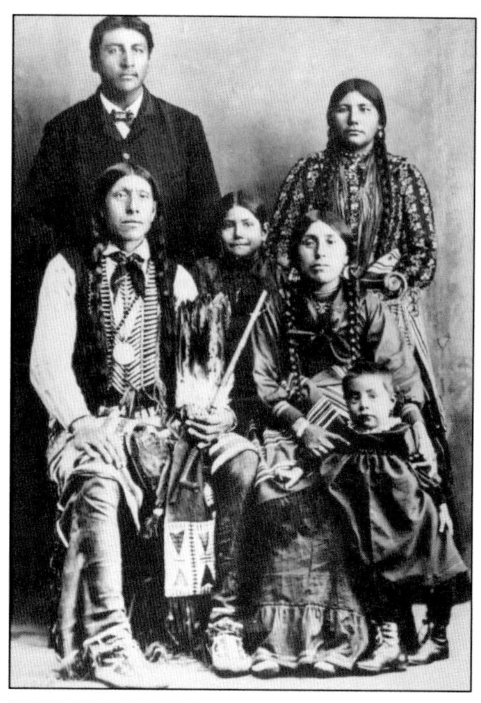

By the time of their removal to present-day Pawnee County, the Pawnee were torn between their tribal traditions and pressure to adjust to American culture. In the left rear, Stacy Matlock wears a suit popular at the beginning of the 20th century, while his wife, Ella, wears a traditional Pawnee dress. Their daughter, Cecilia, stands between them. In the front row is Phillip, also called Brigham Young, his wife, Lulu, and their son Sam. (Courtesy of the Field Museum of Natural History.)

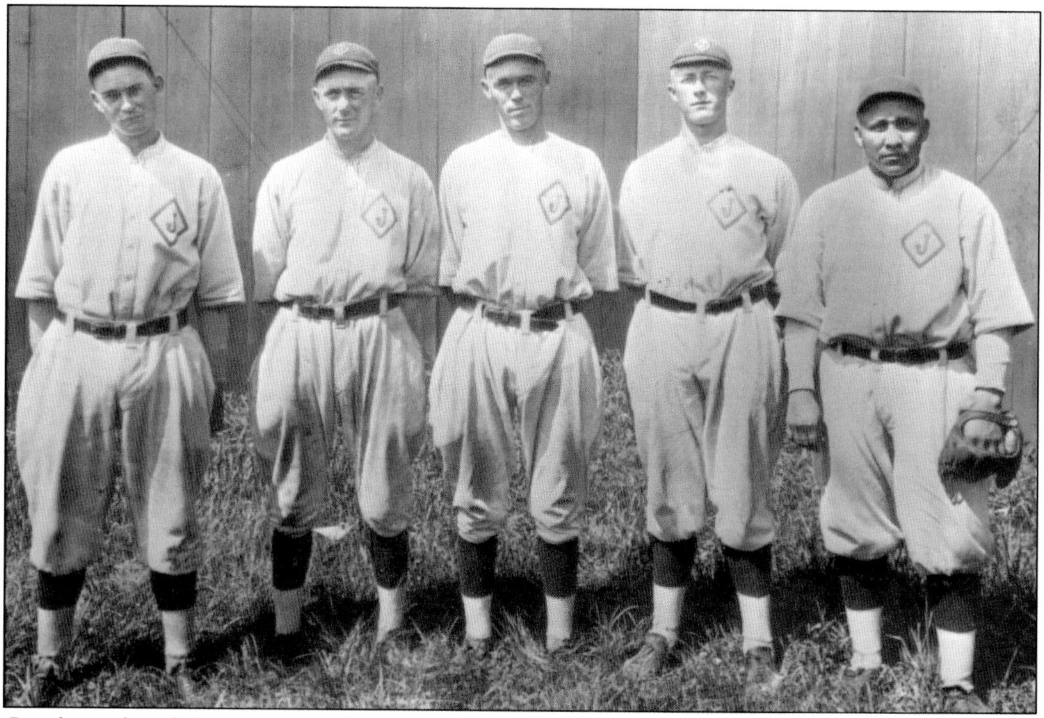

On the right of this photograph is Mose Yellowhorse, a Pawnee and a major-league baseball player. He is wearing his Joplin, Missouri, team uniform of the Western Baseball Association. Yellowhorse played major-league ball with the Pittsburgh Pirates. Others in the photograph are Johnny Bishop, in the center, Loyd Bruington, second from the right, and Pete Elmore, second from the left. (Courtesy of the Pawnee County Historical Society.)

Two

Outlaws and Lawmen

Pawnee County was a mecca for early outlaws. Among them were the Doolin and Dalton Gangs. Bill Doolin worked as a cowboy and frequently was in Pawnee County. It was Doolin who named Hell Roaring Creek: Doolin and some other cowboys were bedded down near the creek when they were struck by a sudden rainstorm. One of the cowboys yelled at Doolin that the "creek is high." Doolin replied, "Yes, it's hell roaring high."

Doolin's outlaw career started one Fourth of July when he and some friends were drinking beer at their camp outside of town. Two deputy sheriffs rode up and attempted to confiscate the beer. A gunfight broke out, the two deputies were shot, and Doolin was blamed.

Doolin joined the Dalton Gang headed by Grat, Bob, and Emmett Dalton. On October 5, 1892, the gang struck the bank in Coffeeville, Kansas. The robbery was botched, and all members of the Dalton Gang were killed except Doolin, who had been left behind when his horse went lame, and Emmett, who was wounded, captured, and sent to prison. Doolin then organized his own gang, which included Bill Dalton; George "Red Buck" Waightsman; George "Bitter Creek" Newcomb; "OL" Yantis; "Little" Bill Raidley; "Little" Dick West; "Dynamite" Dan Clifton; Roy Daugherty, alias "Arkansas Tom" Jones; and William "Tulsa Jack" Blake.

In January 1894, Doolin, Newcomb, and Tulsa Jack planned to rob the Farmers and Citizens Bank of Pawnee. About 3:00 p.m. on Tuesday, January 23, the outlaws rode into Pawnee and dismounted in front of Stewart's Hotel. Newcomb held the horses while Doolin and Tulsa Jack rushed into the bank, only to discover the vault was on a time lock. Realizing they could not wait, Doolin and Tulsa Jack scooped up $262.24 from the cash drawers and headed out of town. A posse led by Pawnee County sheriff Frank Lane and chief deputy Frank Canton chased the outlaws to the Arkansas River, where they lost the trail.

One of the last gasps of the Wild West in America was in Pawnee County.

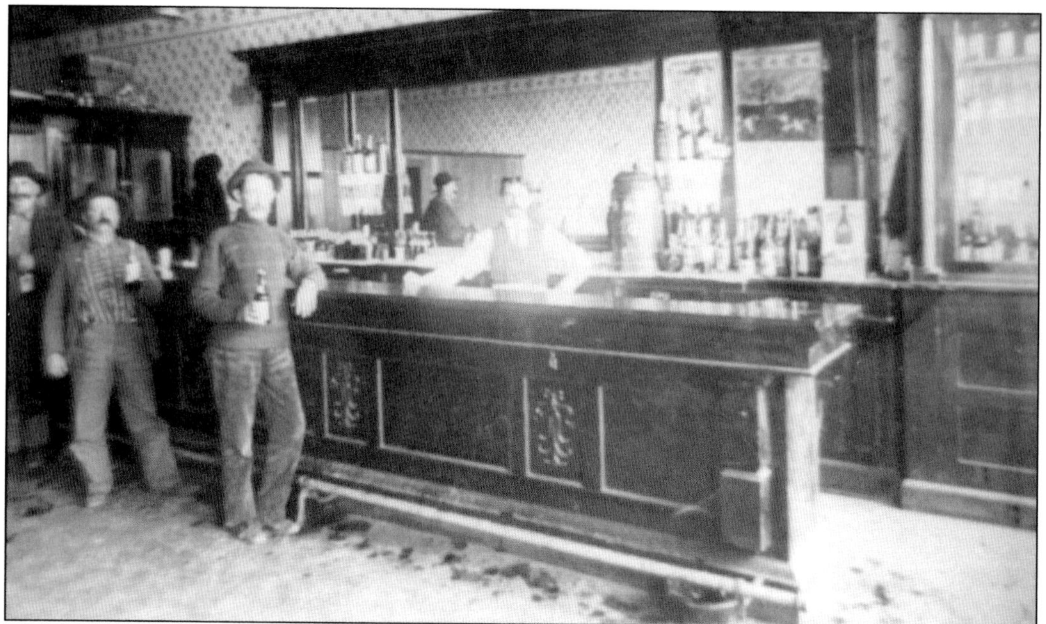

Fred Boggs is standing behind the bar at the Silver Dollar Saloon in Cleveland, Oklahoma. The three customers are drinking bottled beer. A keg of beer and several liquor bottles are sitting on the back bar. Although there is a spittoon on the floor on the right end of the bar, notice the chewing tobacco stains on the floor itself. (Courtesy of Evelyn "Zeke" Cheek.)

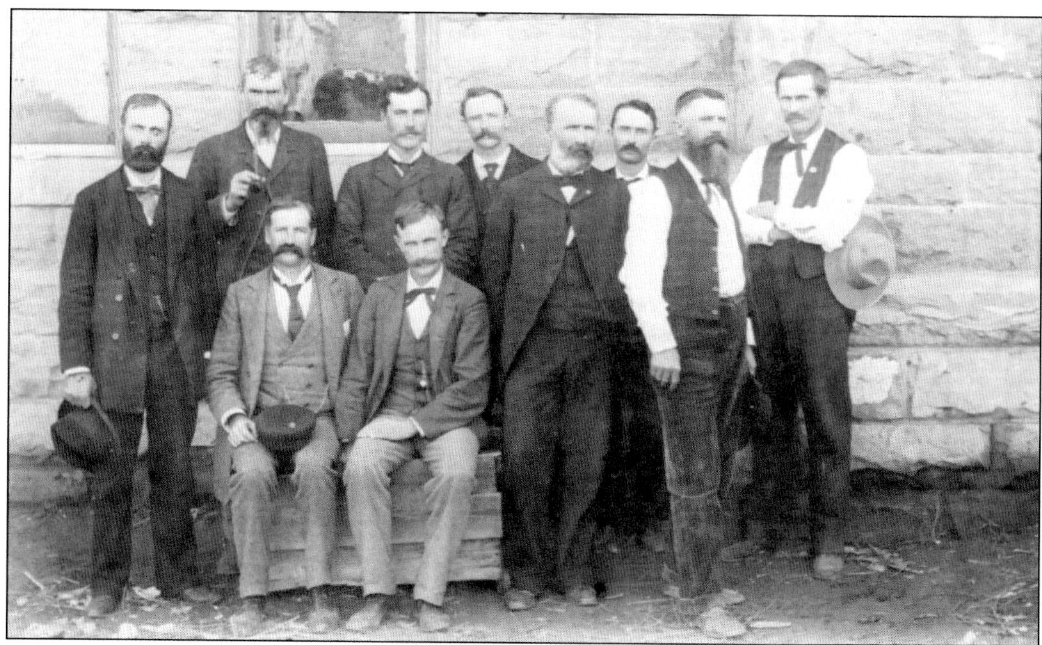

Pictured here, the first elected officials of Pawnee County are, from left to right, (first row) Charles M. Hill, county clerk; C.A. Houston, county attorney; O.M. Lancaster, county treasurer; unidentified; M.F. Lake, county sheriff; and K.H. Hulls, deputy county sheriff; (second row) J.H. Burkholder, registrar of deeds; F.M. Beavers, county superintendent; George Seldomridge, deputy registrar of deeds; and S.J. Tucker, deputy sheriff. (Courtesy of Bill Lake.)

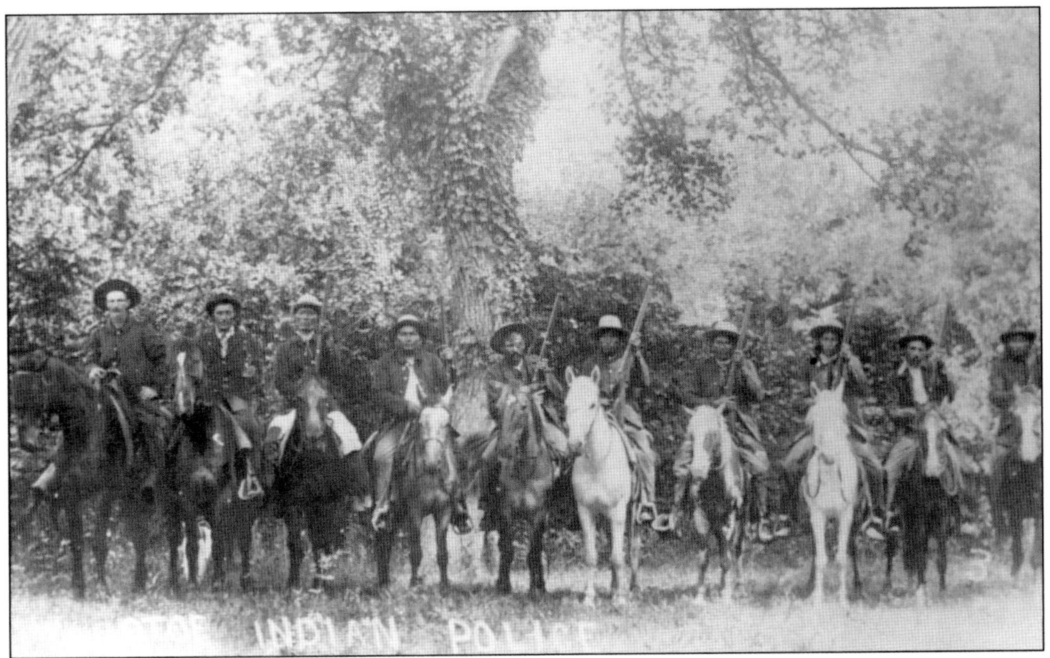

The Otoe tribe's Indian police were kept busy in the county. Located outside of the jurisdiction of lawmen from the surrounding states and subject only to federal deputy marshals out of Fort Smith, Arkansas, and tribal police who had jurisdiction over Indians only, Pawnee County had some of the worst outlaws in the West. (Courtesy of the Oklahoma History Center.)

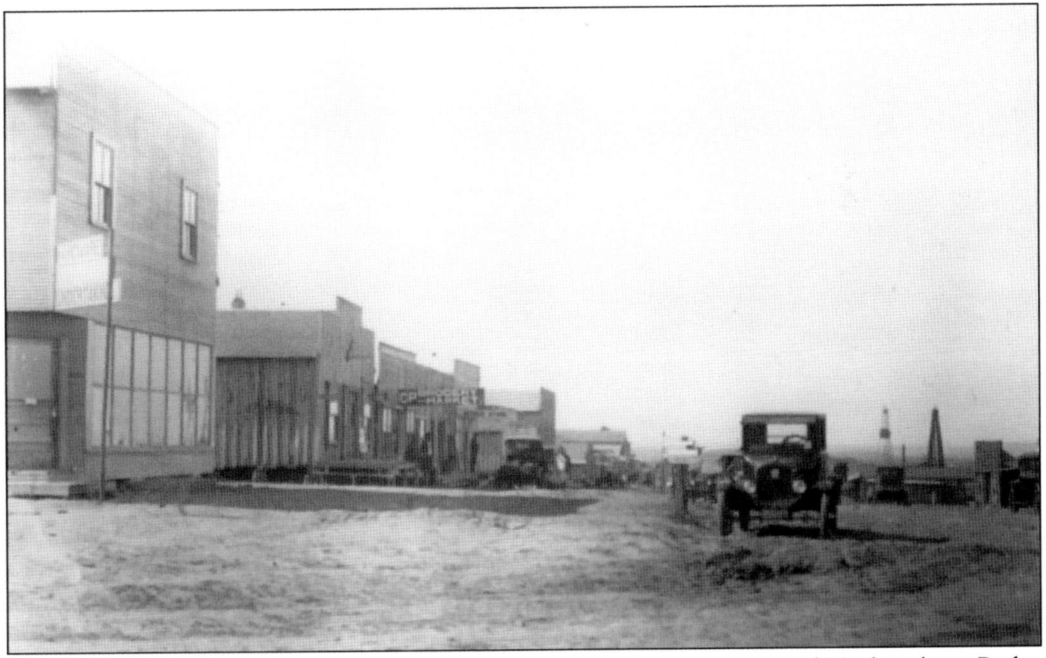

A photograph of early Watchorn shows Bruington's Hardware Store and Undertaking Parlor on the corner of the street. The C.P. Grocery and Brock's Drug Store are next door. The local undertaker was often one of the busiest businesses in town during the early days of Pawnee County's oil boom. (Courtesy of the Pawnee County Historical Society.)

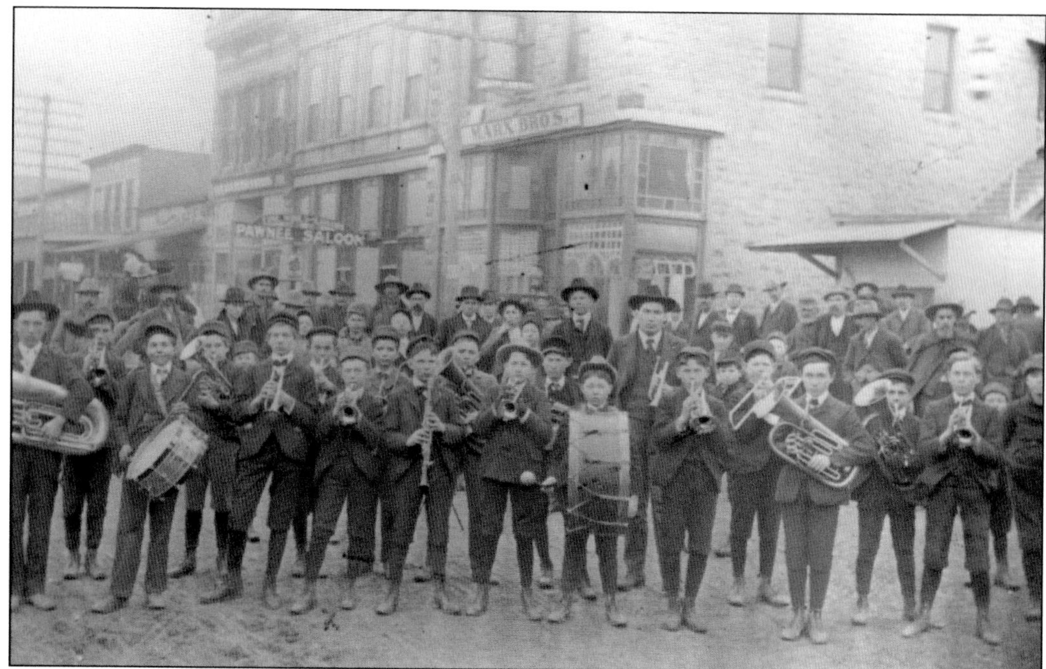

The Pawnee School band is performing on the main street. Just to the rear of the band is the Pawnee Saloon offering "fine wines and liquors." It was one of 13 saloons in the town. Located in wet Oklahoma Territory but close to the dry Osage and Creek Nations, Pawnee did a booming business in the liquor trade before statehood and Prohibition. (Courtesy of the Pawnee County Historical Society.)

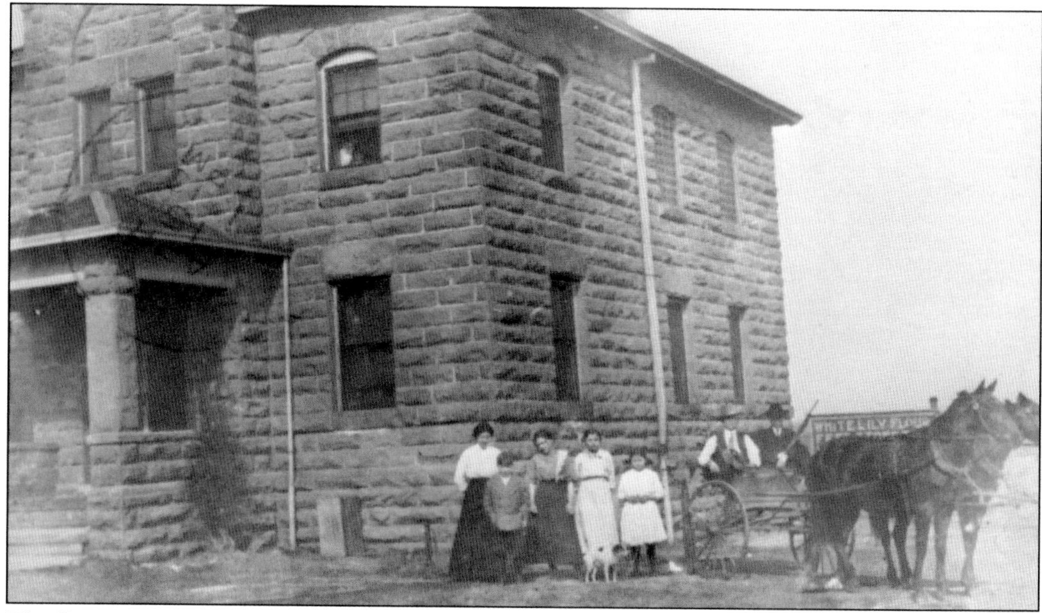

The Pawnee County Jail was a two-story structure on the northeast corner of the courthouse square. Note the man on the right in the wagon is carrying a 12-gauge pump shotgun. Prisoners were kept on the second floor at the rear of the building, where the windows are barred. (Courtesy of the Pawnee County Historical Society.)

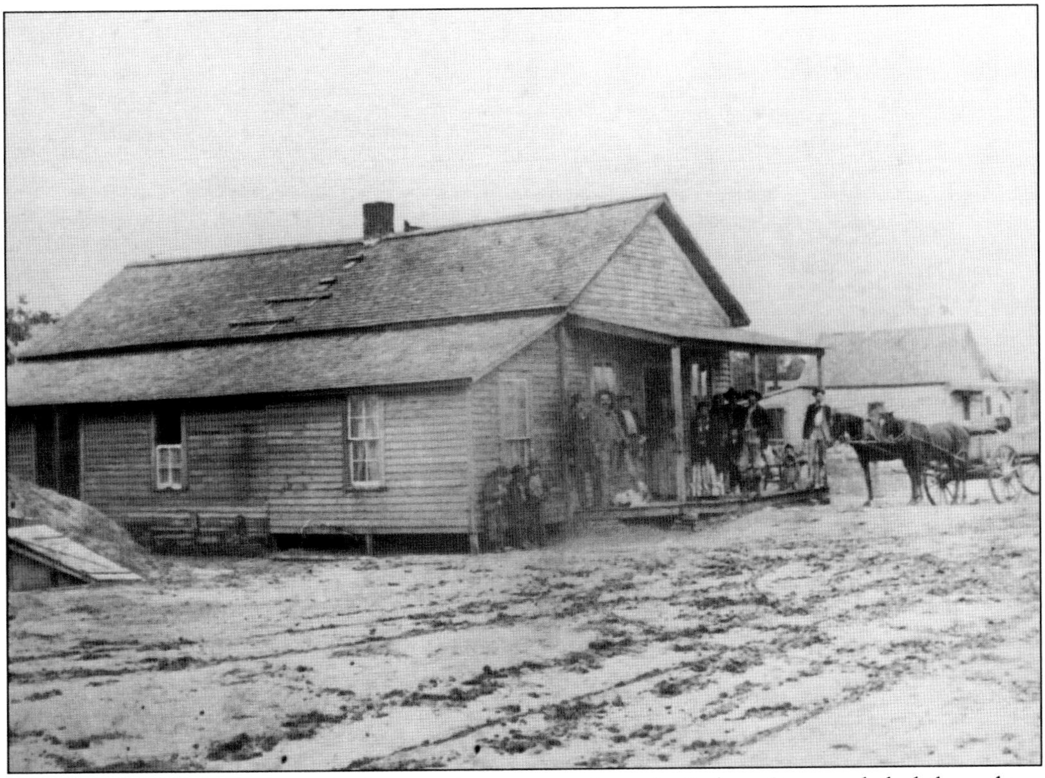

Charles Vandervoort's store at the Pawnee Agency was where the Dalton Gang traded while working for the Bar X Ranch. The ranch ran cattle near the mouth of Black Bear Creek where it entered the Arkansas River. Grat, Bob, and Emmett Dalton often stopped at the store before going on a "scout," which meant hiding from lawmen. (Courtesy of the Pawnee County Historical Society.)

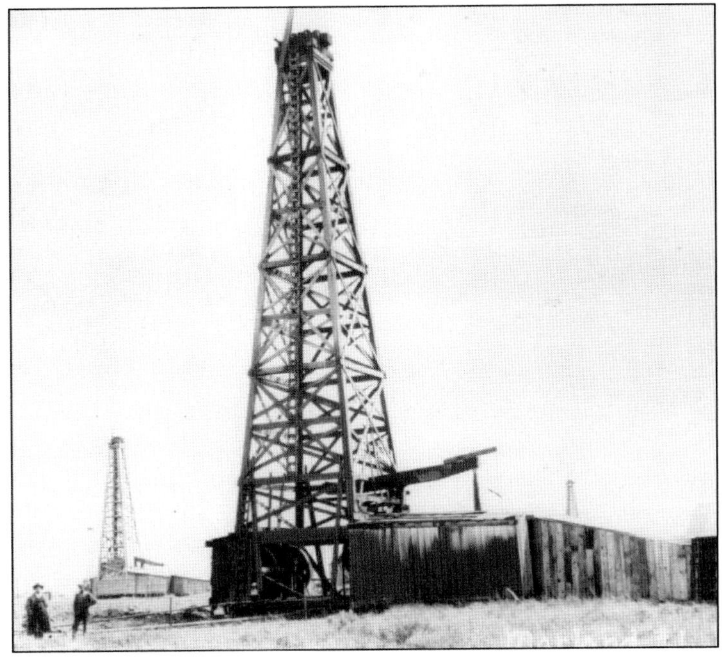

A typical cable tool rig sits in Pawnee County. Powered by a steam boiler, it was connected by a series of belts to the bull wheel, which moved the walking beam up and down. The walking beam, which was attached to the bit by a cable, raised and lowered the bit in the hole. The drill hole was often 24 inches wide and provided a convenient place to dispose of an unwanted body. A corpse would be thrown down the hole and pulverized as the bit moved up and down. (Author's collection.)

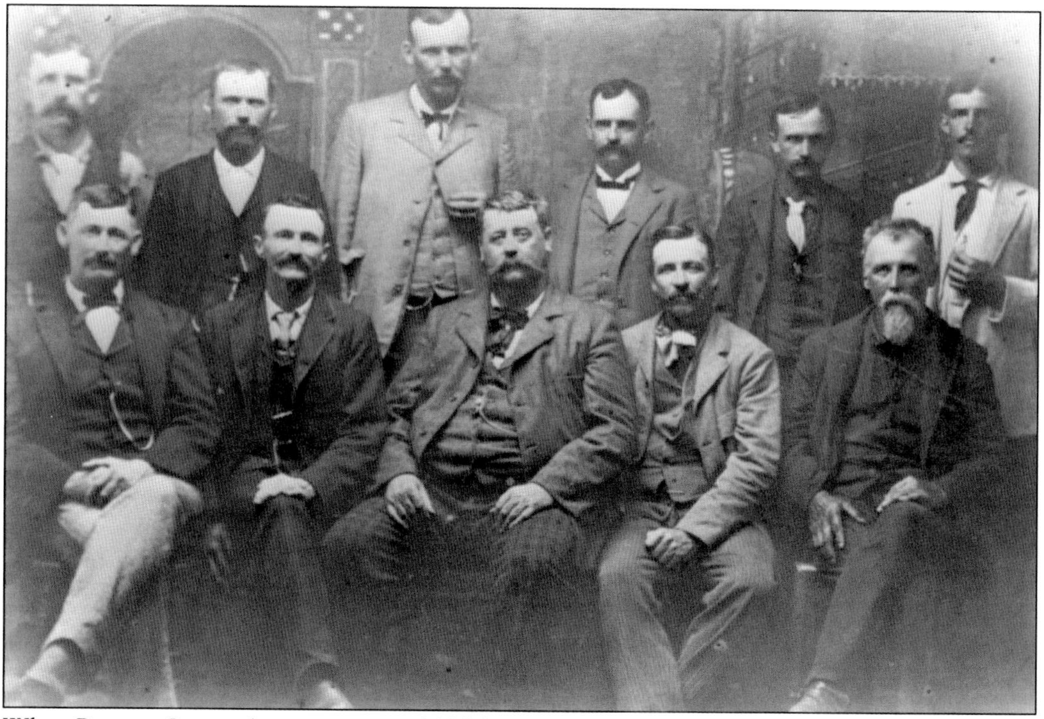

When Pawnee County became a part of Oklahoma Territory, local officials brought law and order to the community. This is a photograph of Pawnee's town officials in 1894. Town Marshal J.W. Perry is fourth from left in the back row. Cook Horton is standing on the right of the second row. Pictured are, from left to right, (first row) J.S. Annawalt (Ward Three councilman), J G. Drake (Ward Five councilman), G.W. Lewis (mayor and Ward One councilman;), G.W. Reid (Ward Four councilman), and J.A. Overton (Ward Two councilman); (second row) C.W. Dunn (assessor), O.M. Lancaster (treasurer), C.P. Mosur (police judge), Perry, J.J. Corbet (town clerk) and Horton. (Courtesy of the Pawnee County Historical Society.)

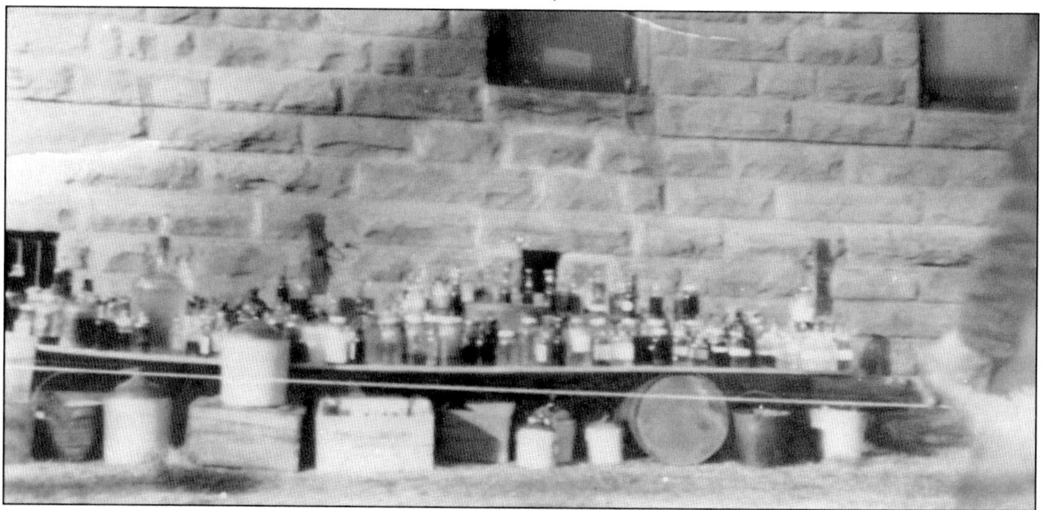

This is a display of illicit liquor beside the Pawnee County Courthouse after a raid on a bootlegger's joint in 1924. Bottles, casks, and jugs of whiskey are shown. Hard liquor became illegal after voters ushered in Prohibition at statehood. (Courtesy of the Pawnee County Historical Society.)

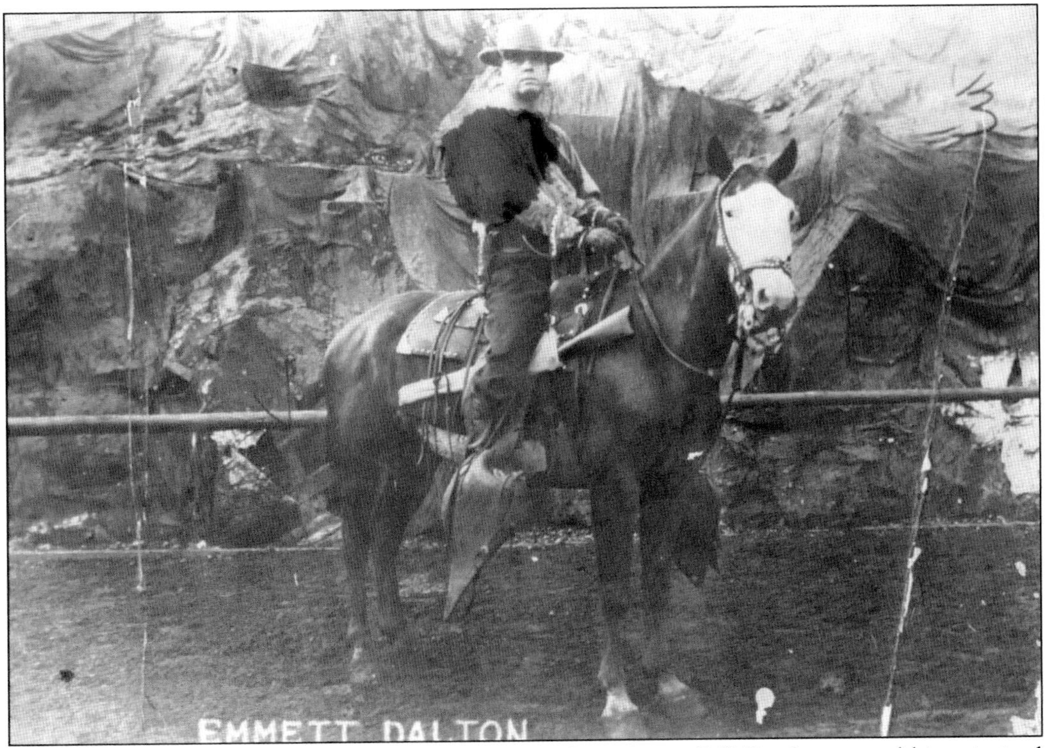

Emmett Dalton was a member of the infamous Dalton Gang. Bill Doolin started his criminal career as a member of the Dalton Gang but formed his own gang of outlaws when all the members of the Dalton Gang were killed or captured trying to rob a bank in Coffeyville, Kansas. Emmett was captured in the shoot-out that followed the attempted robbery. Doolin escaped because his horse went lame, and he had been left behind by the other gang members. (Courtesy of the Pawnee County Historical Society.)

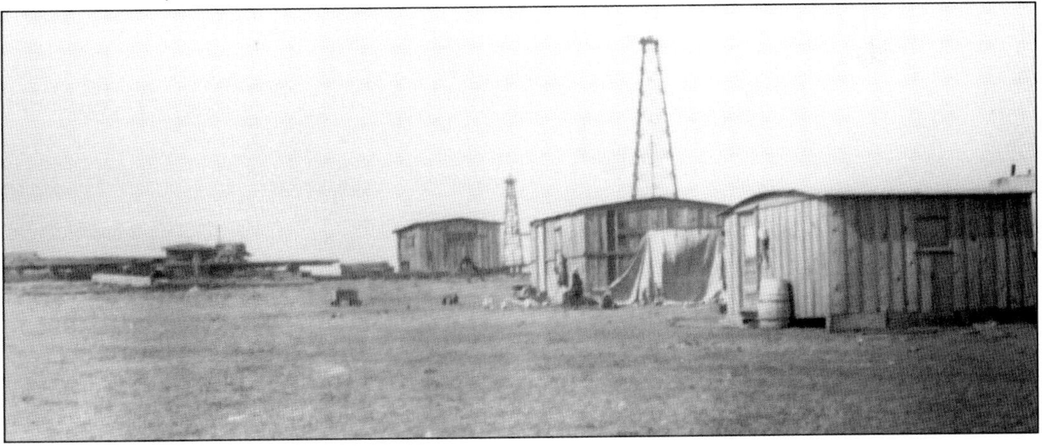

Pawnee County's oil-boom era was among the last throes of the Wild West. Thousands of honest workers as well as prostitutes, gamblers, bootleggers, hustlers, conmen, and other outcasts rushed to the oil field in dreams of riches. Many workers found it easier to rob and steal than live in such primitive housing as these shotgun houses at Watchorn. Note that the residents in the middle house have a flock of chickens scrounging for food in their front yard to supplement their meager rations. (Courtesy of H.P. Laird.)

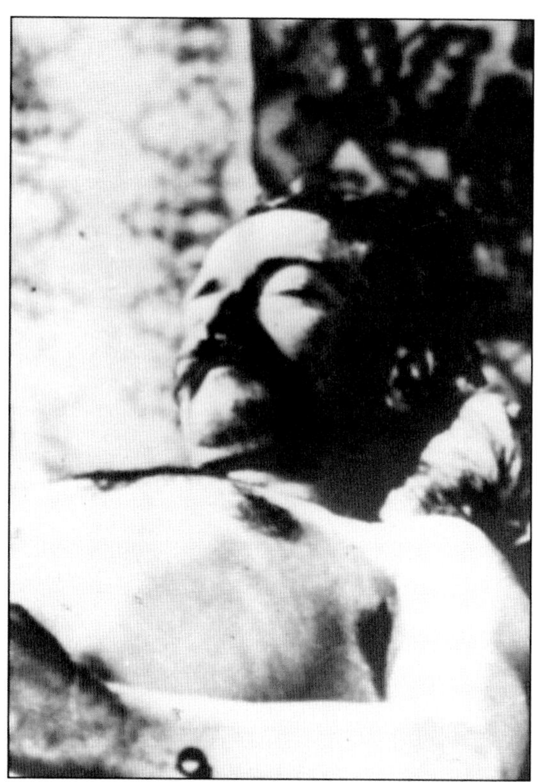

George "Bitter Creek" Newcomb was a member of the Bill Doolin Gang that robbed Pawnee's Citizen's and Farmer's Bank in January 1894. Newcomb was shot on May 2, 1895, by two brothers of 14-year-old Rose Dunn, with whom he was having a romantic relationship. Newcomb was ambushed as he rode up to the Dunn Ranch on the Cimarron River, south of Pawnee. After the shooting, the brothers threw Newcomb's body into a wagon to take him in for the reward. When he moaned, they shot him again. (Courtesy of the Pawnee County Historical Society.)

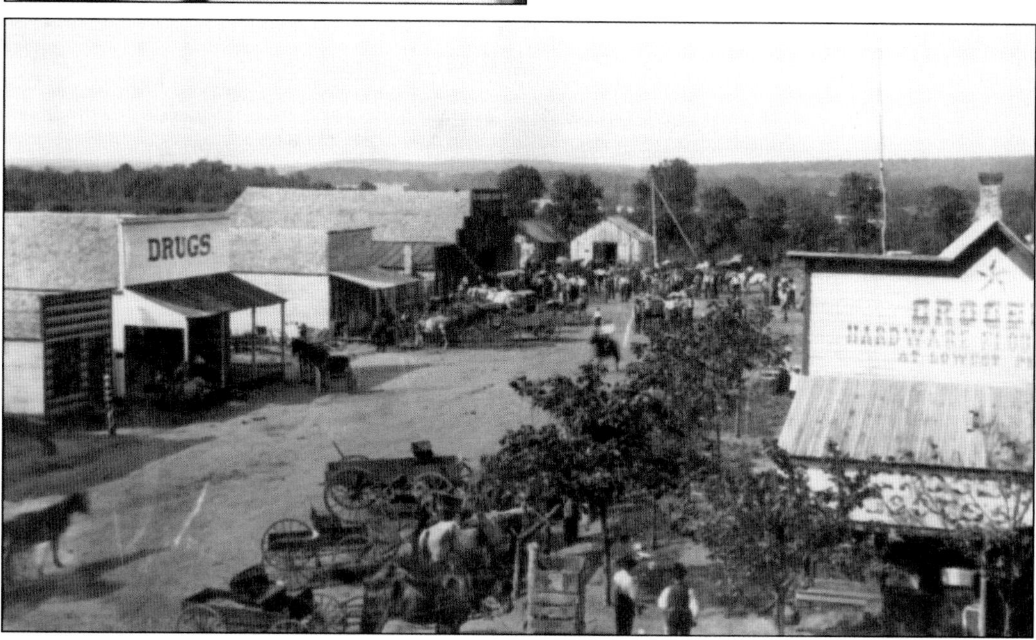

As seen here, the main street of Blackburn boasts a barbershop, drugstore, and the local saloon on the left, and on the other side is the Star Grocery and Hardware. In the background is the Arkansas River, which separated Pawnee County from the Osage Reservation. It was a simple matter for residents of the Osage Reservation, where liquor was illegal, to cross the river into Blackburn and frequent the local saloons. (Courtesy of the Pawnee County Historical Society.)

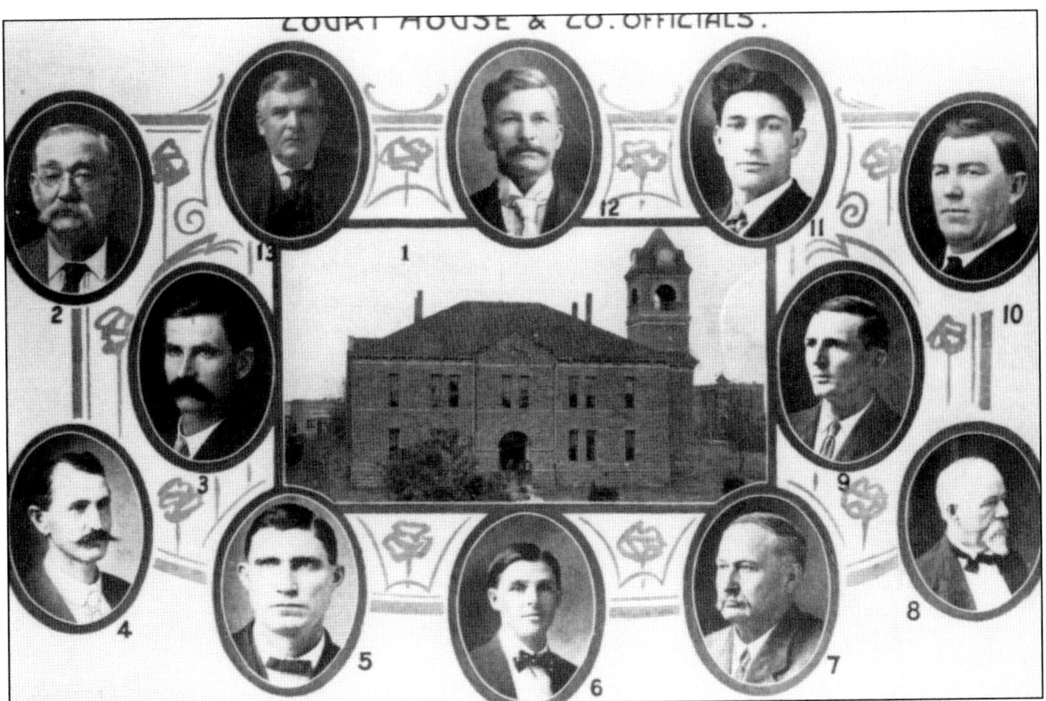

Pawnee County sheriff C.I. Pumroy can be seen in the lower left (No. 4) in this group photograph of early-day Pawnee County officials. The county courthouse is in the center of the image. The Pawnee County Jail was built on the northeast corner of the courthouse square. (Courtesy of the Pawnee County Historical Society.)

These lawmen are destroying contraband liquor, seized from bootleggers, on the east side of the courthouse square in Pawnee. The booze ran down the side of the hill into Black Bear Creek. The man with his back to the photographer and a gun on his belt is Dave Boren. Note the Bull Durham Chewing Tobacco advertisement painted on the side of the building across the street. (Courtesy of the Pawnee County Historical Society.)

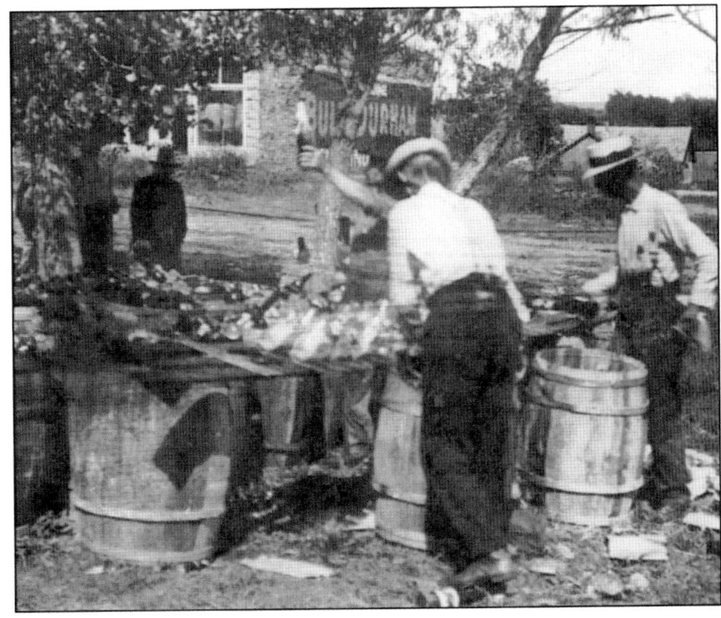

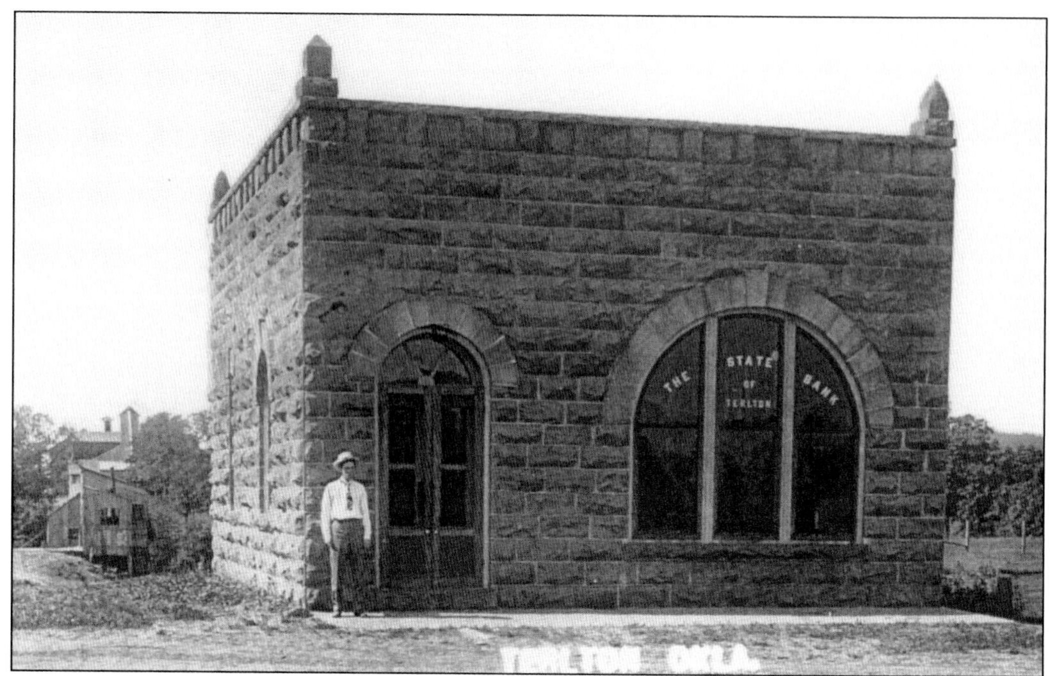

The oil boom attracted a multitude of outlaws to Pawnee. This is a photograph of the Terlton State Bank, which was robbed by three gunmen on January 13, 1915. As they fled the town, a gunfight ensued, and William Inhof, one of the robbers, had his horse shot out from under him and was captured. (Courtesy of the Pawnee County Historical Society.)

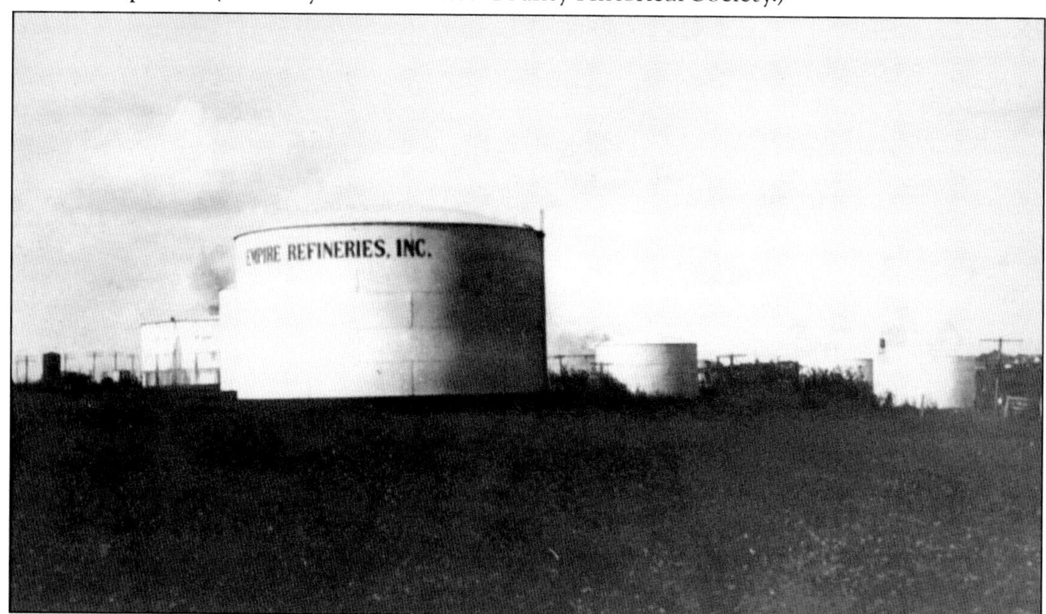

This is the Empire Oil Company's tank farm in Cleveland. The 55,000-barrel tanks had a floating top that moved up and down as oil was pumped in or drawn out of the tank. The tanks were an ideal place to get rid of a murder victim. There was an entrance in each tank's top, which provided easy access. Once the body was hidden in the tank, it could be months before it was discovered, and if it was found, there would be little left of it. (Courtesy of the Oklahoma History Center.)

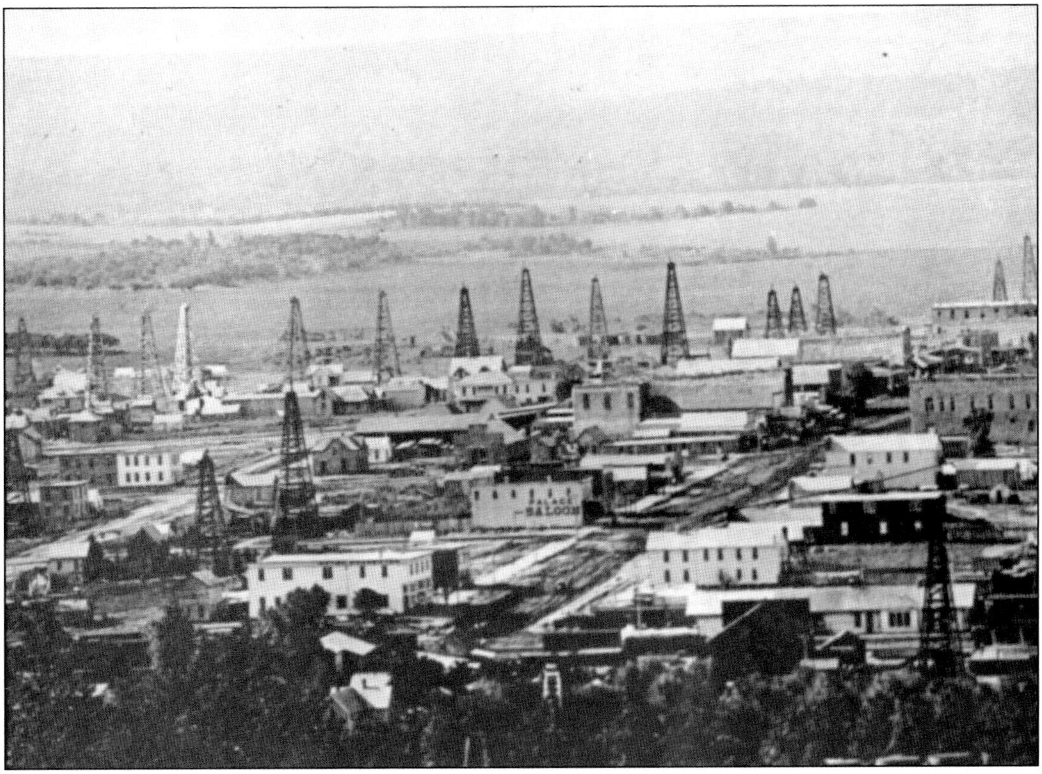

The Palace Saloon, in the center of this photograph and a Cleveland social center during the oil boom, was a frequent gathering place for the myriad oilfielders in and around the town. It offered just the kind of entertainment and excitement that the young and unmarried workers craved, especially after a payday. (Courtesy of McFarlin Library, University of Tulsa.)

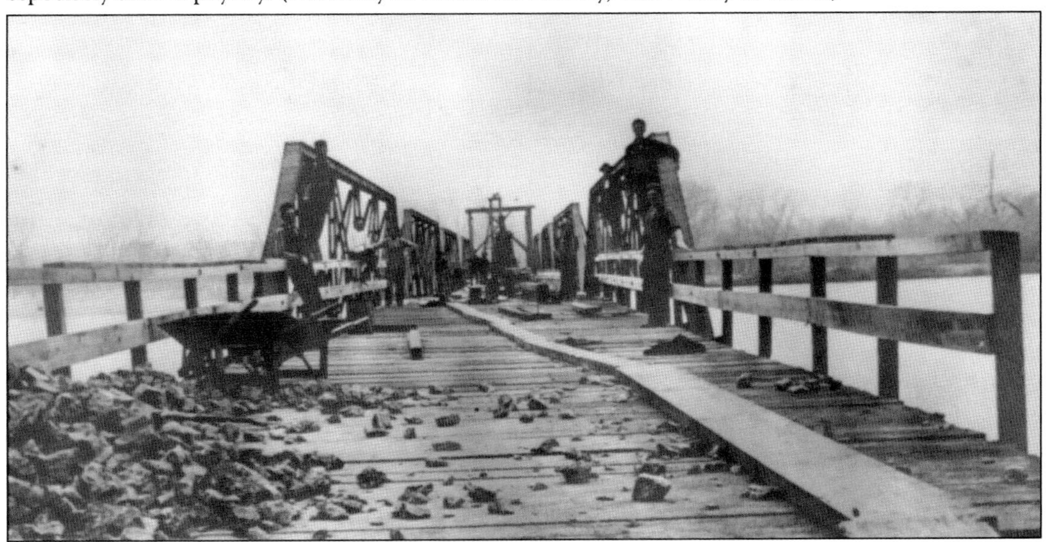

Workers are completing the bridge across the Arkansas River between Ralston in Pawnee County and Fairfax in the Osage Nation. One of the county's whiskey towns, Ralston catered to Osages, who were prohibited by federal law from purchasing liquor in the Osage Nation. The bridge gave them easy access to Ralston's liquor trade. (Courtesy of the Pawnee County Historical Society.)

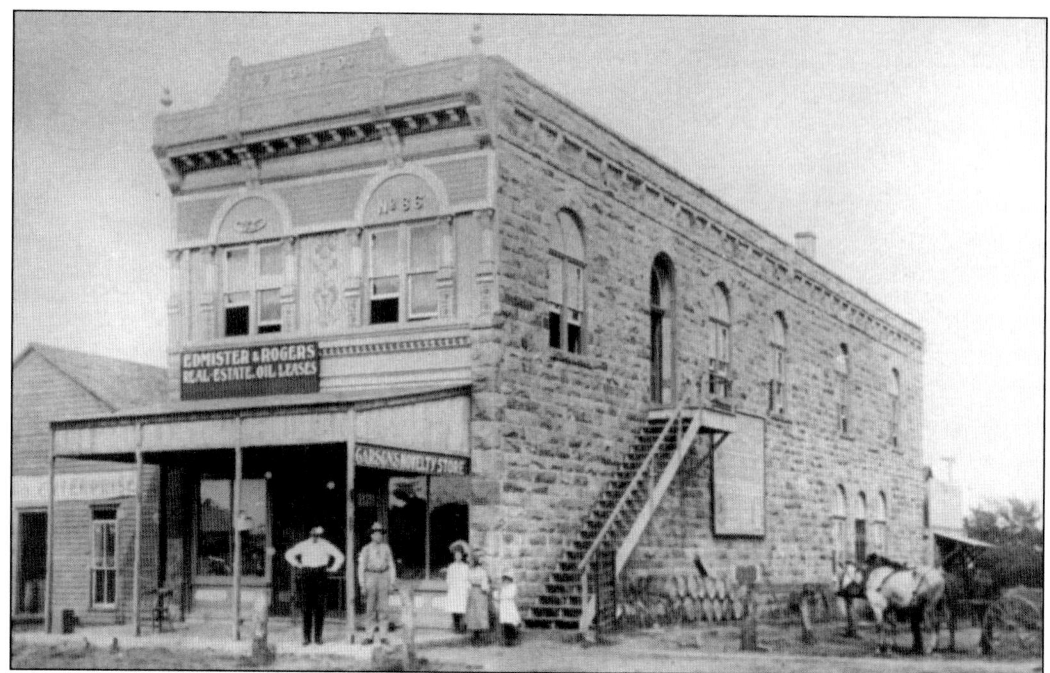

Constructed in 1888, the Independent Order of Odd Fellows Lodge was at the corner of Broadway and Delaware Streets in Cleveland. Access to the fraternal gathering was by the stairs on the side of the native-stone building and the only entrance to the lodge. Once safe from lawmen in their lodge, the Odd Fellows could indulge in whatever they wished. Underneath the stairs are stacked beer barrels. An oil-lease company maintained its offices on the first floor. (Author's collection.)

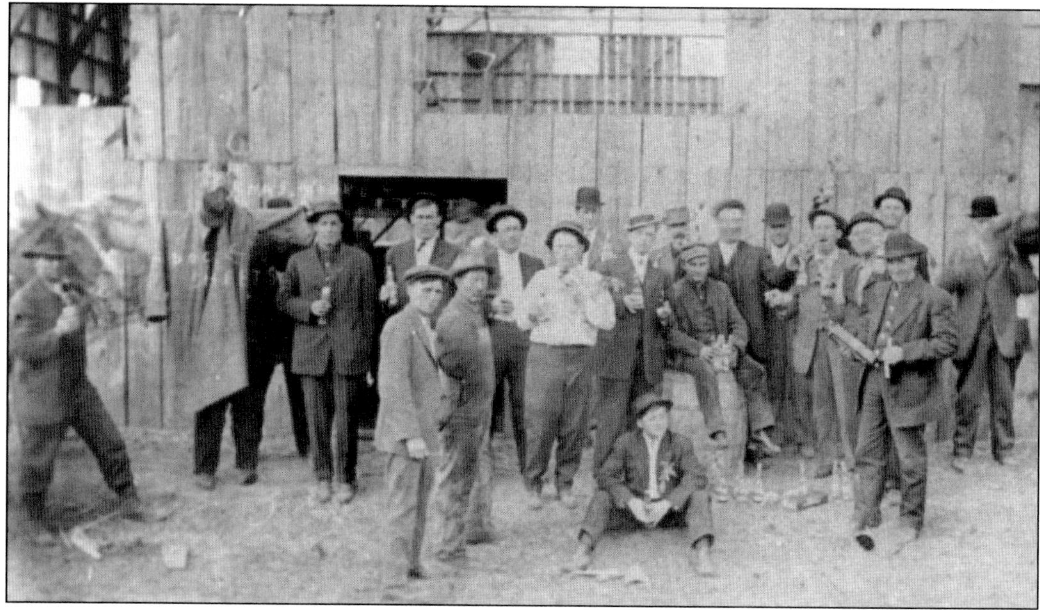

At the south end of Cleveland's main street was a half-completed livery stable that was the place of business for the town's bootleggers. In this photograph, obviously made before statehood and Prohibition, men standing in front of the livery are holding bottles of beer and pints of hard liquor. (Courtesy of Robert Jordan.)

Three

CATTLE AND AGRIBUSINESS

Pawnee County was a part of the Cherokee Outlet. During the late 19th century, the buffalo were killed off, and Texas cattlemen quickly drove herds north to graze on the rich grasslands they leased from the Indians. From 1883 to 1893, the members of the Cherokee Strip Live Stock Association leased the entire Cherokee Outlet. Three of the leases were in Pawnee County: the Bennett and Dunham Lease, McClellan Cattle Company Lease, and the Berry Brothers Lease. The Berry brothers—King, William, and Thomas—played a prominent role in the early development of Pawnee County. Their lease consisted of 60,000 acres and supplied the beef for the Pawnee Agency.

Witnessing the success of the Cherokees, the Otoes also leased their land. C.M. McClellan & Company was the largest lease holder in the Otoe Reservation in Pawnee County. After allotment, many Otoes continued to lease the land to cattlemen.

The cattle were driven to the Pawnee stockyards for shipment. Often, the herds were forced to cross the swinging bridge at Black Bear Creek. Once, a herd of cattle was about halfway across when an automobile started across from the west. When the cattle saw the auto, they bolted, with many jumping over the side of the bridge into the water. The result was chaos.

It was not unusual for herds to be driven down Pawnee's streets, often to the consternation of local residents. In 1902, a herd of Texas cattle was being driven from the Pawnee stockyard to the Pawnee Bill's Ranch, when the cows spooked. Three women were caught in the street, and one was trampled before she could escape.

In 1906, Push Garner was driving a herd through Pawnee to the depot for shipment. One of the nervous steers broke loose. Stampeding down the street, it charged two men. One managed to escape. The other was gored to death. Cattle ranching and agriculture continues to play a major role in Pawnee County's economy. It remains a central marketing center for livestock and much of western Pawnee County is still covered by ranchland.

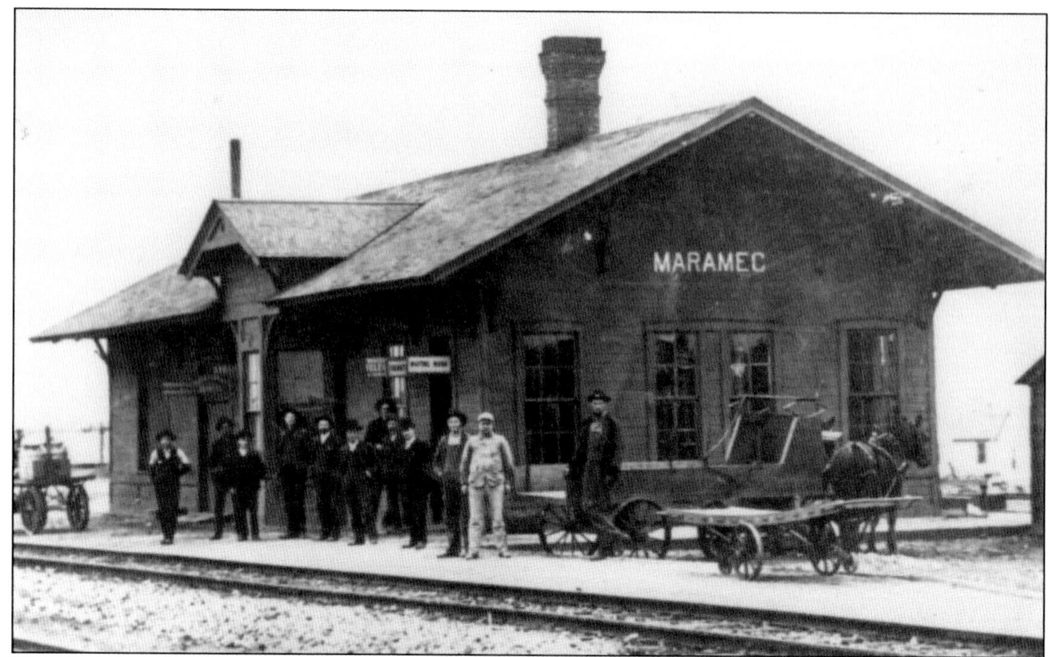

The Atchison, Topeka & Santa Fe was the main north-south rail line through Pawnee County and offered cattlemen access to packing plants in the north. This is the railroad's depot in Maramec. The cattle herds were generally driven overland to the rail station. (Courtesy of the Oklahoma History Center.)

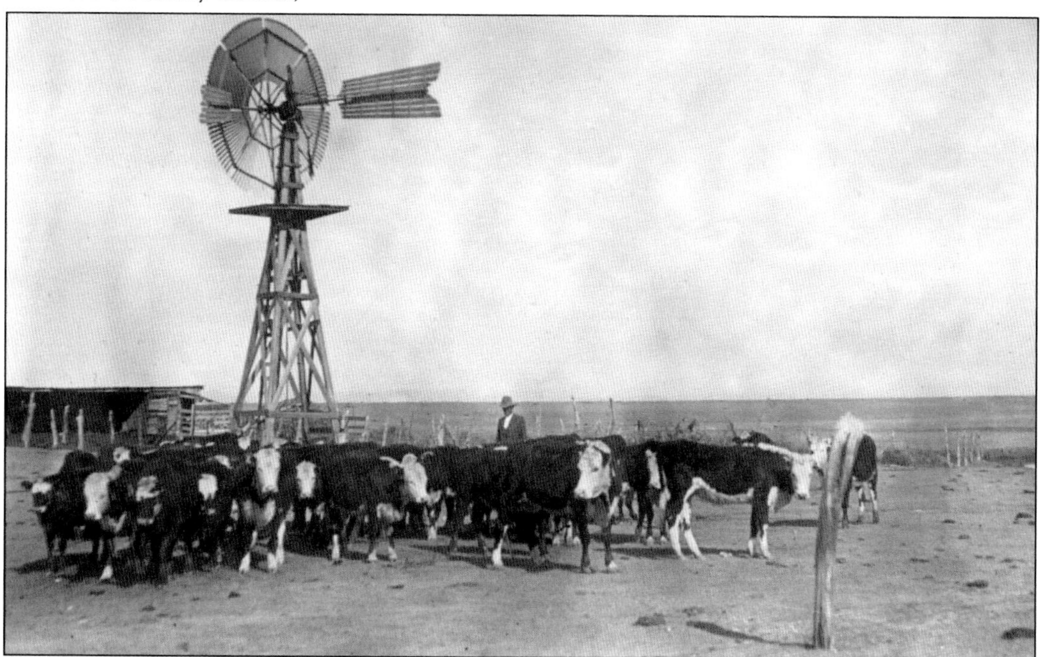

Cattle are gathered around a water trough near Ralston. The pump filling the trough with water was powered by a windmill. In the background is a cattle shed. The view is toward the north, because the south side of the shed is open while the north side is enclosed to protect the cattle from winter weather. (Courtesy of the Pawnee County Historical Society.)

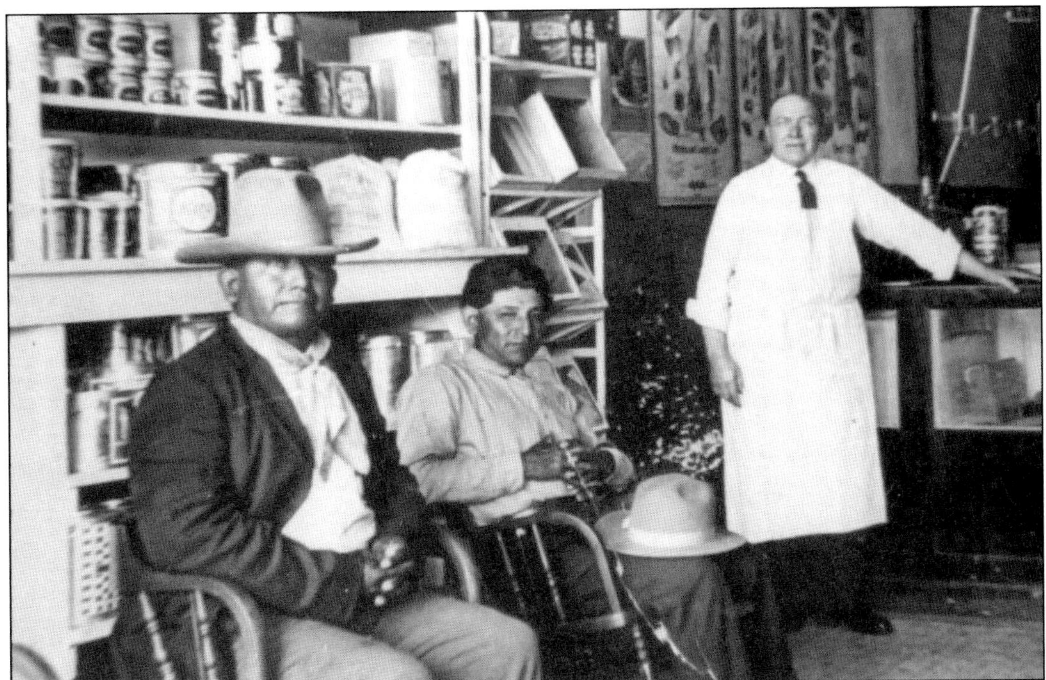

Gregor's Meat Market also offered a local outlet for cattlemen. Note the diagrams on the wall behind the man standing showing the different cuts of beef. Other dry goods are displayed on the shelves for sale. Two men are lounging in the store while the butcher is waiting for an order. (Courtesy of the Pawnee County Historical Society.)

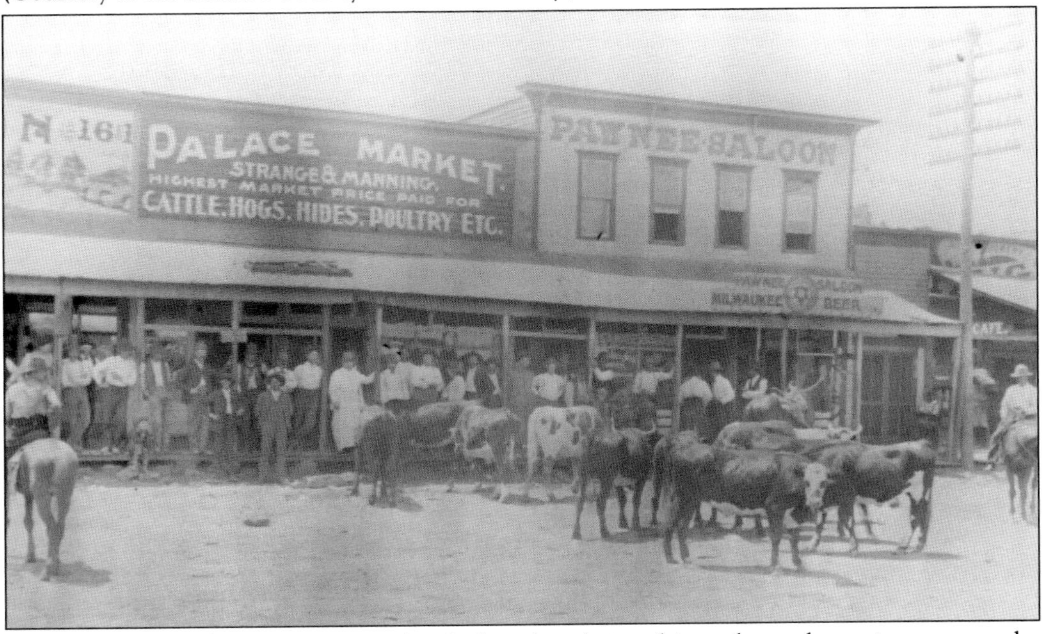

A once common sight in Pawnee, a herd of cattle is being driven down the main street on the way to the railroad depot. Two cowboys are herding 10 head of cattle while local residents watch from the wooden sidewalks. Behind them is the Pawnee Saloon advertising Milwaukee Beer. (Courtesy of the Pawnee County Historical Society.)

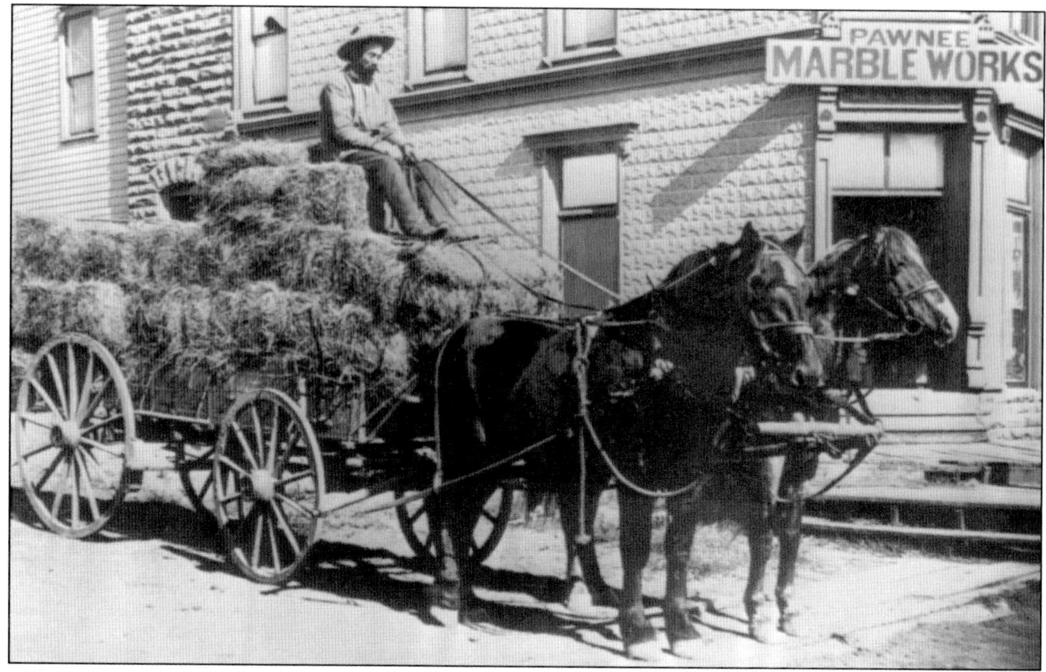

Adam Welch is driving a wagon filled with hay into Pawnee for sale. Welch has filled the wagon with as much hay as possible by putting it not only in the wagon bed but also on the wagon seat. Pawnee County's cattle industry not only benefited ranchers but also provided farmers a market for their hay. The wagon is parked in front the Pawnee Marble Works. (Courtesy of the Pawnee County Historical Society.)

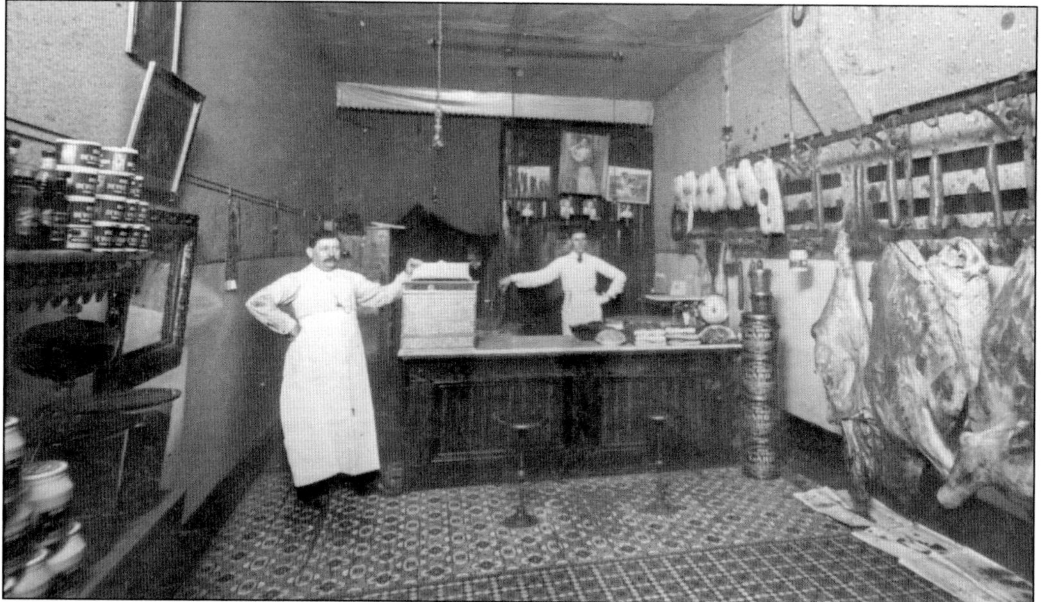

John's Meat Market was located on the north side of Pawnee's courthouse square. While most of Pawnee County's locally raised beef was shipped to markets in Kansas City, Missouri, and other meatpacking centers, some was cut to order by local butchers, as were these sides of beef hanging at the right of the photograph. (Courtesy of the Pawnee County Historical Society.)

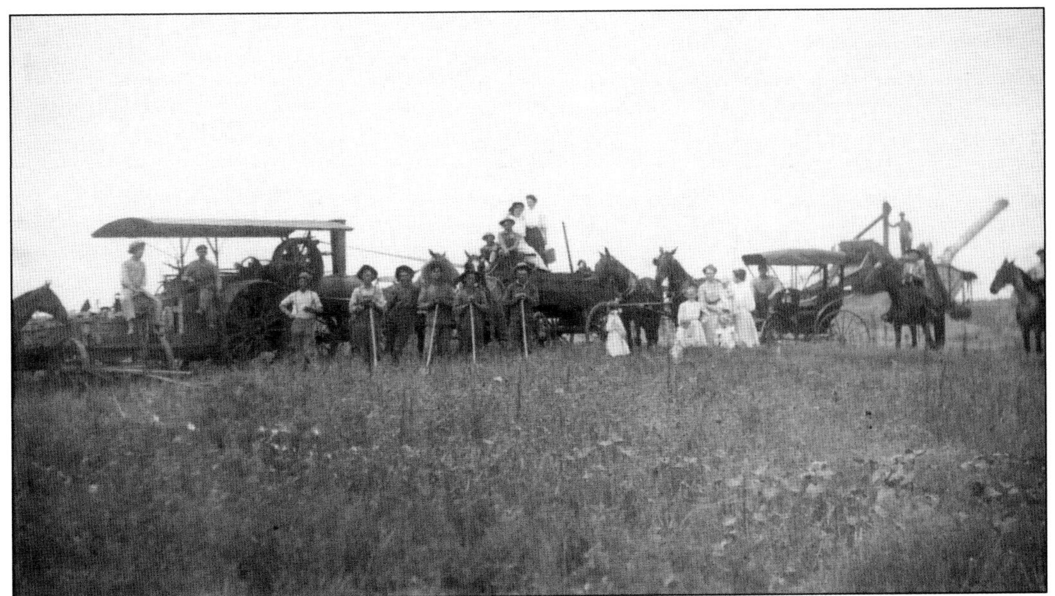

Pictured here is an early-day threshing crew in Pawnee County. The steam-powered tractor is on the left, with a belt connecting it to the thresher on the right. Between the two is a water wagon used to supply water for the tractor's boiler. Note the women and children, especially the woman with a basket, atop the water wagon. It probably is mealtime, and they have brought the meal to the workers. It was the duty of the landowner to feed the threshing crew. (Courtesy of the Pawnee County Historical Society.)

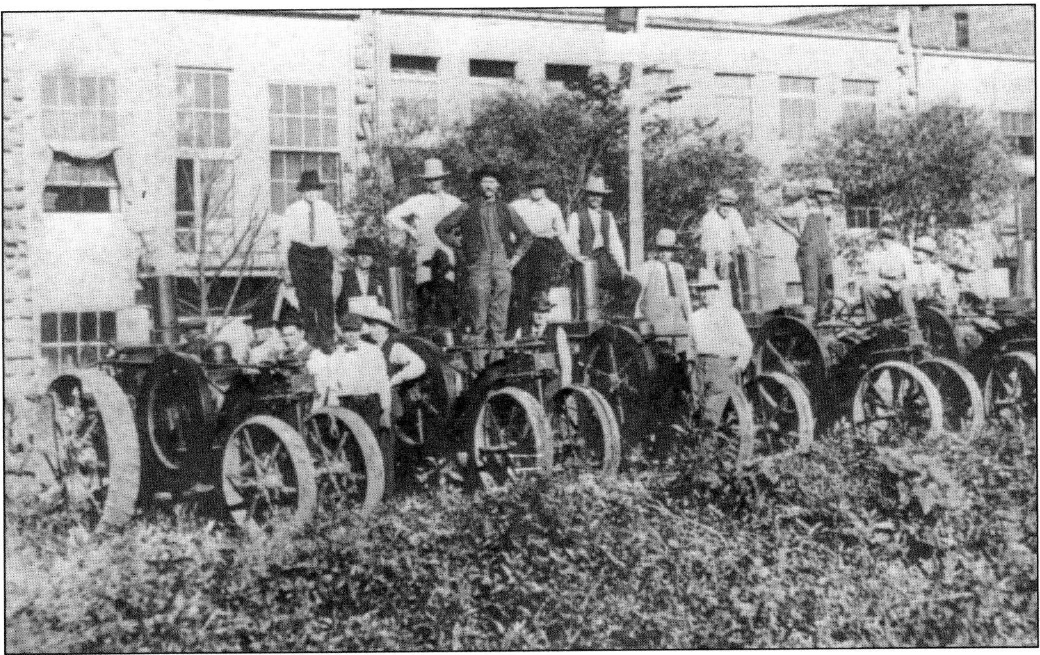

Steam tractors offered a great advantage over horse- or mule-pulled farm implements. These steam-powered tractors are being displayed in Pawnee. However, they quickly went out of style when the Hart-Parr Engine Manufacturing Company introduced gasoline-powered engines in the first decade of the 20th century. (Courtesy of the Pawnee County Historical Society.)

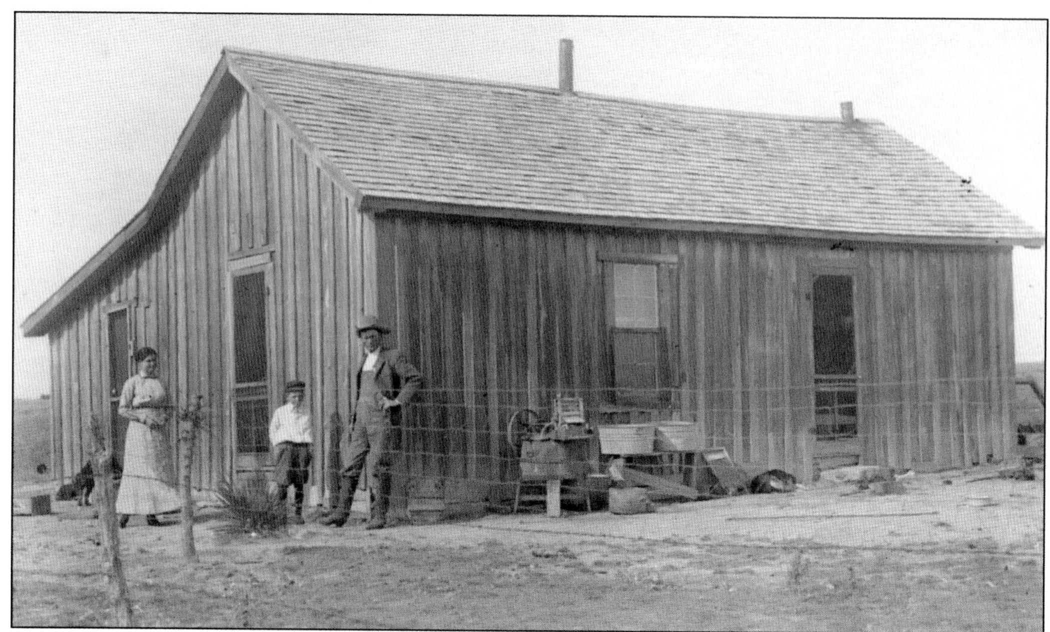

A typical farm family poses at their home near Ralston in Pawnee County. The house is surrounded by a fence to keep farm animals out of the yard. The man, his wife, and son are on the left. In front of the house is a hand-powered washing machine. The tubs to the right of the washing machine hold rinse water. The doors are covered with screens so that when they are left open to let in the air, insects cannot enter the house. (Courtesy of the Pawnee County Historical Society.)

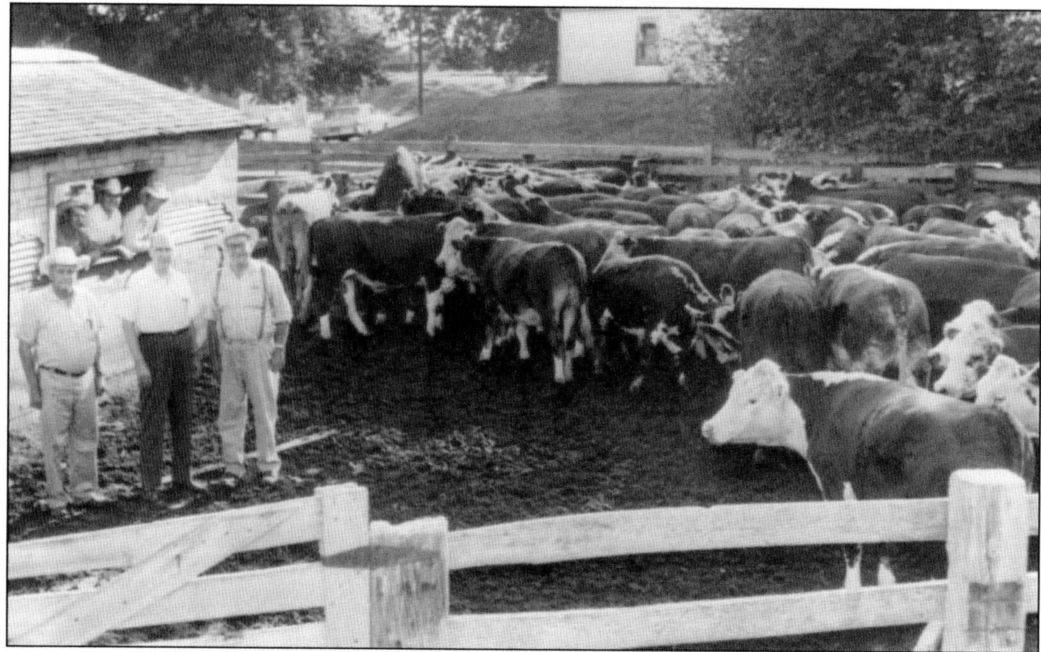

Pawnee County sheriff Charlie Burkdoll, (left) banker Don Hudson (center), and D. Burkdoll, the sheriff's son, are checking over Burkdoll's cattle. The sheriff's son-in-law Nolan Dunn is in the center of the cowboys in the window, peeking out. (Courtesy of the Pawnee County Historical Society.)

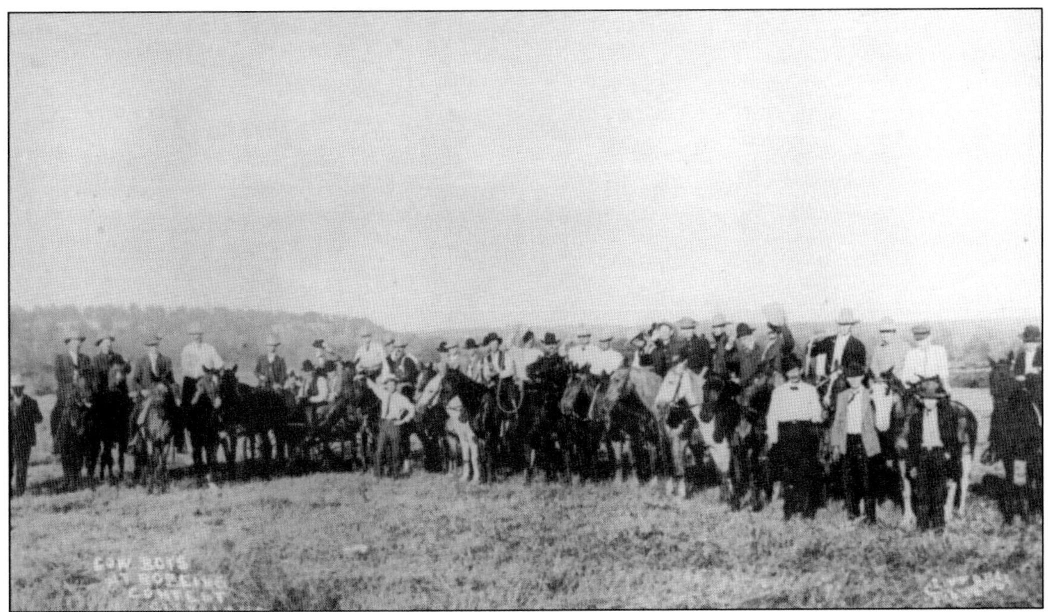

Cowboys from surrounding ranches gather for a roping contest at Cleveland in October 1906. The fifth mounted cowboy from the right is using his hat to shield his eyes from the sun. The man in the center is carrying a rope. Cowboy hats predominate, but a few derbies and caps can be seen. (Courtesy of the Pawnee County Historical Society.)

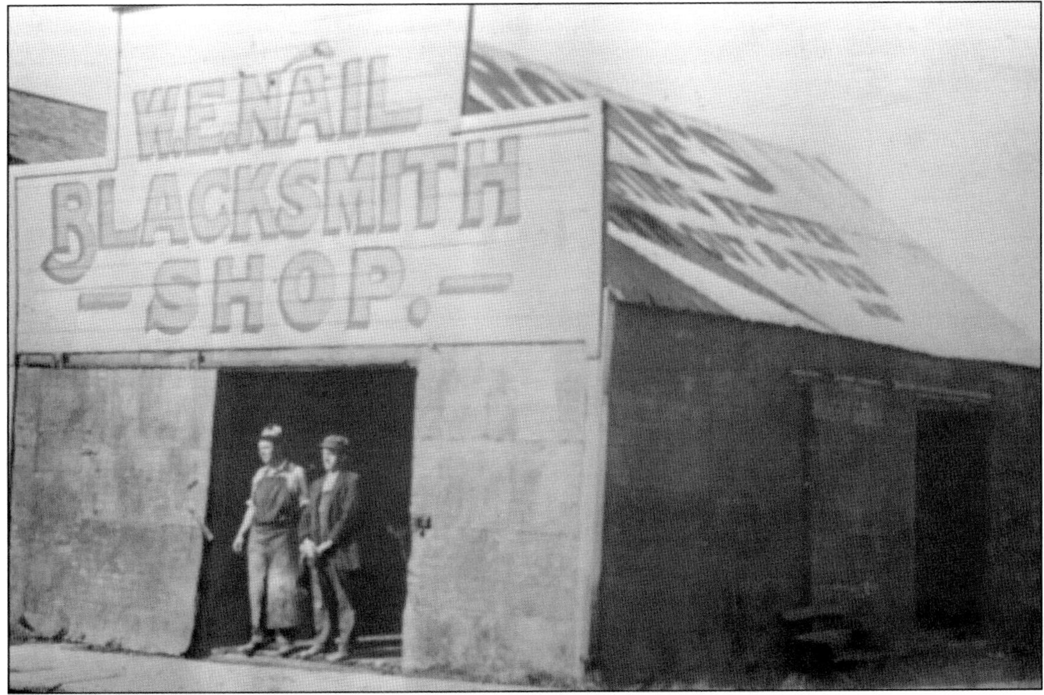

Farmers depended on local blacksmiths such as the W.E. Nail blacksmith shop in Pawnee to keep their farm implements in working order. The working blacksmith is the man wearing the leather apron in the doorway. The apron protected him from flying sparks and hot iron. (Courtesy of the Pawnee County Historical Society.)

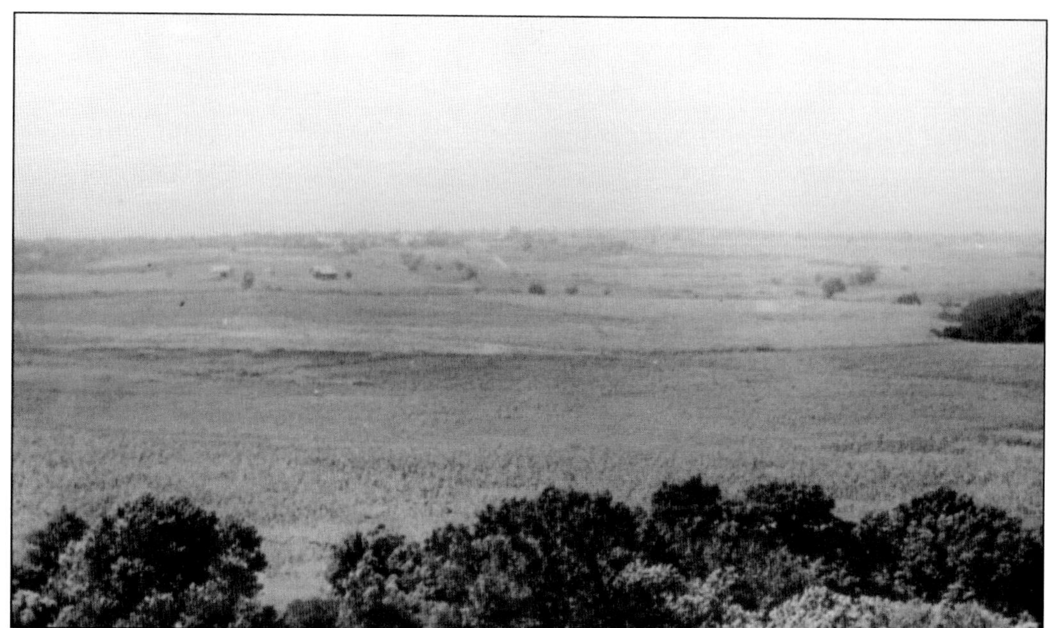

The open spaces and rich grassland attracted cattlemen to Pawnee County. As early as 1880, much of the ranchland in Texas had been grazed bare. Lease arrangements were quickly made with the Indians of Indian Territory to lease grazing rights. In 1883, the Cherokee Strip Live Stock Association, a consortium of cattlemen, paid the Cherokees $500,000 for a five-year lease to six million acres in the Cherokee Outlet. (Author's collection.)

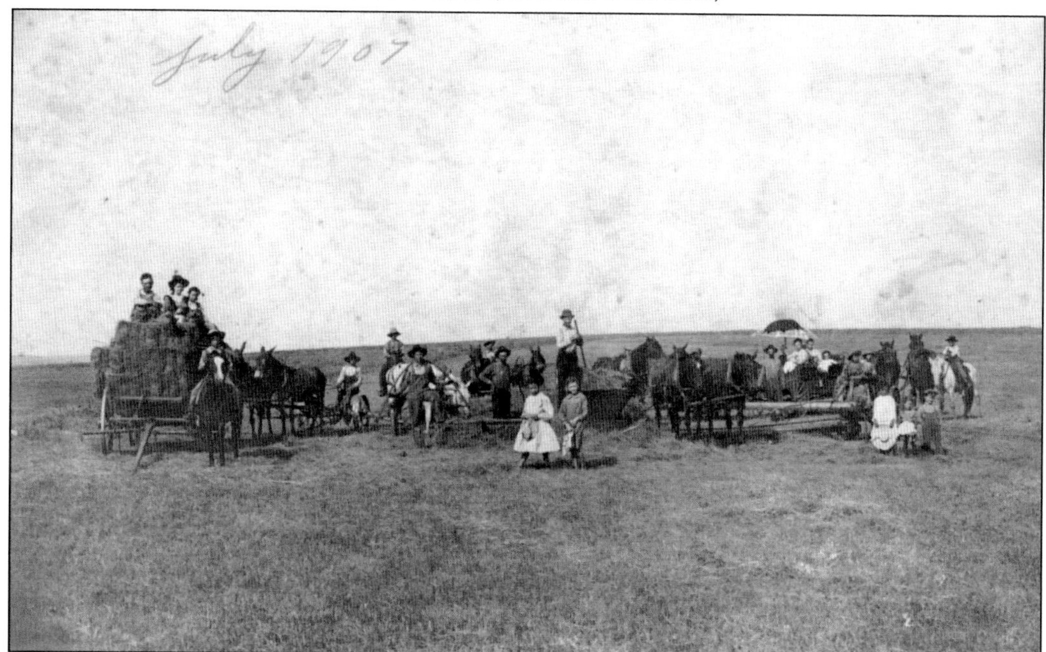

A farm family is seen cutting hay in Pawnee County in July 1907. The hay is cut, and then the rake, on the right, piles it into rows. The hay is gathered in piles and then fed into the baler in the center of the photograph. Once it is baled, it is loaded on the hay wagon on the left and either hauled to a barn for storage or market for sale. (Courtesy of the Pawnee County Historical Society.)

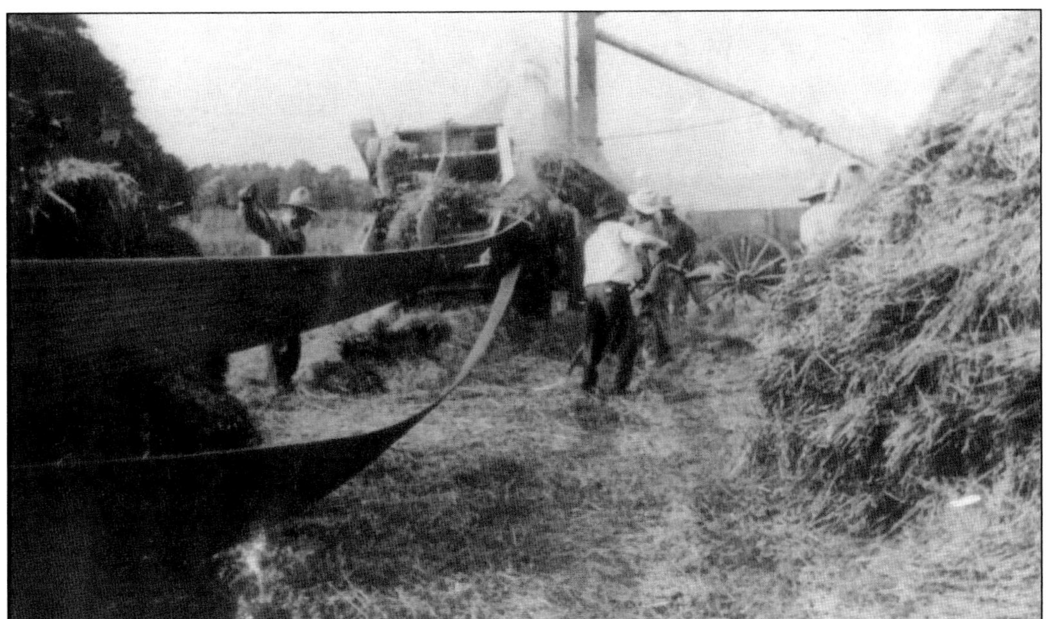

A steam-powered threshing machine is pictured here in operation in rural Pawnee County. The wheat was cut in the field and then hauled to a central location where the steam tractor was located. The boiler was fired up and power transferred to the threshing machine by the belt running from the tractor's power wheel to the thresher. Farmworkers then used pitchforks to throw the wheat into the thresher. (Courtesy of the Pawnee County Historical Society.)

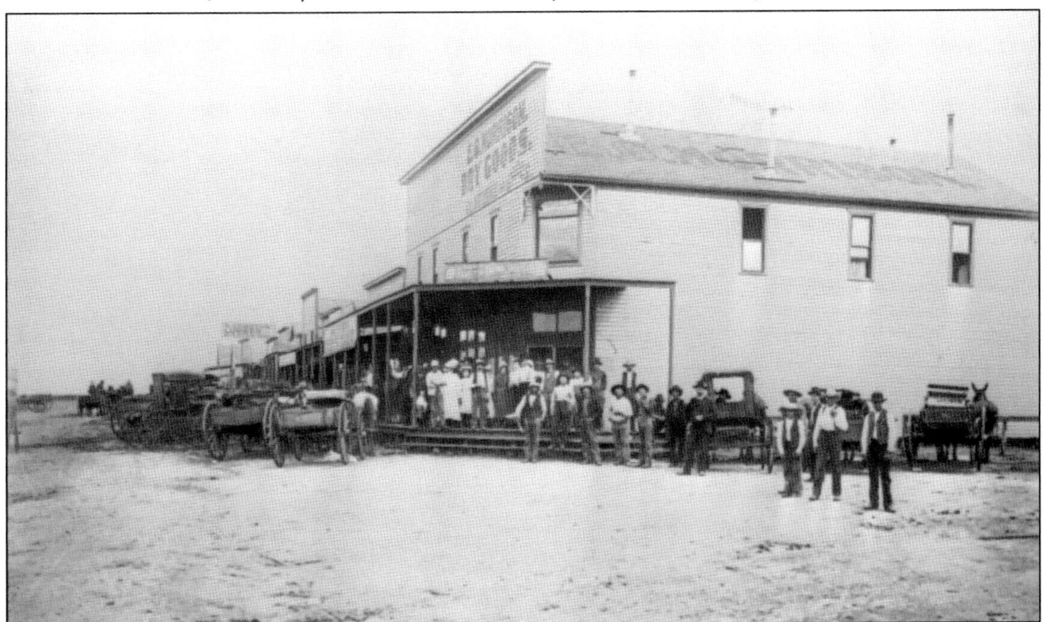

The E.G. Morrison dry-goods store was located in Pawnee. Note the farmers' wagons and people gathered in front of the store. Saturdays were usually given over by farmers dressing in their finest and making a trip into town to purchase supplies for the week. The wooden sidewalks are crowded with people taking the opportunity to visit with friends. (Courtesy of the Pawnee County Historical Society.)

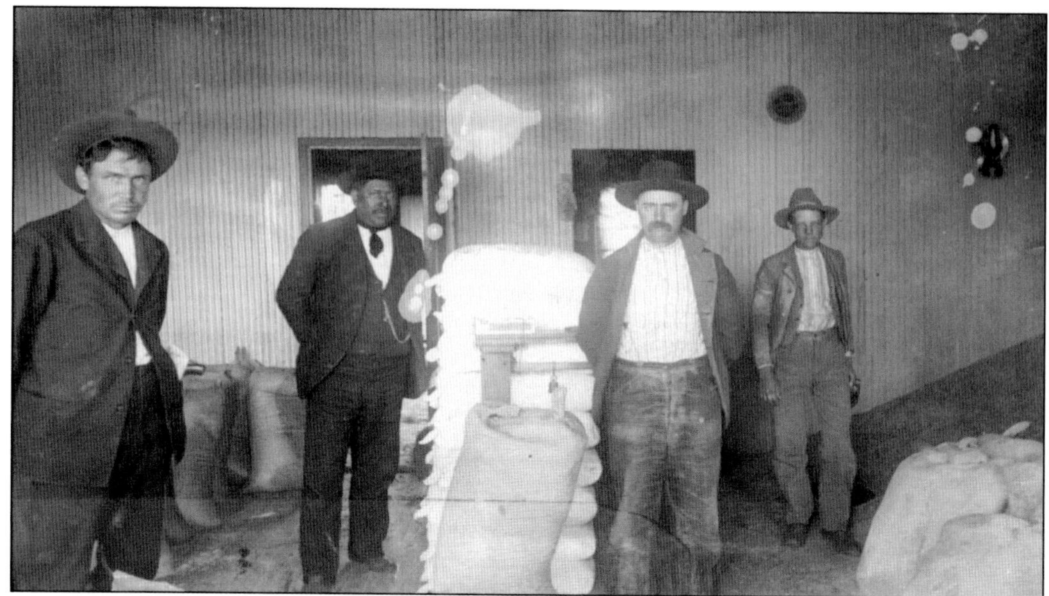

George E. Clark, owner of the feed store in Pawnee, purchased the produce of local farmers and then shipped it to market. The men are, from left to right, Jack Nail, John Morris, George E. Clark, and Carl Dunbar. Sacks of feed and seed can be seen stacked around the store's floor. (Courtesy of the Pawnee County Historical Society.)

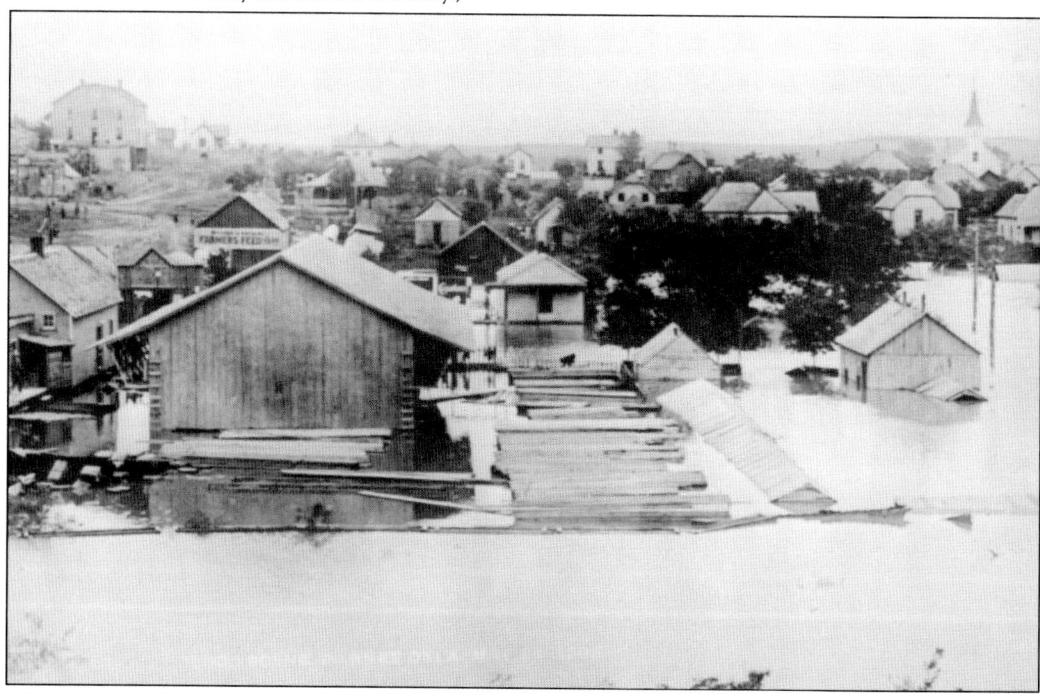

The Farmer's Feed Store in the center right of this photograph supplied farmers and ranchers in central Pawnee County with their agricultural needs. It barely escaped being swept away by the flood of 1908, in which Black Bear Creek flooded into eastern Pawnee. Note the people standing on the hill in the upper left watching to see how high the water would go. (Courtesy of the Pawnee County Historical Society.)

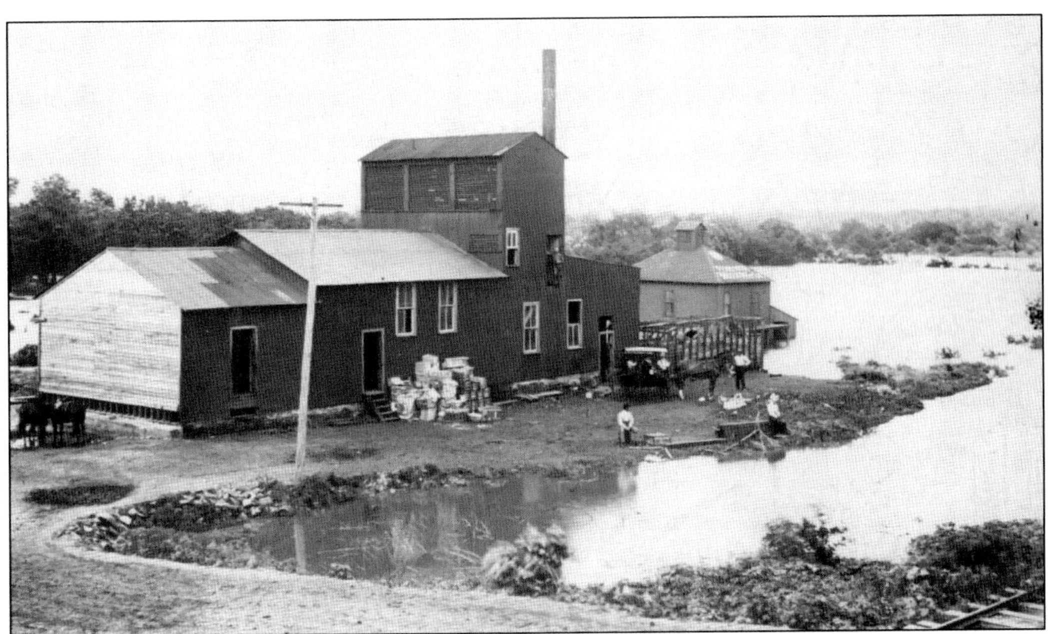

Harvested cotton was hauled to the Pawnee Cotton Gin in cotton wagons with high sides covered with wire. When the wagons arrived at the gin, a suction tube was used to empty the cotton from the wagons into the gin. Once inside the seeds were separated from the bolls of cotton and the cotton was then compressed into bales for shipment, usually by railroad. Note the railroad tracks in the lower right. (Courtesy of the Pawnee County Historical Society.)

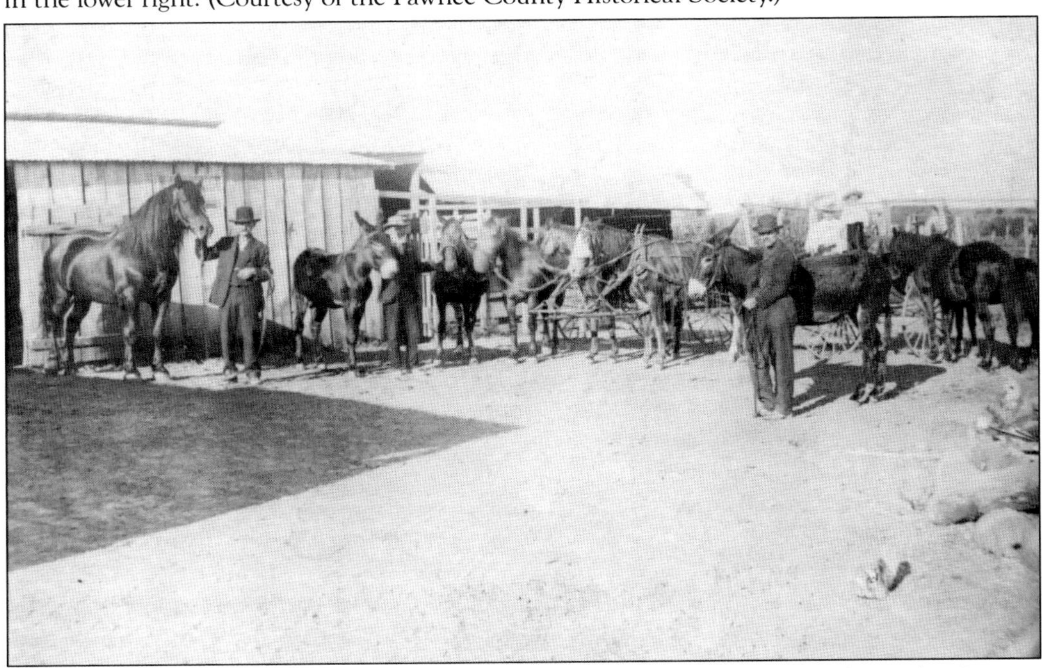

Bill and John Weeks of Skedee bred and sold many of the farm horses and mules used in Pawnee County. The man on the left of the photograph is holding the reins of a working horse; the man at center, a mule and a horse; and the other man, a mule. Draft animals preformed much of the work on many Pawnee County farms. (Courtesy of the Pawnee County Historical Society.)

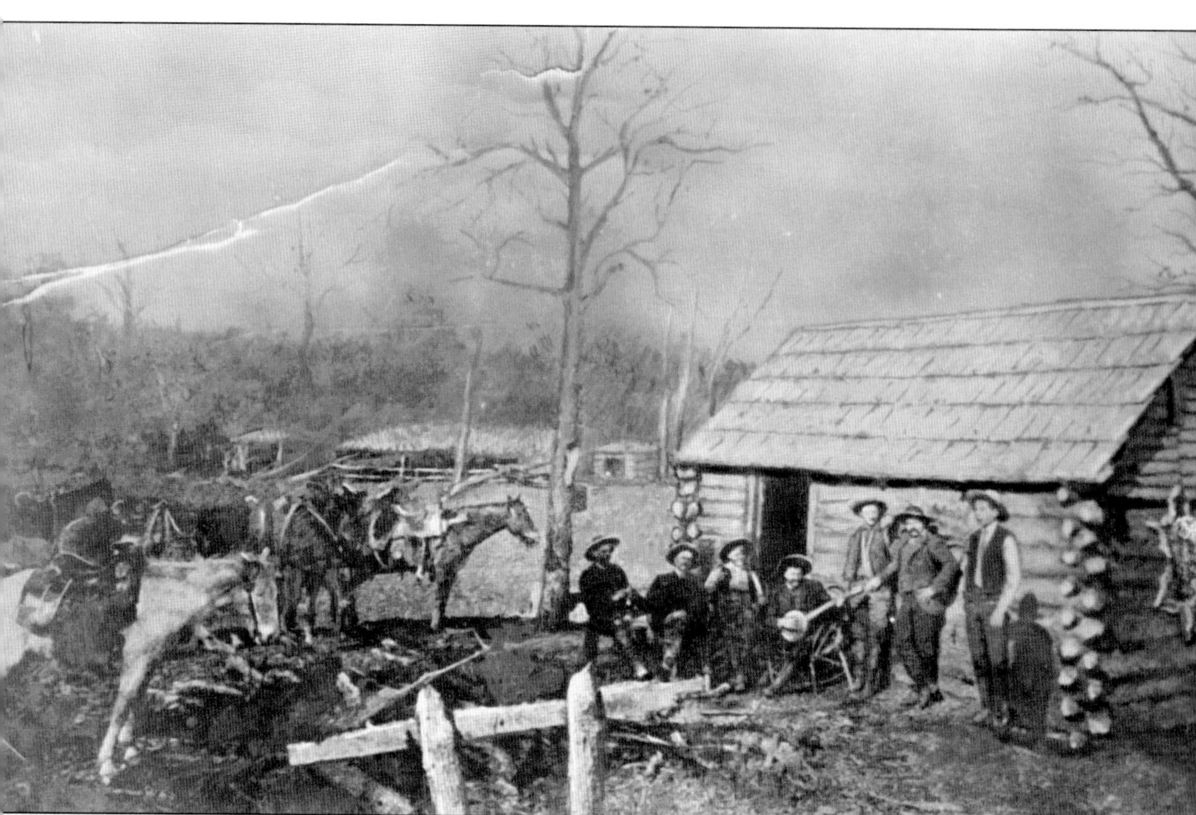

The day's work done, the cowboys of the Bar X Ranch are gathered in front of the bunkhouse, where they are being entertained by one of them playing a banjo. Note the animal pelts nailed to the side of the bunkhouse. The man on the far left of those sitting is rolling a cigarette from a pouch of tobacco. (Courtesy of the Pawnee County Historical Society.)

Four

Q County

In October 1891, the Pawnees agreed to accept individual allotments, and two years later, on September 16, 1893, Pawnee County and the rest of the Cherokee Outlet were thrown open to homesteaders by the Land Run of 1893. Now a part of Oklahoma Territory, what later became Pawnee County was given the designation of Q County, which included the townships of Banner, Burnham, Liberty, Hoke Smith, and Jordan Valley.

On April 21, 1904, Congress ordered the allotment of Otoe-Missouri land and the dissolution of their tribal government. The Otoe-Missouri Reservation was then divided between Noble and Pawnee Counties.

Townsite No. 13 was named the seat of Q County until November 1894, when voters chose between Pawnee and Queen for a permanent name. Pawnee won by a 2-1 vote, and on January 12, 1894, a petition was filed to name Pawnee the permanent county seat. Post offices quickly were established in Pawnee, Herbert (Cleveland), Jennings, Riverside (Ralston), Blackburn, Basin, Bedford, Bryan, Casey, Chilco, Crystal, Dixie, Edgar, Filson, Hallett, Keystone, Lela, Leroy, Lawson (Quay), Masham, Maramec, Osage City, Rambo, Schley, Sinnett, Skedee, Terlton, and Valley.

At the transition from territory to statehood, there was a movement, headed by Cleveland leaders, to join a portion of eastern Pawnee County and southeastern Osage County to form a new county, with Cleveland as the county seat. The plan was thwarted when the Oklahoma Enabling Act required the Osage Nation to be a single county.

In 1916, another attempt was made to alter the boundaries of Pawnee County. With the development of the Cushing Oil Field, residents of the oil-rich area around Oilton wanted to take 45 square miles of Creek County and add it to Pawnee County. However, the area was separated from Pawnee County by the Cimarron River, and the high cost of bridging the river, coupled with the fact some of the land to be annexed was Indian land and not taxable, resulted in the effort being defeat by voters 866 to 555.

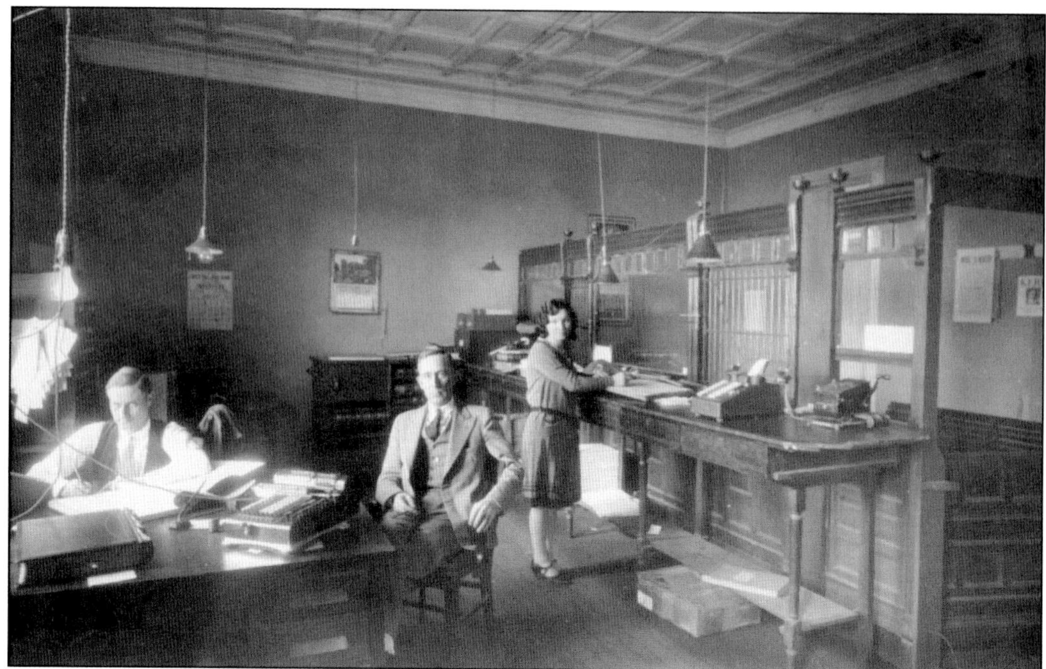

This photograph is of the office of the Pawnee County treasurer in the county courthouse in 1931. Charles P. Livesary, the county treasurer, is in the center. His two deputies, Wilma Culver Bradley (right) and Leo Hampton, can be seen working. People would pay their taxes at the windows on the right, and then Hampton would enter them by hand in the ledger books. (Courtesy of the Pawnee County Historical Society.)

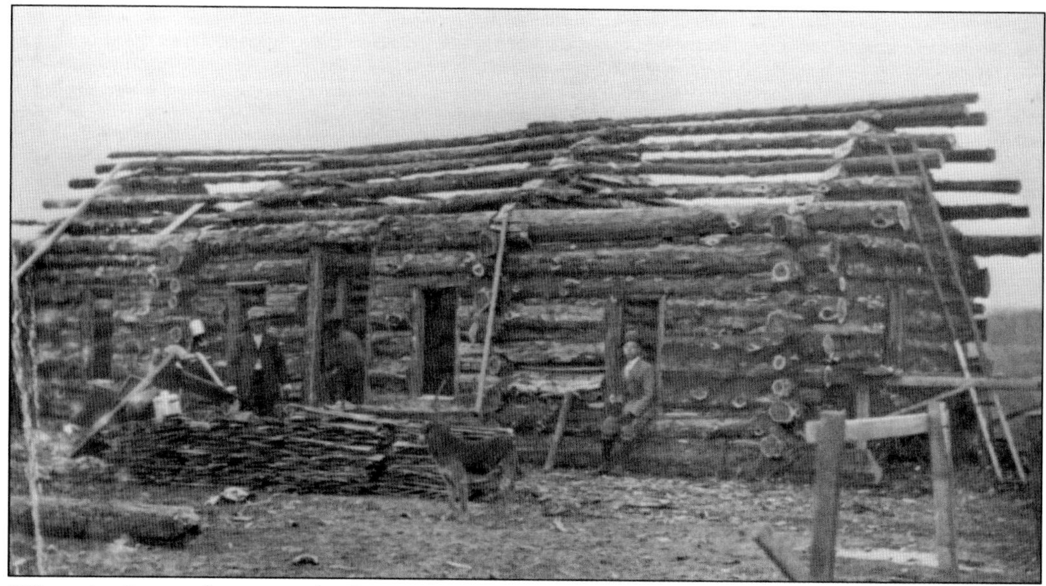

When the first settlers arrived in Pawnee County, they used the region's plentiful supply of trees to construct log cabins such as this. The cedar logs have been cut, notched to fit together, and stacked to form the cabin's walls. The chinking has not yet been placed between the logs to make the cabin airtight. Rafters have been laid to form the backbone for a roof, and shingles are stacked in front of the cabin, waiting to be installed. (Courtesy of the Pawnee County Historical Society.)

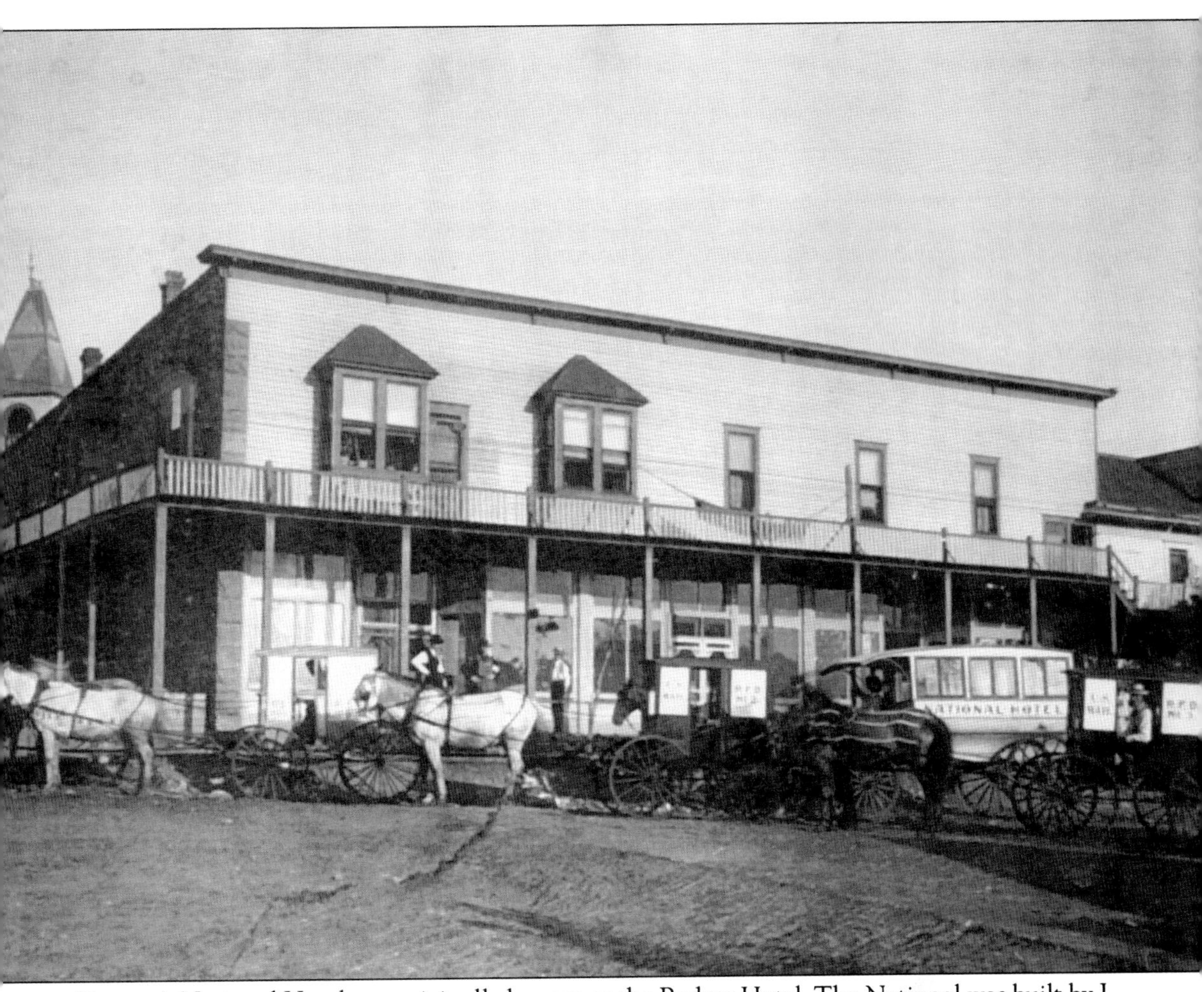

Pawnee's National Hotel was originally known as the Badger Hotel. The National was built by J. S. Badger in 1893 and eventually contained 40 rooms. Note the hotel's hack parked in front. It was used to convey guests from the hotel to the railroad depot. Also in front are three US mail hacks from the rural free delivery mail service. They carried the mail from Pawnee throughout the nearby farming area. (Courtesy of the Pawnee County Historical Society.)

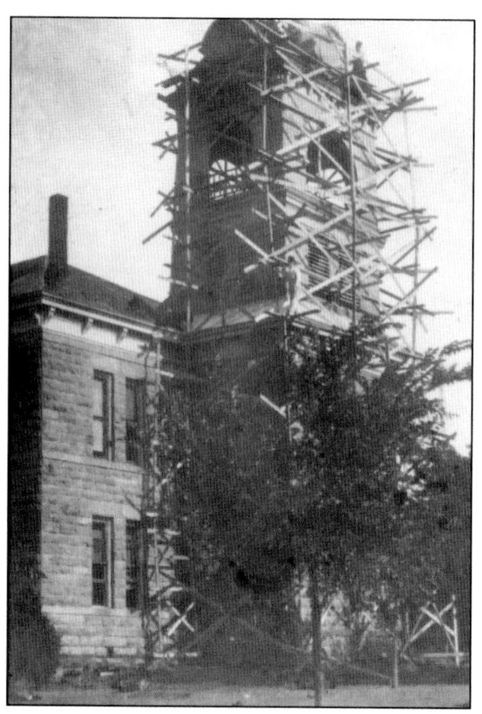

Scaffolding surrounds the tower on the east side of the cut-stone original Pawnee Courthouse. The tower was the last part of the courthouse to be completed before its opening in 1895. Before the courthouse could be built, prison laborers had to fill in a large gully on the west side of the courthouse square. When the courthouse was completed, the county jail was moved to a two-story building on the northeast corner of the courthouse square. (Courtesy of the Pawnee County Historical Society.)

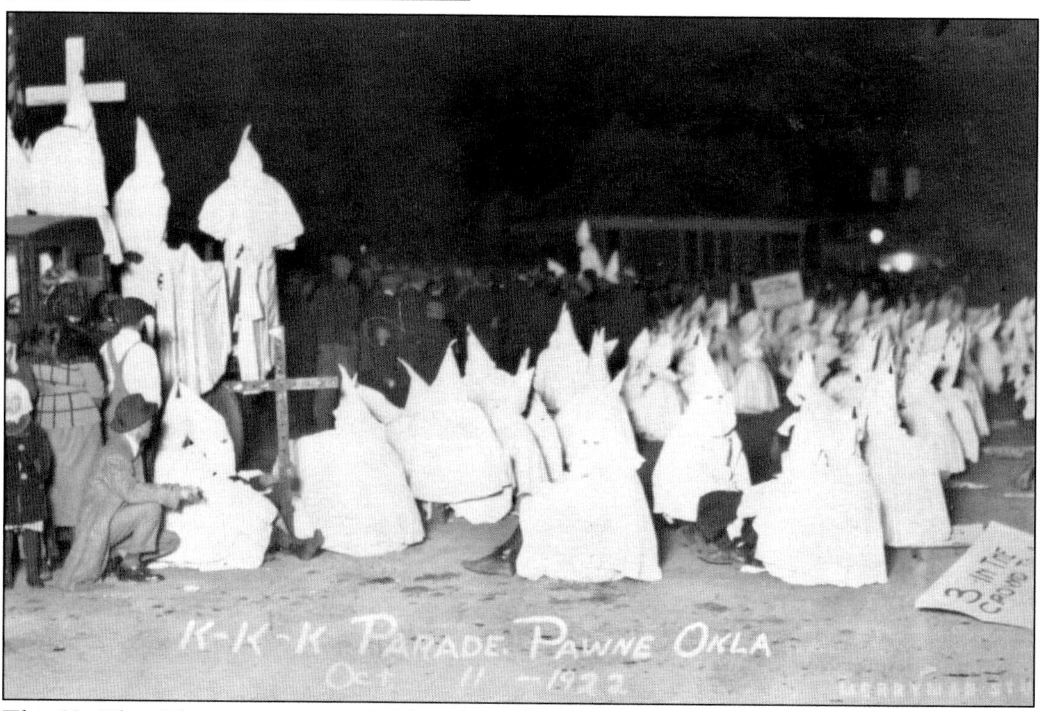

This Ku Klux Klan meeting was held in the town of Pawnee. The Kluxers, as KKK members were called, were active throughout Pawnee County. Note the women and children attending the meeting. The Klan had a ladies auxiliary and a "Kiddie Klan" open to females and children. The cross being held in the left foreground is made of two yardsticks fastened together. (Courtesy of the Pawnee County Historical Society.)

The Eastern Oklahoma Railroad, which became a part of the Atchison, Topeka & Santa Fe, maintained a concrete coal chute at Skedee. Coal would be hauled to the facility and stored inside. The chute sat across the railroad tracks so that trains that needed to replenish their supplies of coal could simply stop beneath the chute and refill their coal cars. (Courtesy of the Pawnee County Historical Society.)

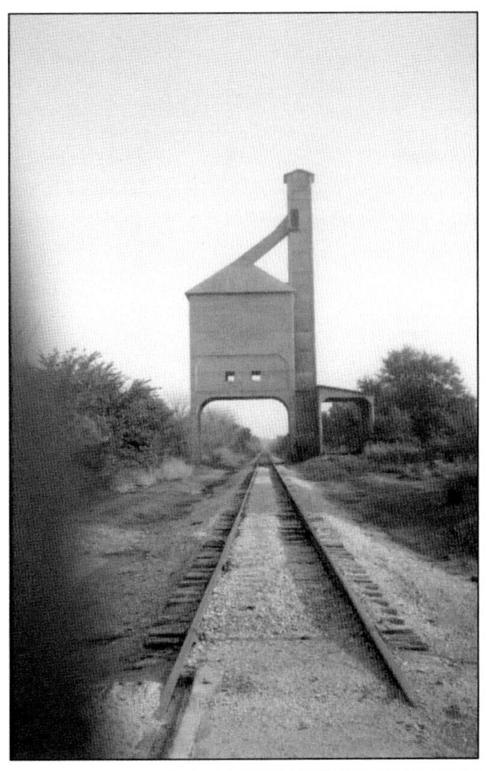

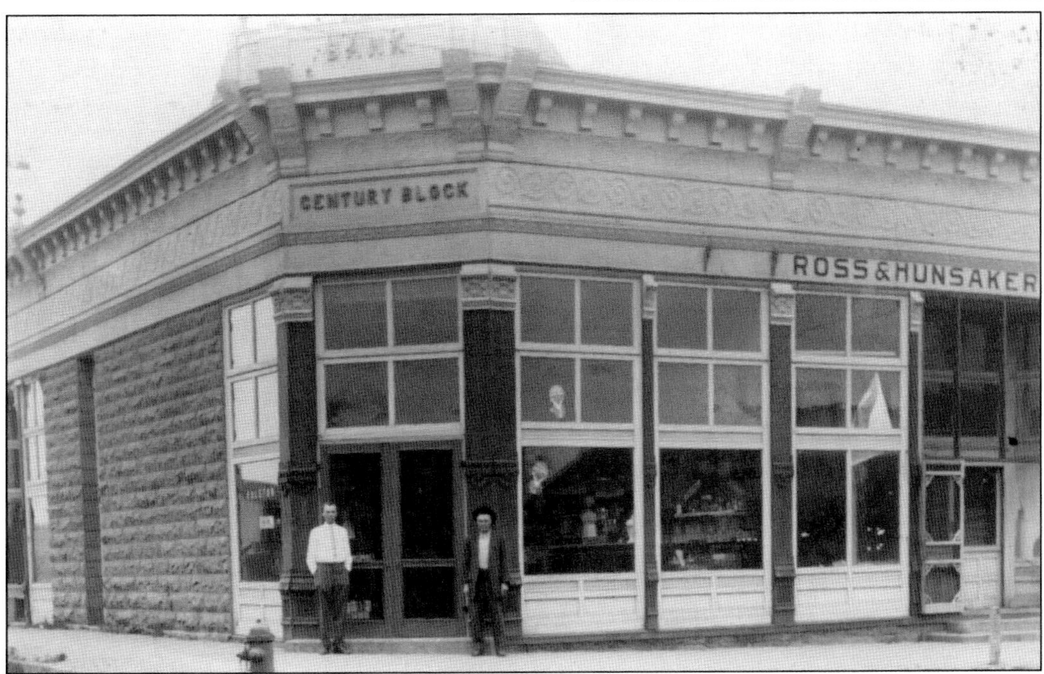

The Exchange Bank was in the Century Block in downtown Ralston. The town's early wooden sidewalks have been replaced by concrete ones in this photograph. The door to the bank is angled to provide access from both streets in the intersection. Next door is the Ross & Hunsaker dry-goods store. (Courtesy of the Pawnee County Historical Society.)

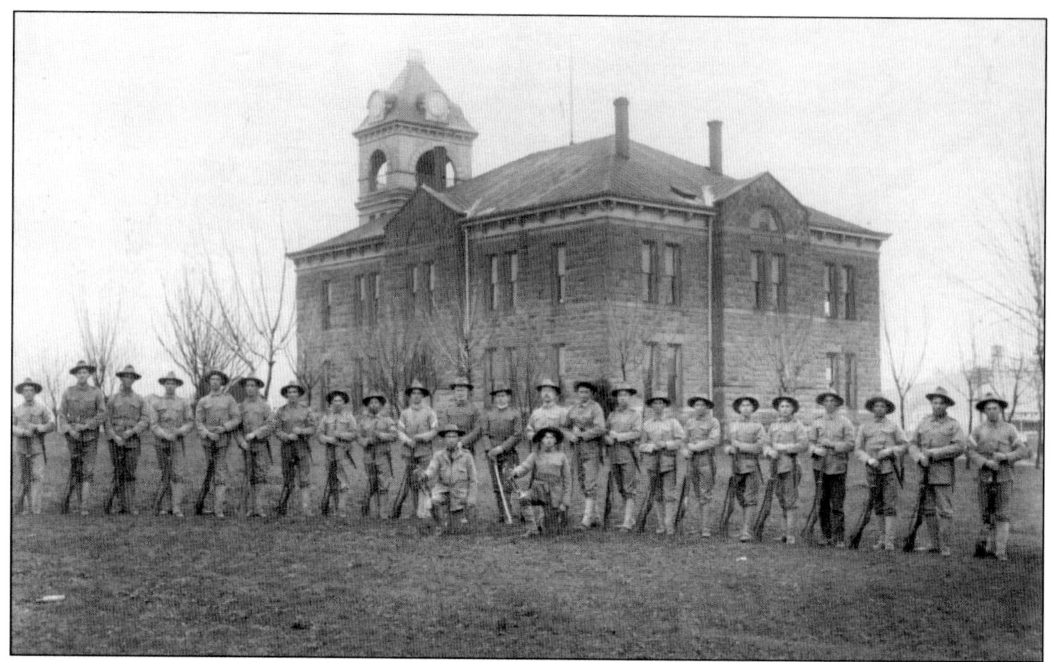

Members of Troop D of the Rough Riders are posing before the Pawnee County Courthouse. Their commanding officer was Lt. Charles Stewart. Kneeling in front of Stewart are the troops two buglers. The men are equipped with Krag-Jorgensen rifles and are wearing khaki uniforms issued for field duty. (Courtesy of the Pawnee County Historical Society.)

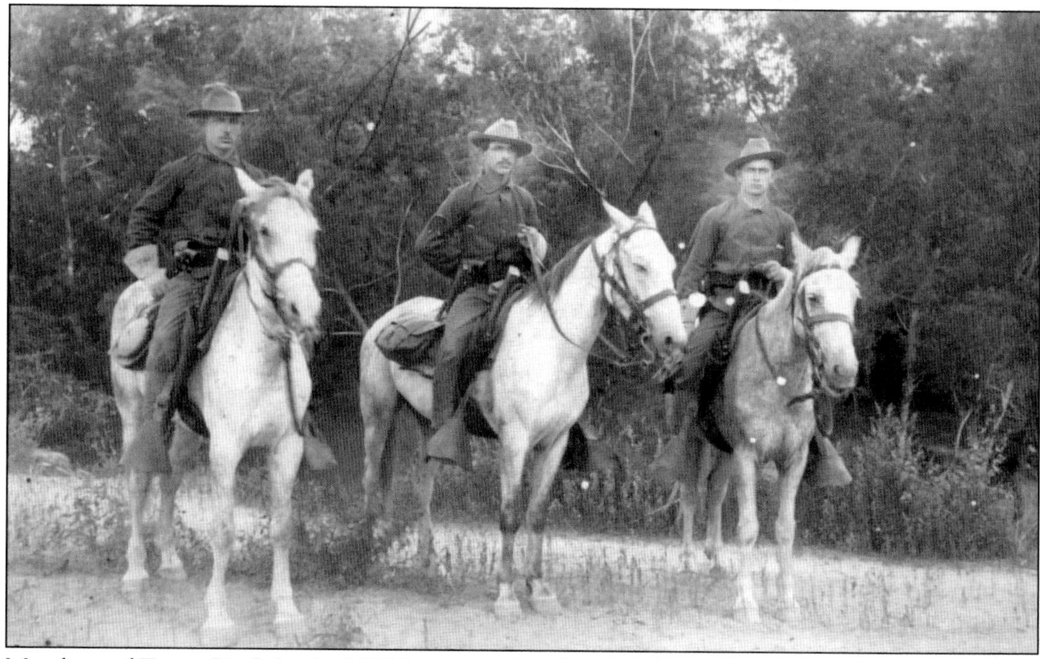

Members of Troop D of the 1st US Volunteer Cavalry were better known as the Rough Riders, organized by Lt. Col. Theodore Roosevelt to serve in the Spanish-American War. Most Troop D members were raised in Pawnee County. Pictured here are, from left to right, Clyde H. Stewart, Arthur G. Luther, and Claire H. Stewart. (Courtesy of the Pawnee County Historical Society.)

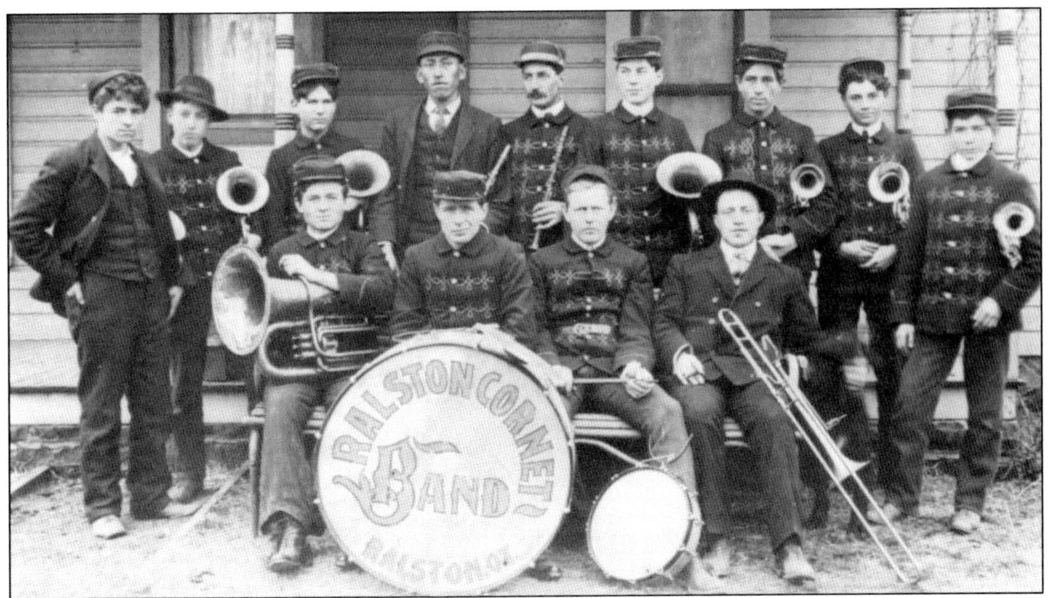

The 12-member Ralston Cornet Band was formed as Ralston progressed from a frontier community to a modern town. One of Ralston's premier attractions was its annual corn carnival, which attracted thousands of visitors. The completion of the Gulf Oil Company's pipeline from El Dorado, Kansas, through Ralston, to Beaumont, Texas, helped the local economy boom when oil was discovered nearby in 1909. (Courtesy of the Pawnee County Historical Society.)

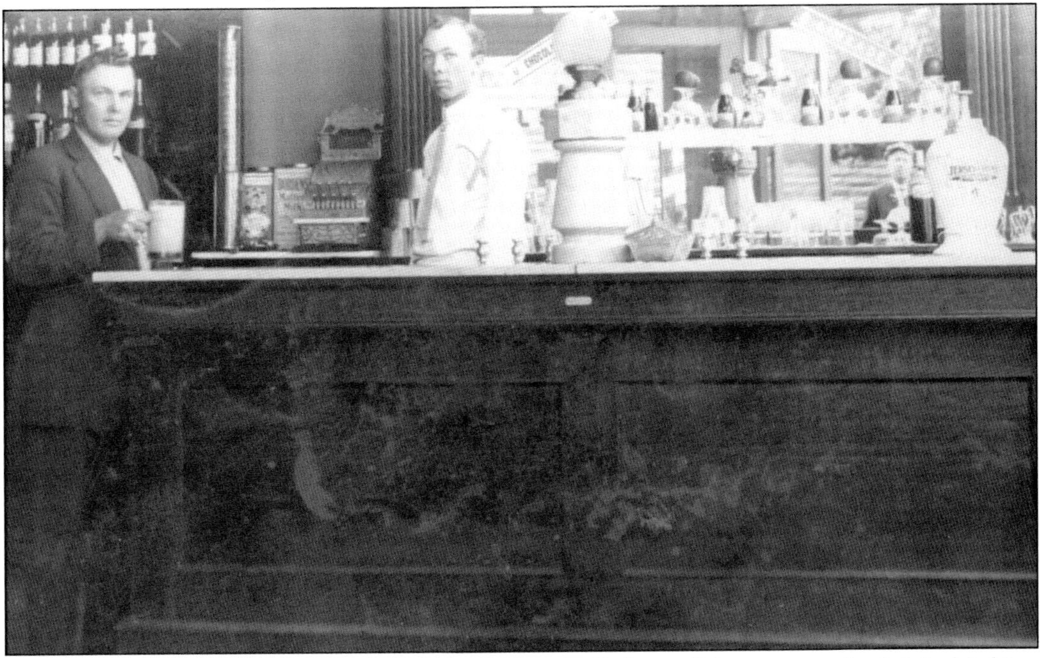

The Ralston Confectionery was located in downtown Ralston. The man on the left is drinking a soda. The dispenser on the right offers Jersey cream, as does the container next to the large dispenser in the center. To the left of the cash register are containers of malted milk and cocoa. The soda jerk would use the various ingredients to individually mix drinks to order. (Courtesy of the Pawnee County Historical Society.)

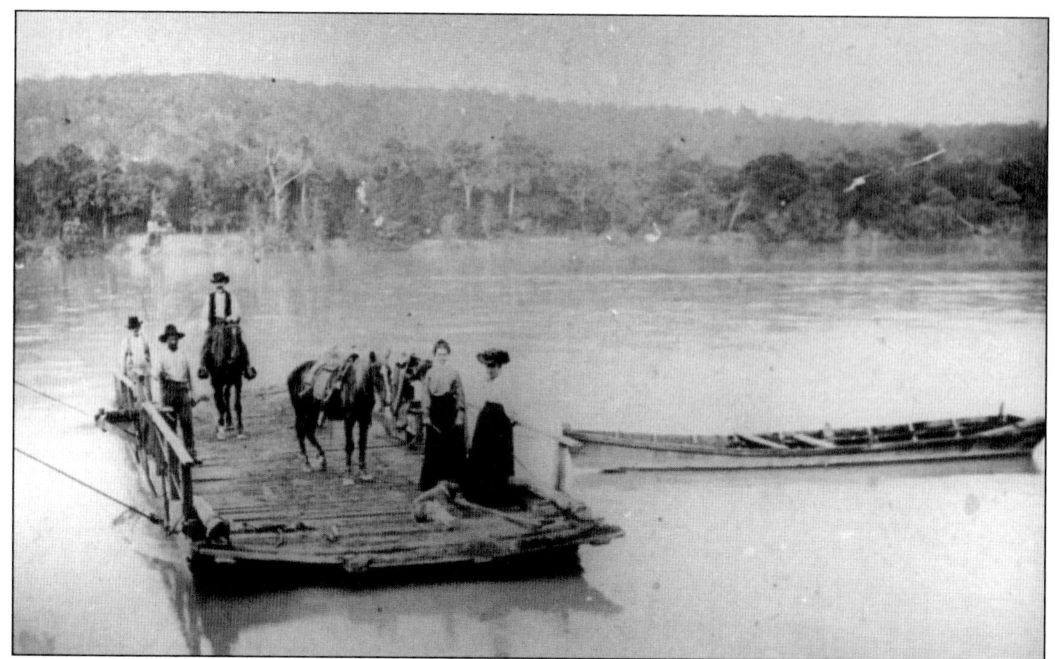

Stout's Ferry was just to the northeast of Cleveland across the Arkansas River to the west. A cable, used to pull the ferry across the river, was stretched across the waterway. The ferry was attached to the cable on the downstream by two other cables seen on the left of the photograph. (Author's collection.)

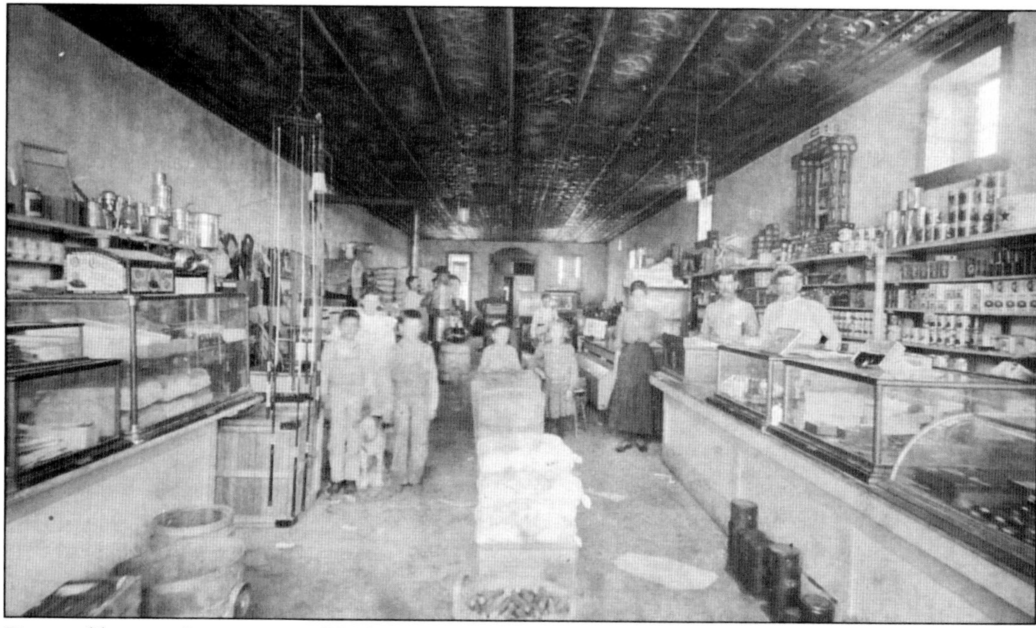

Pictured here is the interior of T.H. Cox's Staple and Fancy Grocery store in Skedee. In addition to ordinary grocery supplies, Cox's store offered other items such as the fishing poles hanging from the ceiling on the left. Note the decorative tin ceiling in the store. Cox was one of the founders of the *Skedee Hustler*, a weekly newspaper started in 1904. (Courtesy of the Pawnee County Historical Society.)

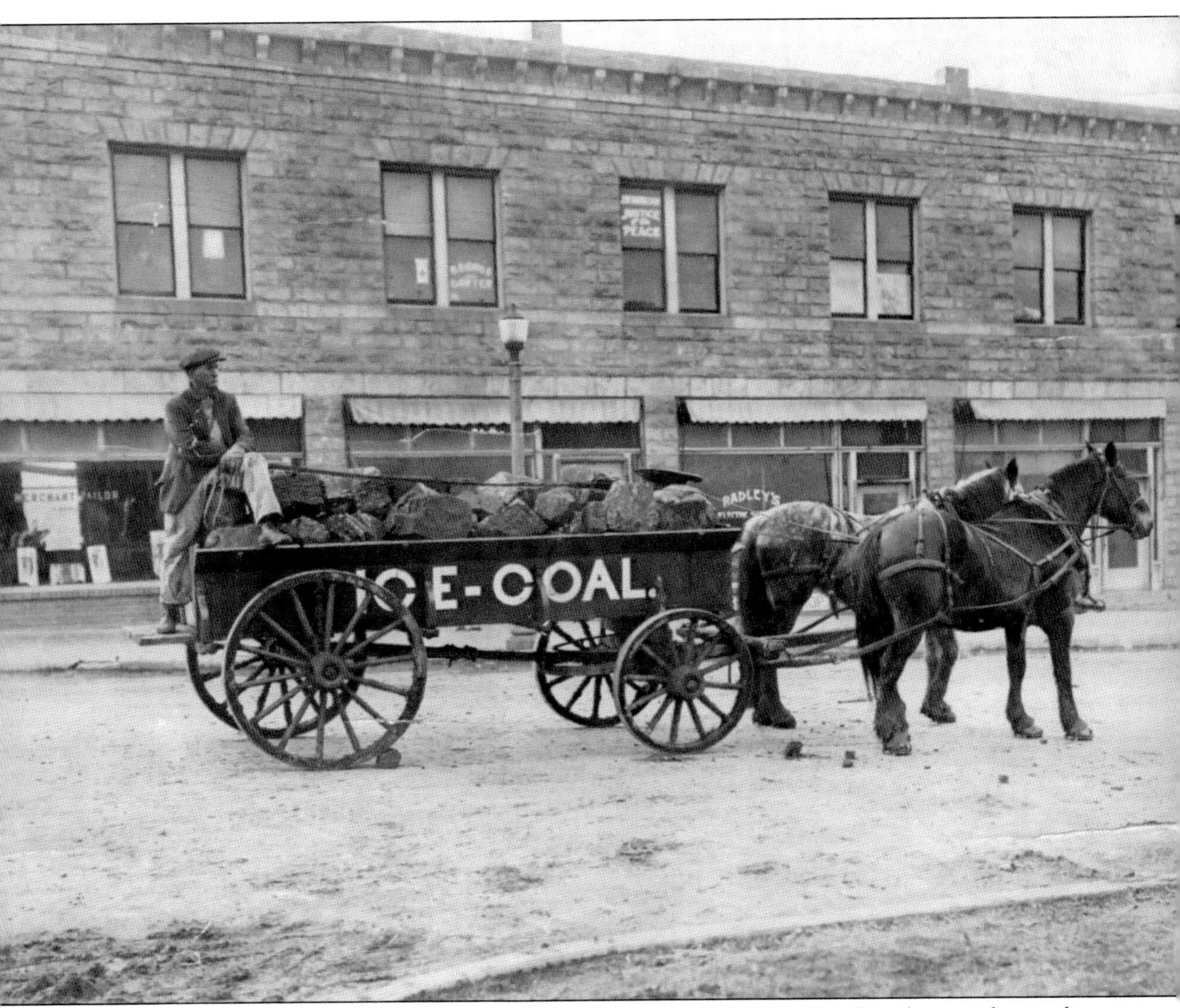

Heat was provided by coal or woodstoves. This coal wagon sold chunks of coal to residents who would break the chunks into smaller pieces to be fed into stoves. A piece of coal has been placed beneath the rear wheel to keep the wagon from moving. On the second floor of the building is the office of Pawnee's justice of the peace. He handled small offenses, and his salary was based on the money he collected in fines. (Courtesy of the Pawnee County Historical Society.)

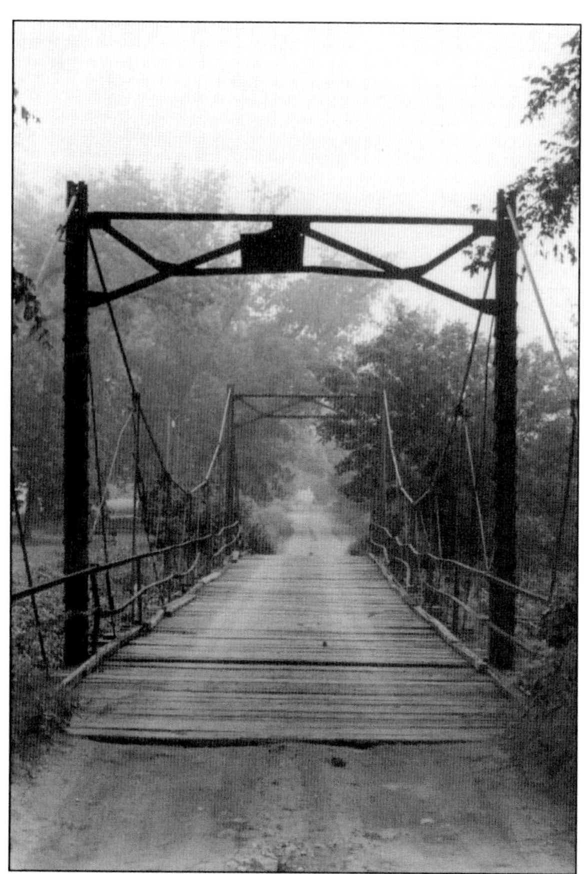

This wood-floored swinging bridge over Black Bear Creek was just to the west of Lela. Located five miles west of Pawnee, on the Pawnee County–Noble County line, Lela was granted a post office in 1894. On October 3, 1905, the post office name was changed to Valeria, only to be changed back to Lela less than a year later. (Courtesy of the Pawnee County Historical Society.)

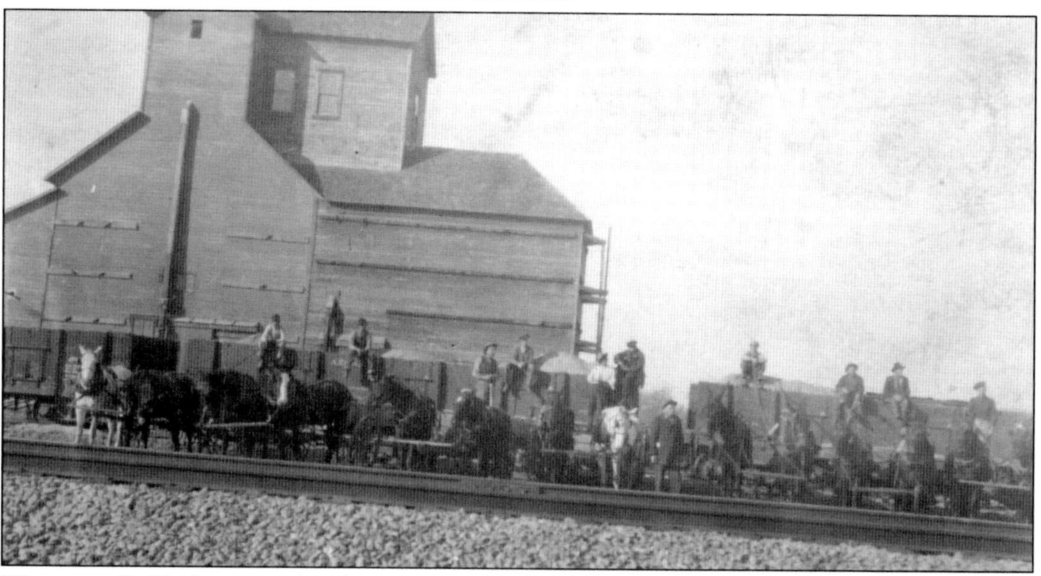

Wagons pulled by horses and mules wait to unload at the Ralston elevator. In the forefront are the Atchison, Topeka & Santa Fe Railway tracks. The railway offered an easy method for farmers to ship their produce to market. The chute on the side of the elevator was used to fill empty wagons. (Courtesy of the Pawnee County Historical Society.)

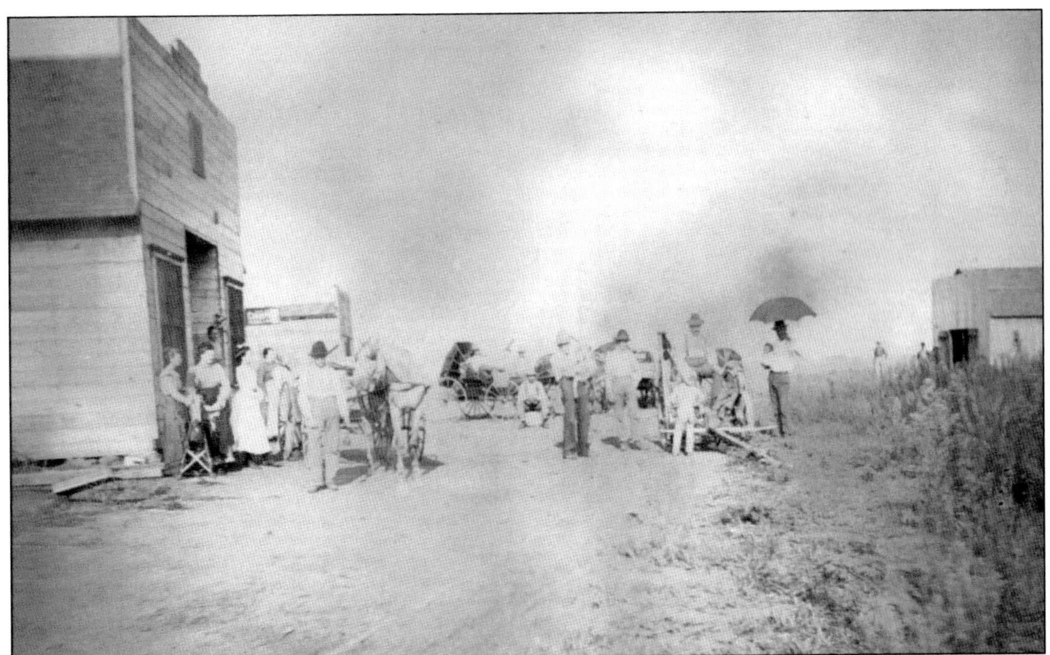

Named for prominent Pawnee County resident Cassius W. Rambo, the town of Rambo was located six miles southwest of Pawnee on the Atchison, Topeka & Santa Fe Railway. Shown in this photograph is the main street of Rambo. Note the man on the right using an umbrella to shield the child he is carrying from the sun. (Courtesy of the Pawnee County Historical Society.)

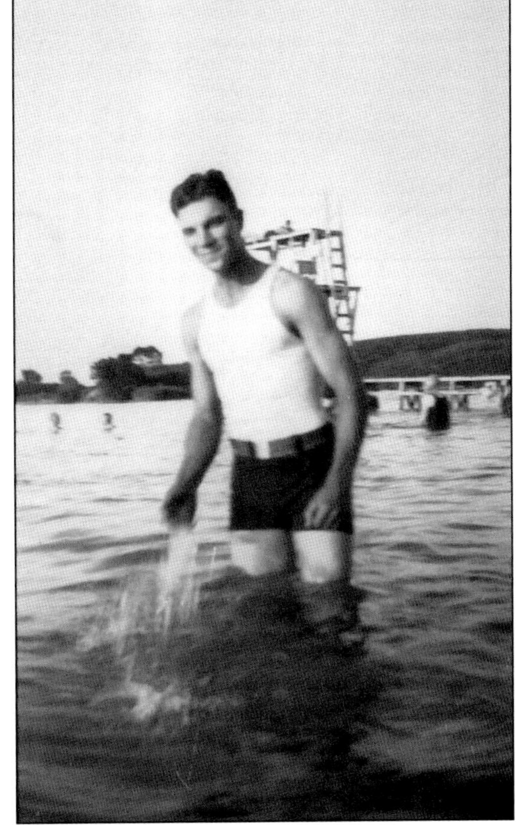

Constructed in 1903 by horse-drawn scoops, Maramec Lake was a popular recreation spot for people in eastern Pawnee County, and many cabins were built around the lake. Note the pier reaching from the shore of the lake to a diving platform. Eventually, the lake homes fell into disrepair, and many of the lake's recreational facilities rotted. (Courtesy of the Pawnee County Historical Society.)

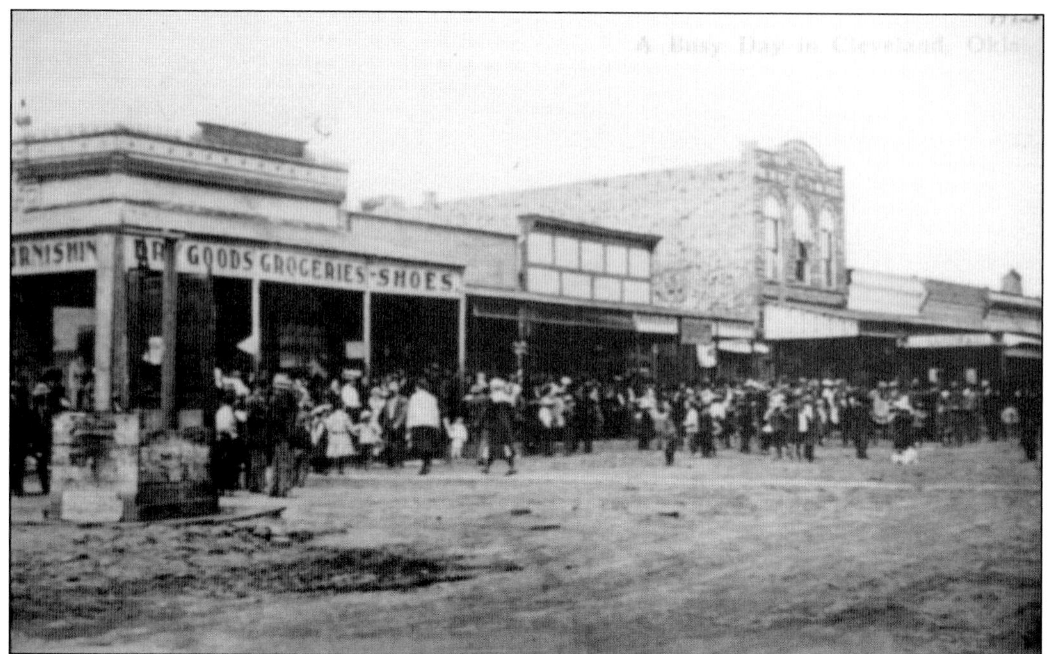

By 1912, concrete walkways had been built across Cleveland's main street to keep pedestrians out of the muddy dirt thoroughfares. The town's well can be seen on the left of this photograph. This is probably a Saturday, when people from the surrounding area flocked to Cleveland to do their weekly shopping. Note the mudhole by the town well. (Courtesy of Evelyn "Zeke" Cheek.)

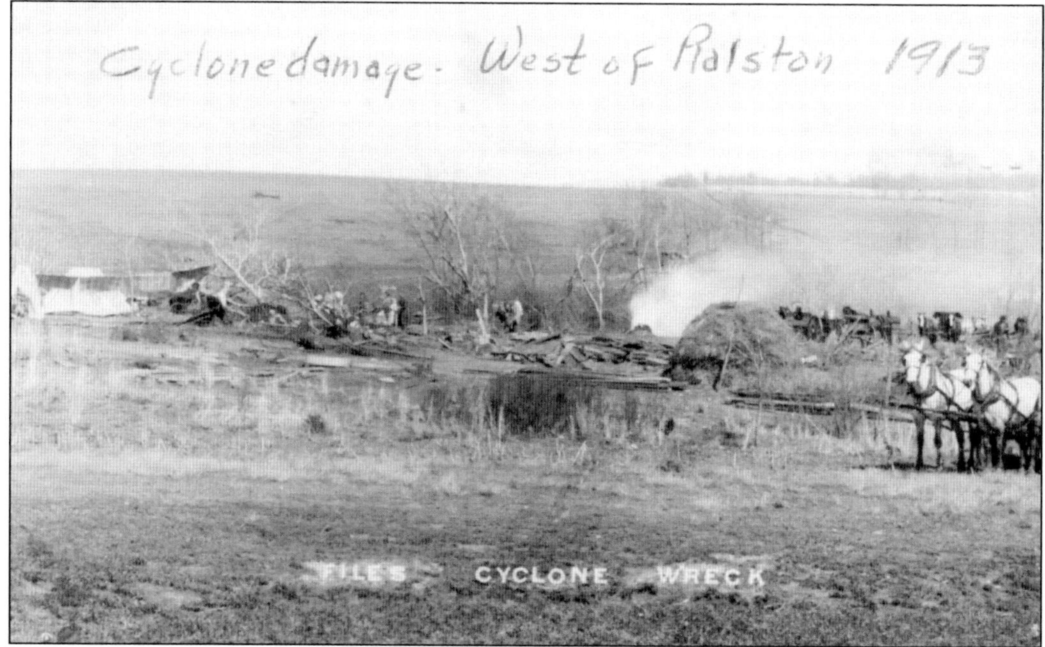

In 1913, a tornado tore through northern Pawnee. This is a photograph of the damage caused by the storm west of Ralston. A haystack remains on the right of the photograph, but the house on the left has been demolished. Note the uprooted trees in the center. Neighbors have gathered to help recover what they can. (Courtesy of the Pawnee County Historical Society.)

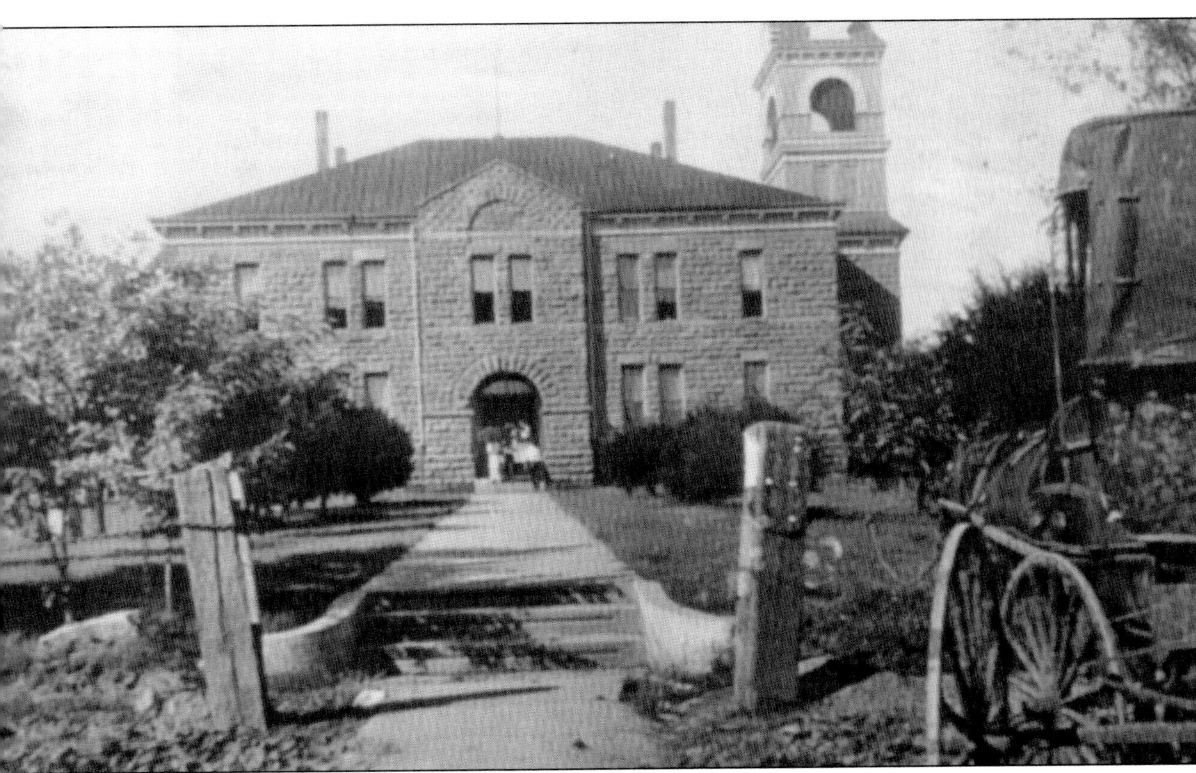

This is the newly completed Pawnee County Courthouse's south entrance. The courthouse was in the center of the town square, which also contained a residence for the county sheriff. A chain surrounded the square, both to keep animals off the grass and to serve as a hitching place for horse-drawn wagons. The name "Pawnee" is engraved in cut stone above the entrance. (Courtesy of the Pawnee County Historical Society.)

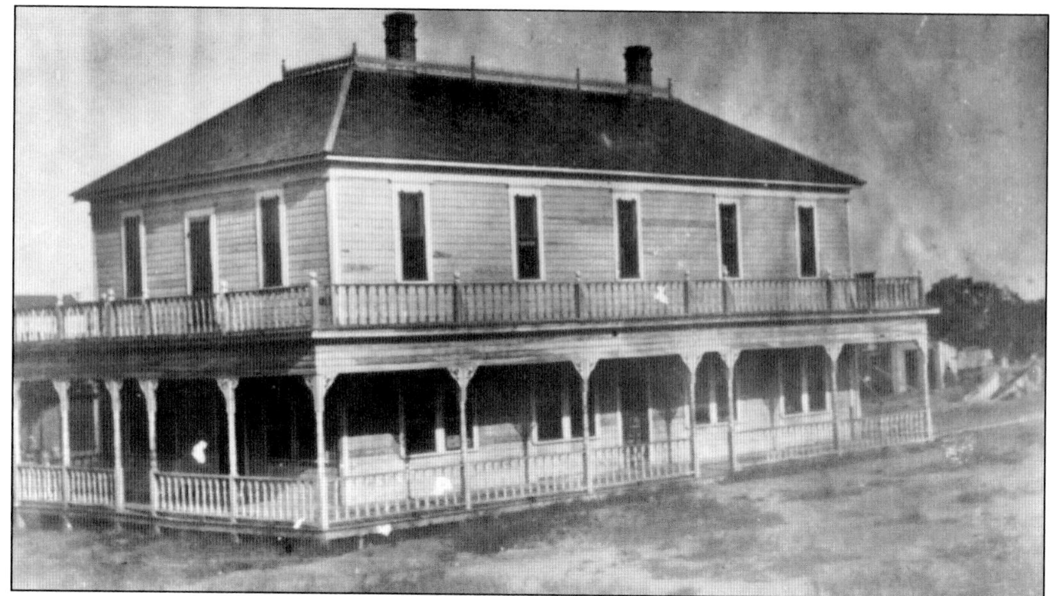

Note the entrance to a storm cave, as storm shelters were called then, at the rear of the Skedee Hotel. Severe storms and tornados were always a threat in Pawnee County during the spring. The underground storm cave gave residents of the hotel a better place to seek cover than the wooden hotel. (Courtesy of the Pawnee County Historical Society.)

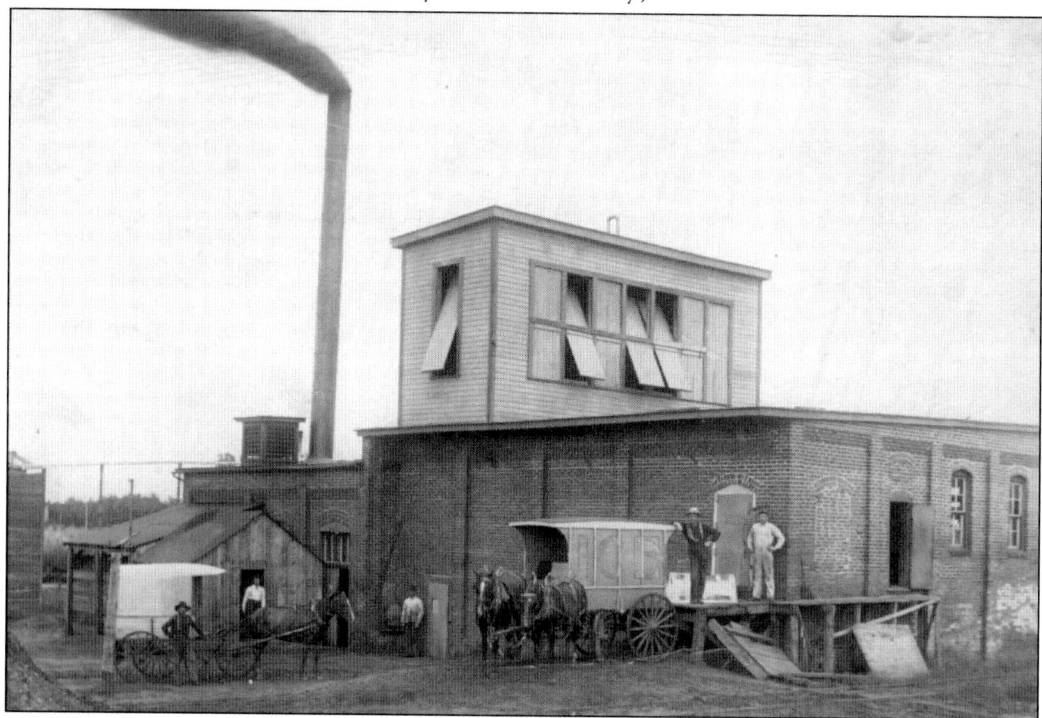

Pictured here is Pawnee's ice plant shortly after statehood. There were no electric refrigerators; instead, people purchased ice and placed it in an insulated wooden icebox. The ice kept the contents of the box cool and prevented them from spoiling. The ice wagons, backed up to the dock on the right, hauled the ice to customers. (Courtesy of the Pawnee County Historical Society.)

Five

Townsite 13

Pawnee's original townsite comprised 200 acres at a horseshoe bend called Rocky Ford across Black Bear Creek. Unfortunately, when the lots were offered for sale, the original plat was missing. Only after C.L. Berry was hurriedly dispatched to the land office in Perry to secure another plat were the sales allowed to resume.

Once Pawnee became the official seat of Pawnee County, federal court was held in a tent pitched on the courthouse square. A federal jail was constructed one block north and east of the square. To finance the courthouse, funds were raised through a company that sold stock to individuals. Once the county's tax base was well established, county officials bought back the stock.

In 1899, the Atchison, Topeka & Santa Fe Railway extended its line to Pawnee, and three years later, the St. Louis–Francisco Railroad arrived. This gave the community both north-south and east-west rail service. Pawnee became a major rail center with four passenger and four mail trains arriving daily.

Many of the pioneer businessmen and residents took advantage of the readily accessible red and brown sandstone, most of which came from F.W. Carlin's nearby quarry. C.A. Bushorr and C.E. Bates were the stonemasons who constructed many of the early buildings. The area north of the courthouse square was reserved for the town's first business district. In 1902, a franchise was granted to supply Pawnee with electricity; all-night service cost subscribers $10 per month.

Work on a new courthouse started in April 1932. Special state legislation allowed the building to be constructed without a bond issue. The county jail was moved to the second floor of the courthouse.

A modern building to replace Pawnee's original eight-room school was constructed in 1912. It was a three-story native-stone structure containing a 700-seat auditorium on the second floor and a gymnasium on the third floor. Later, a junior college was added.

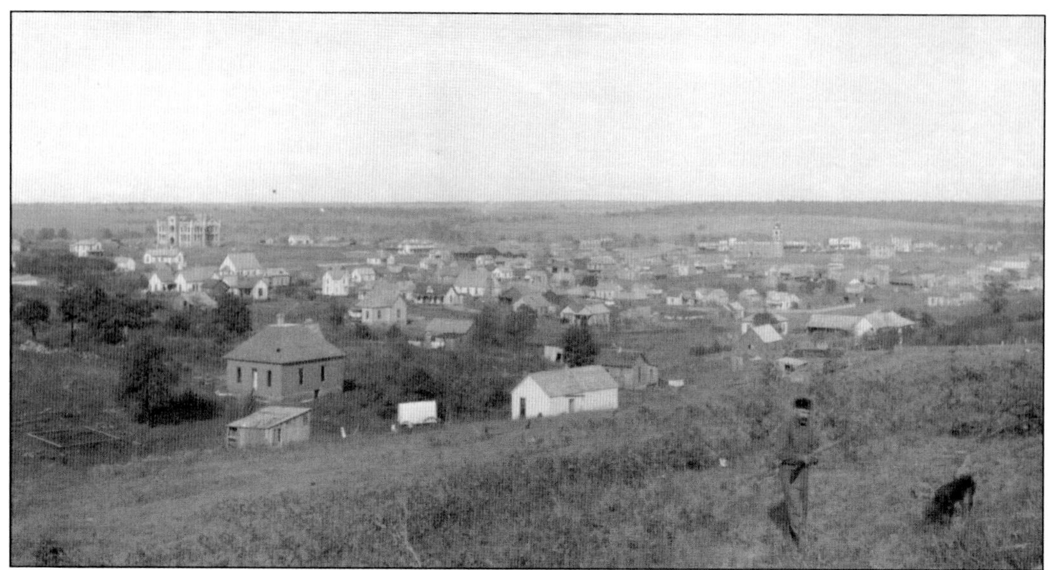

This photograph provides a view looking toward the north from the hills south of Pawnee. The large building in the background is Pawnee High School, which was nicknamed "the Castle." The Pawnee County Courthouse is in the background, on the right. The man is using a double-barreled shotgun to hunt, and his dog is hoping to flush rabbits or perhaps quail. (Courtesy of the Pawnee County Historical Society.)

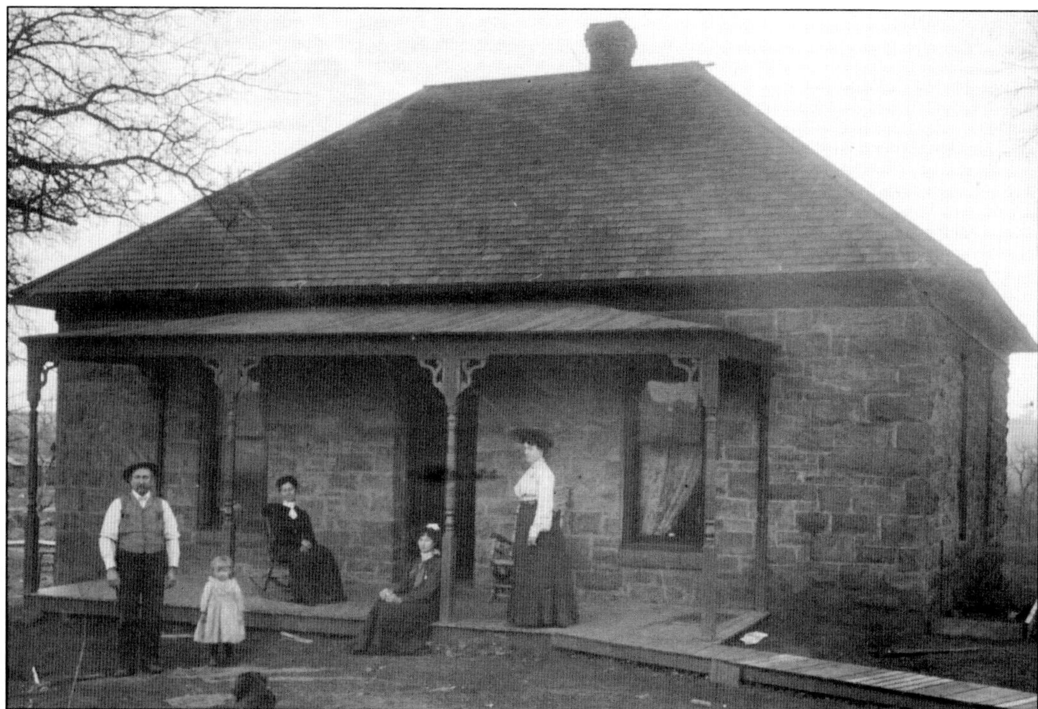

George W. Hughes and his family and dog are posing in front of their home near Pawnee. Like Pawnee's businesses, many early residences around Pawnee utilized the plentiful native stone cut in F.W. Carlin's quarry. There are no steps to the porch, but note the ramp in the lower right. (Courtesy of the Pawnee County Historical Society.)

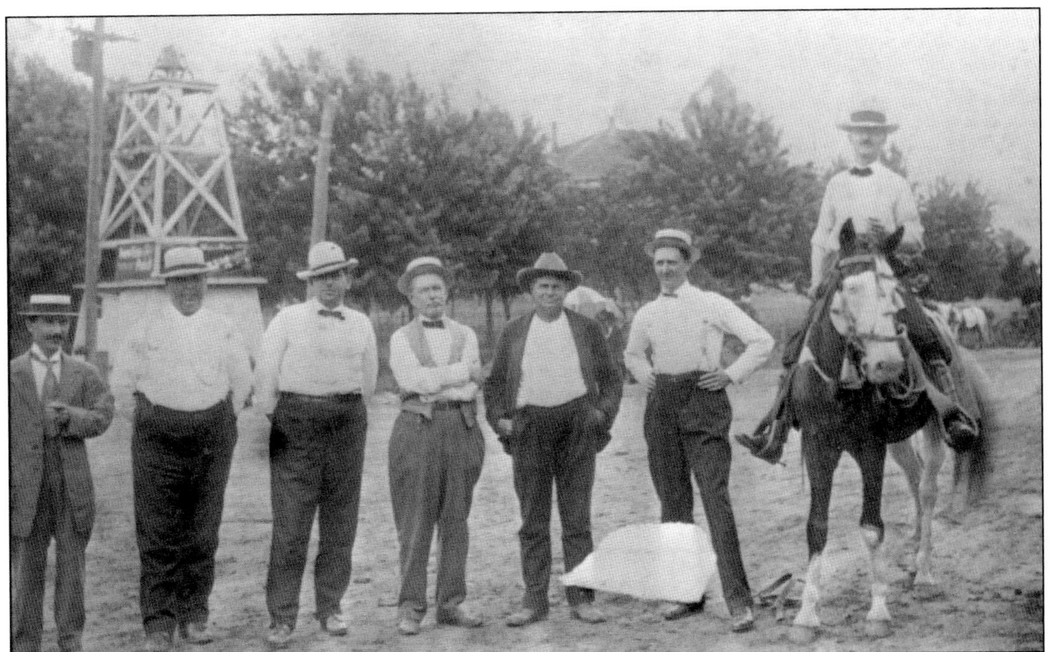

Pictured here, from left to right, are Gus Marx, W.E. Toler, James B. David, Ed Gray, unidentified, Joe Soulsby, and Dr. William Moore in front of Pawnee's fire bell on the courthouse square. The bell was used to summon the town's firemen, who kept the fire cart stored in the structure beneath the bell tower. (Courtesy of the Pawnee County Historical Society.)

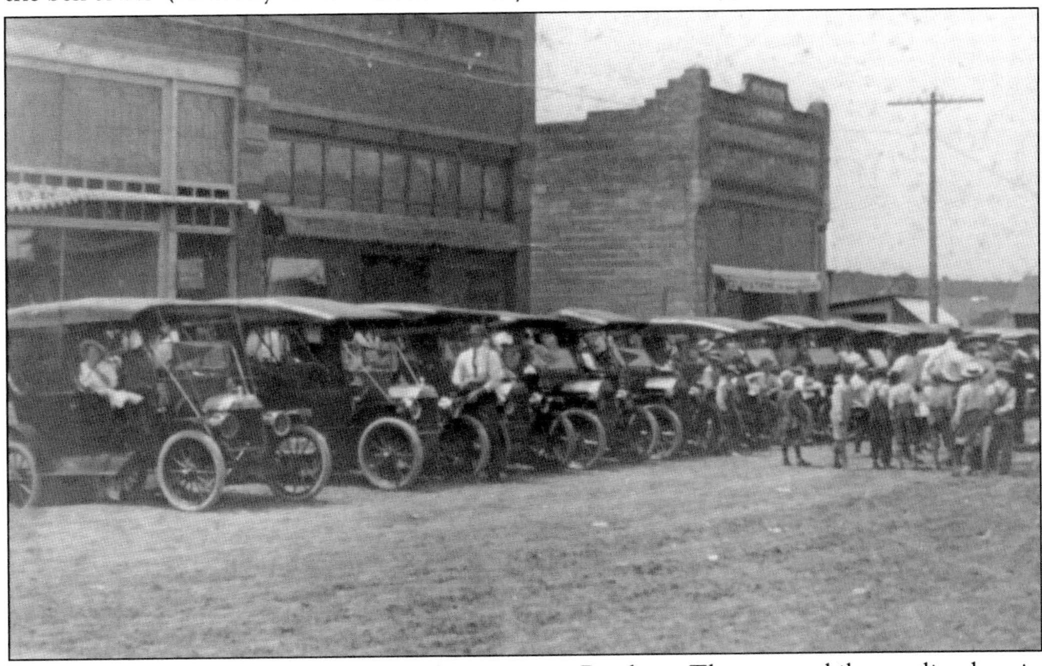

Ford Day, June 10, 1913, was sponsored by Mentzer Brothers. The automobiles are lined up in front of the Mentzer Brothers Hardware Store. Although the automobile age had come to Pawnee, the roads of the town and the surrounding area were still dirt and often turned into impassable quagmires in heavy rain. (Courtesy of the Pawnee County Historical Society.)

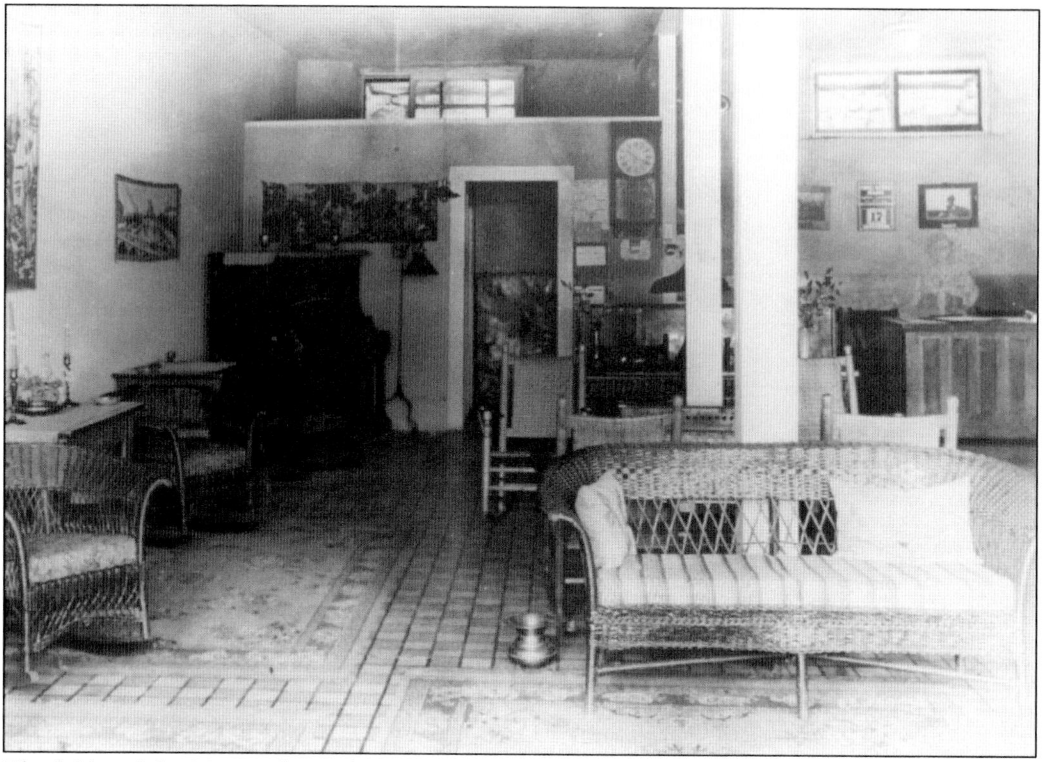

The lobby of the National Hotel in Pawnee, the town's most upscale hotel, was furnished with wicker seating. The tile floor was covered with area rugs. The front desk is on the right and a piano on the left in the photograph. Note the spittoon on the floor by the couch for those guests who chewed tobacco. (Courtesy of the Pawnee County Historical Society.)

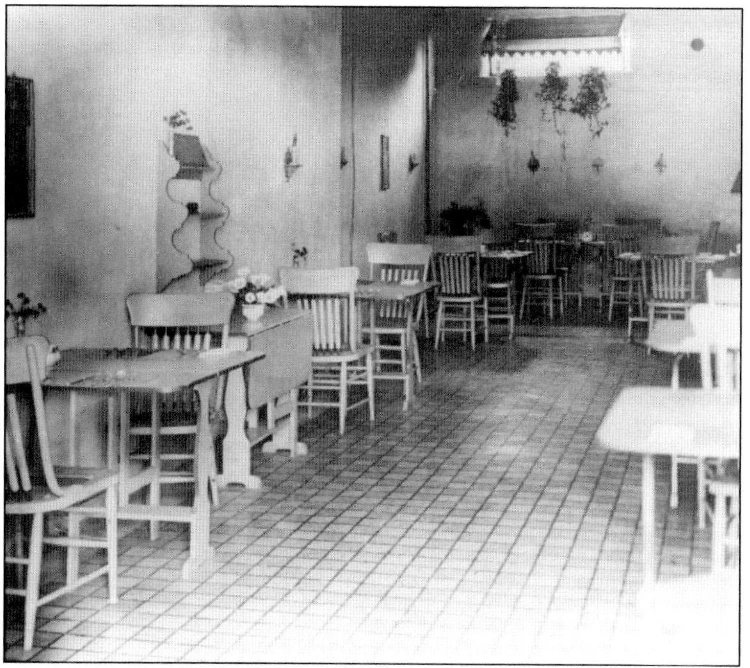

Pawnee's National Hotel not only offered the best rooms in the town, its restaurant, the Coffee Shop, was one of the best places to eat. The Coffee Shop was a favorite place for Pawnee residents to enjoy a morning coffee while getting caught up on local events. Here, the tables have been preset and are waiting for customers to arrive. (Courtesy of the Pawnee County Historical Society.)

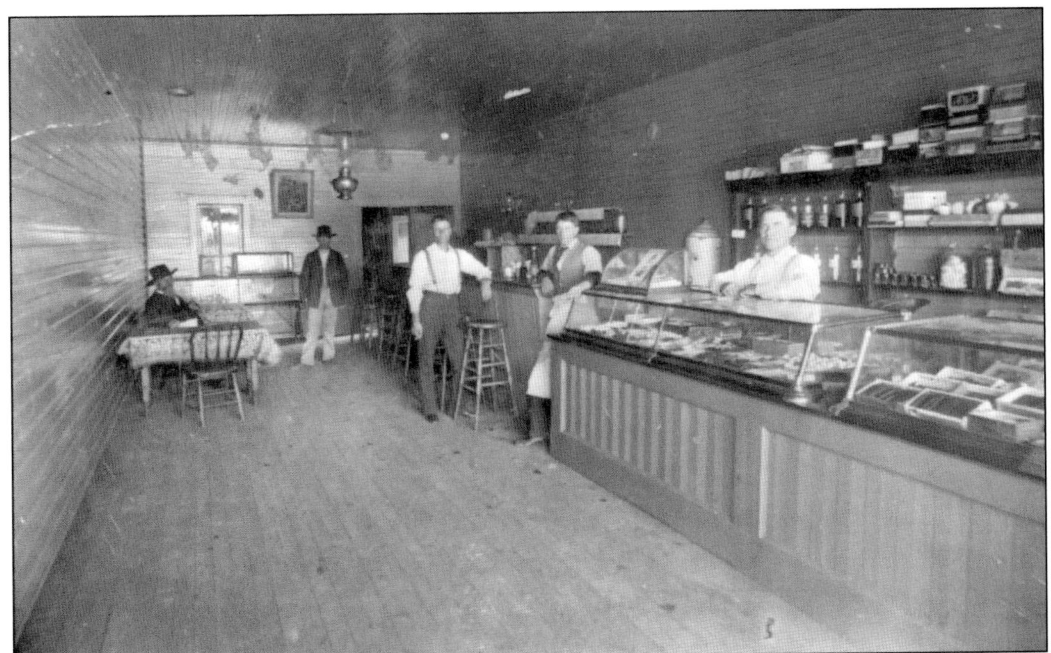

A 1910 view of the interior of Gran Vance's restaurant in Pawnee shows that customers were served on three tables on the left and at a bar with six stools. In the right foreground are counters offering pastries and cigars. Drinks, kept cool with ice, were kept in the container to the left of the man on the right. (Courtesy of the Pawnee County Historical Society.)

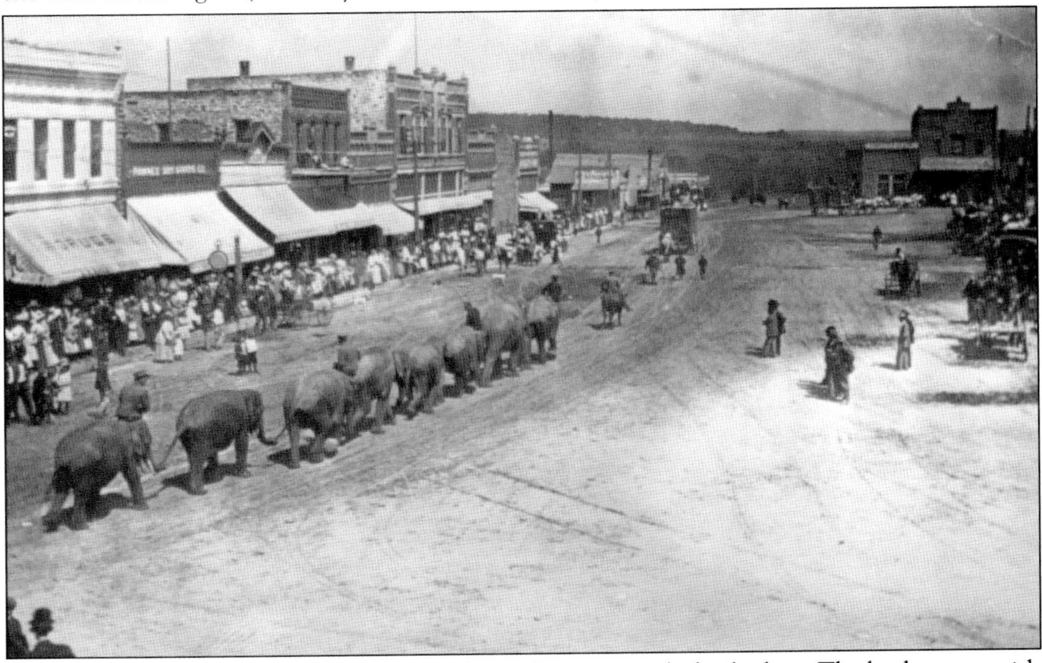

A 1912 circus parade through downtown Pawnee draws a crowd of onlookers. The lead wagon, with matching white horses, is making the turn around the courthouse square. A clock hangs in front of the Pawnee Dry Goods Company. Most of the stores have their awnings pulled out to provide shade for the crowds on the sidewalks. (Courtesy of the Pawnee County Historical Society.)

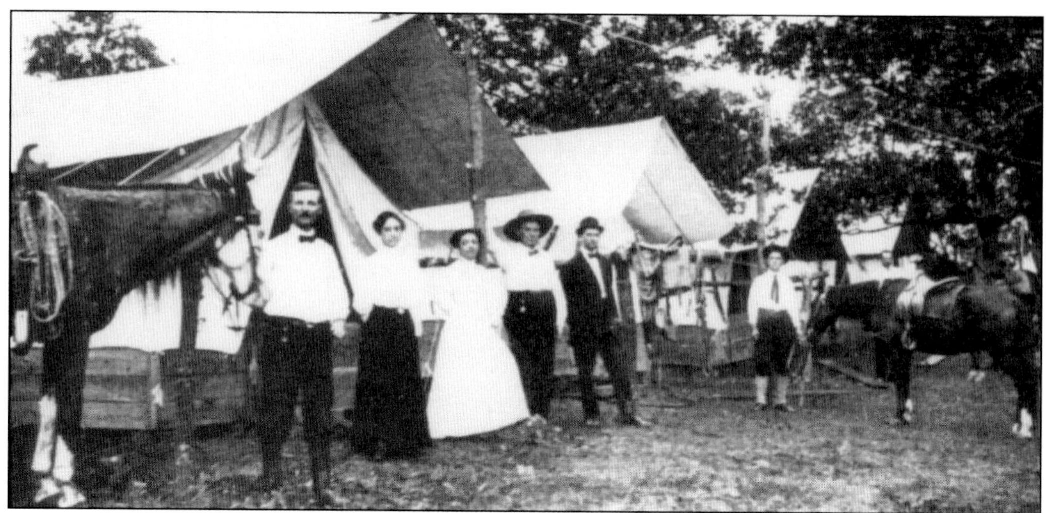

The Buffalo Park Sanitarium, Pawnee's first hospital, was opened by Dr. William M. Moore (standing by the horse on the left) in 1909. It was located to the south of the main part of town in Gordon W. "Pawnee Bill" Lillie's buffalo pasture. The original patients were housed in tents until a building could be constructed. Note that some of the tents are covered with canvas sheeting to provide shelter from the rain. (Courtesy of the Pawnee County Historical Society.)

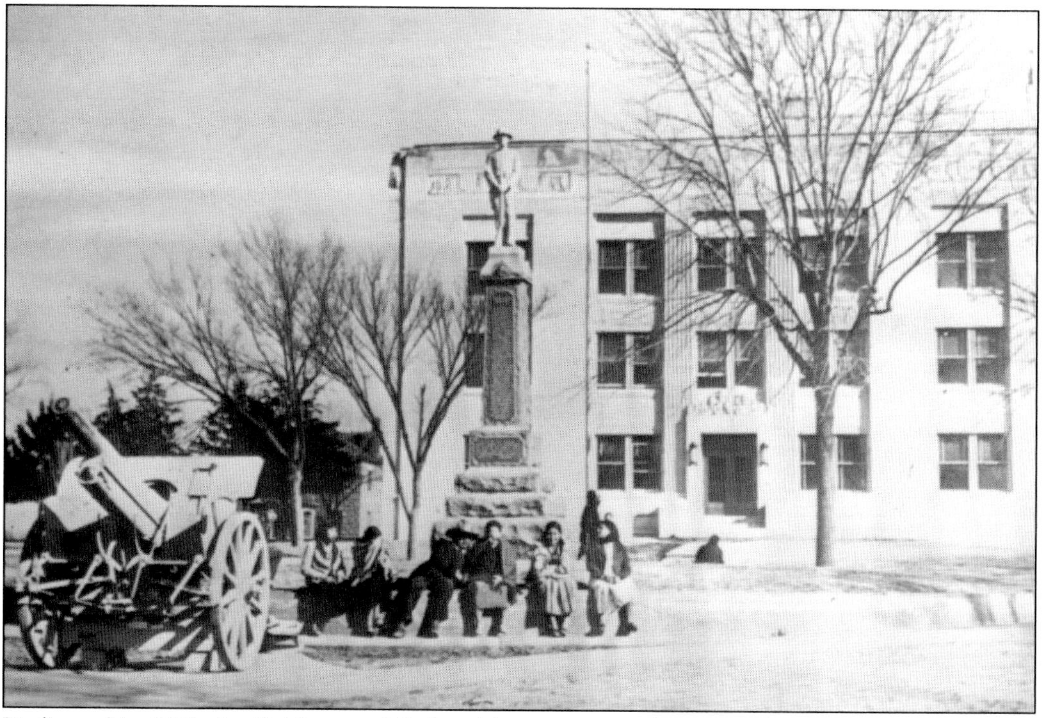

Dedicated in 1922, the Soldiers and Sailors Monument on the west side of the Pawnee County Courthouse was to honor those men from Pawnee County who served in World War I. Pawnee National Guards in the conflict were members of Company E, 1st Oklahoma Infantry Regiment, which became a part of the 36th Infantry Division. (Author's collection.)

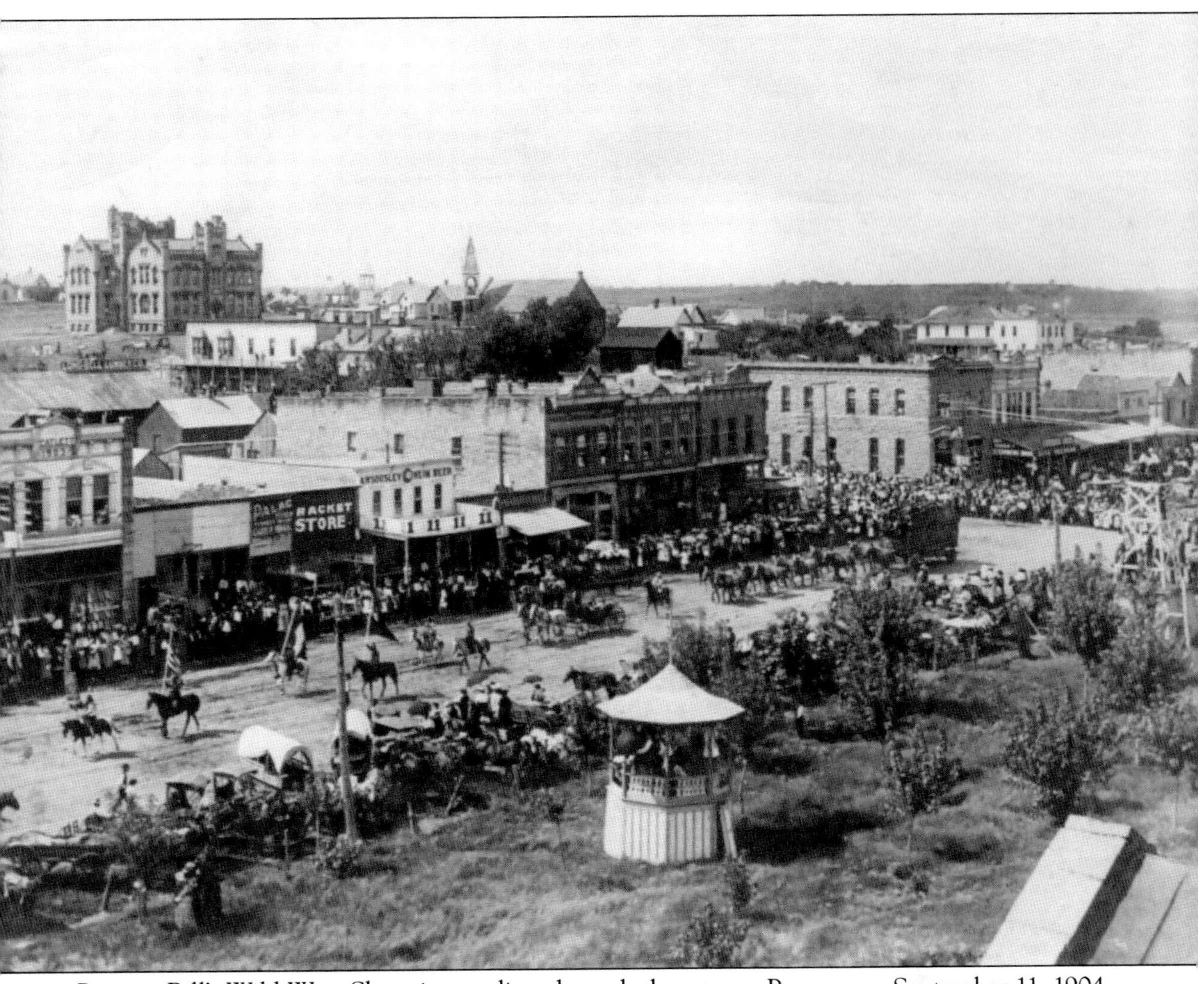

Pawnee Bill's Wild West Show is parading through downtown Pawnee on September 11, 1904. The photograph, with a view looking southwest, was taken from the courthouse. The parade was headed by a flag escort followed by the band on top of a wagon pulled by 10 horses. Pawnee Bill can be seen on horseback in front of the band. Note the men standing on top of the town's fire tower to view the parade. (Courtesy of the Pawnee County Historical Society.)

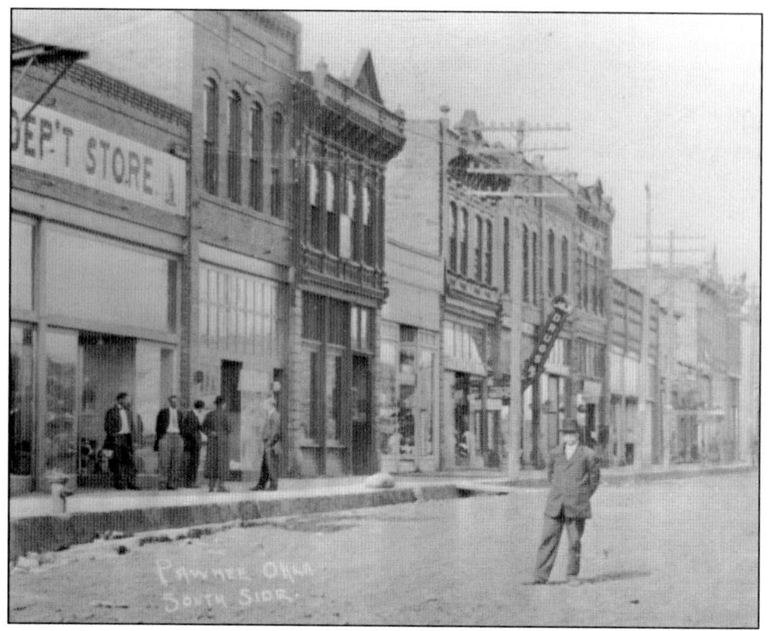

This man is standing in the still-dirt streets of Pawnee's business district on the south side of the courthouse square; however, the wooden walkways have been replaced by concrete sidewalks. Electricity has been provided, and fire plugs protect the town from fires. Open ditches carry off rainwater, but notice the walkway over the ditch. (Courtesy of the Pawnee County Historical Society.)

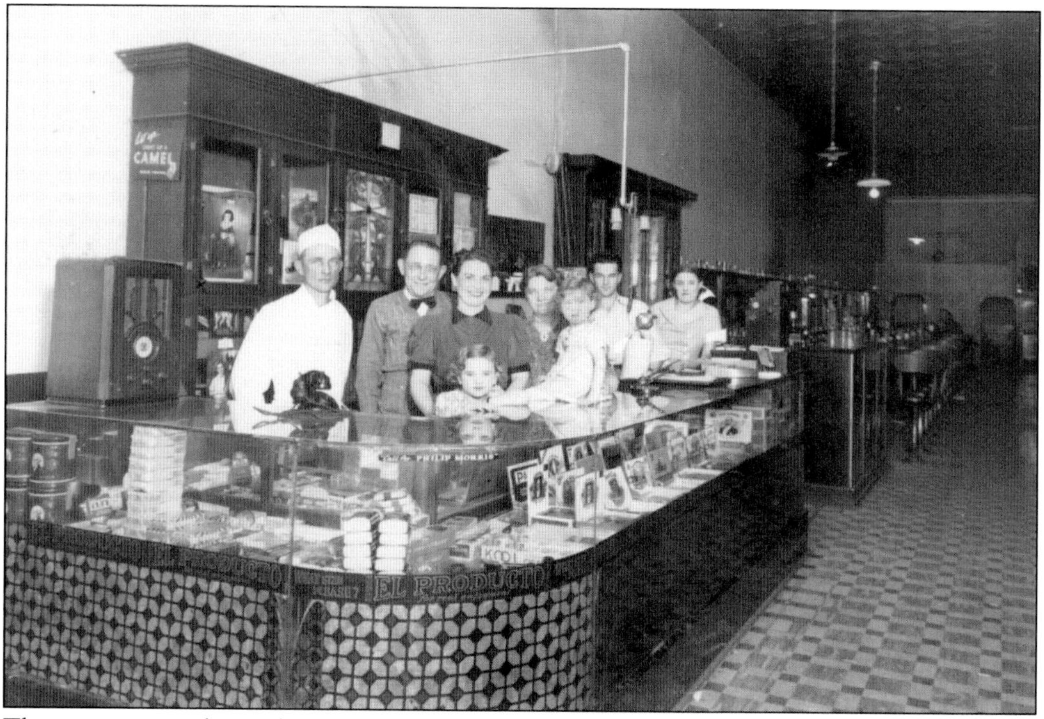

The restaurant in the Graham Hotel in Pawnee was a popular gathering place for businesspeople. Stools provide seats for customers at the counter in the background. A cash register is at the end of the lunch counter. The case in the foreground holds cigars, cigarettes, and chewing tobacco. Over the cigar counter is a cigar lighter. A tube radio provides music to eat by and a telephone, with a long cord, allows customers to make or receive calls. (Courtesy of the Pawnee County Historical Society.)

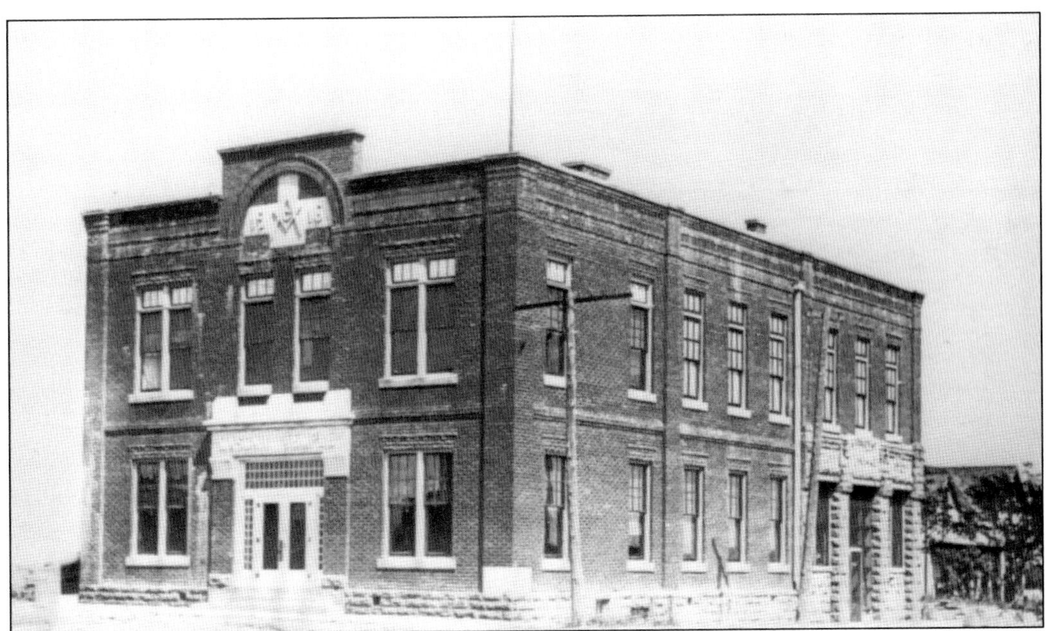

The Masonic Building housed the Masonic lodge on one end of the building and the Lundquest Laundry on the other. The structure, which stood on the northwest side of Pawnee's courthouse square, was built in 1916. The Masons still use the facility today. (Courtesy of the Pawnee County Historical Society.)

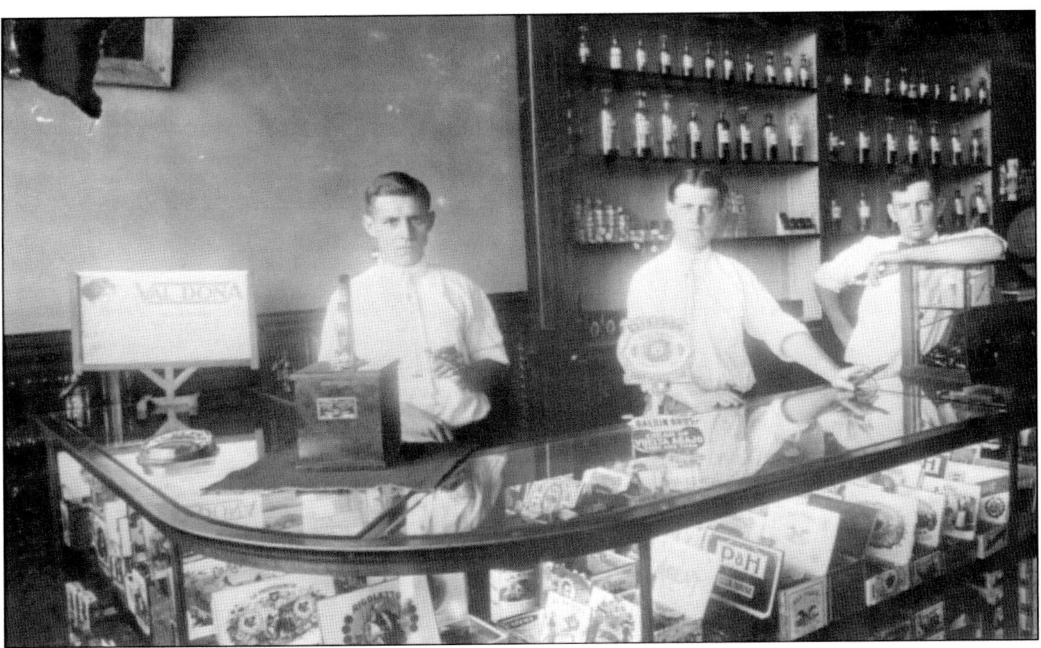

The Jay & Jay Drug Store in Pawnee offered a large selection of fine cigars from its cigar counter. Note that all three salesmen are holding cigars from the selection. The pipe extending from the box in front of the salesman on the left is a natural-gas cigar lighter. A customer would press on the handle, and a spark would ignite natural gas released from the pipe to provide a light for his cigar. (Courtesy of the Pawnee County Historical Society.)

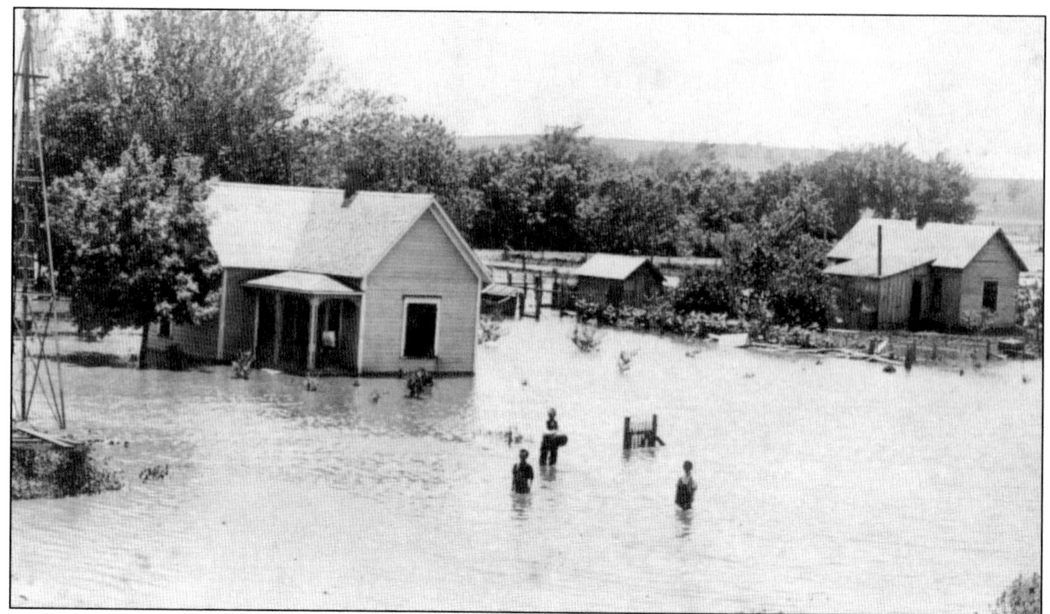

The 1908 Bear Creek Flood in Pawnee inundated many of the homes on the east side of the community. In this photograph, one can see homeowners wading through the water hoping to salvage something from their homes. (Courtesy of the Pawnee County Historical Society.)

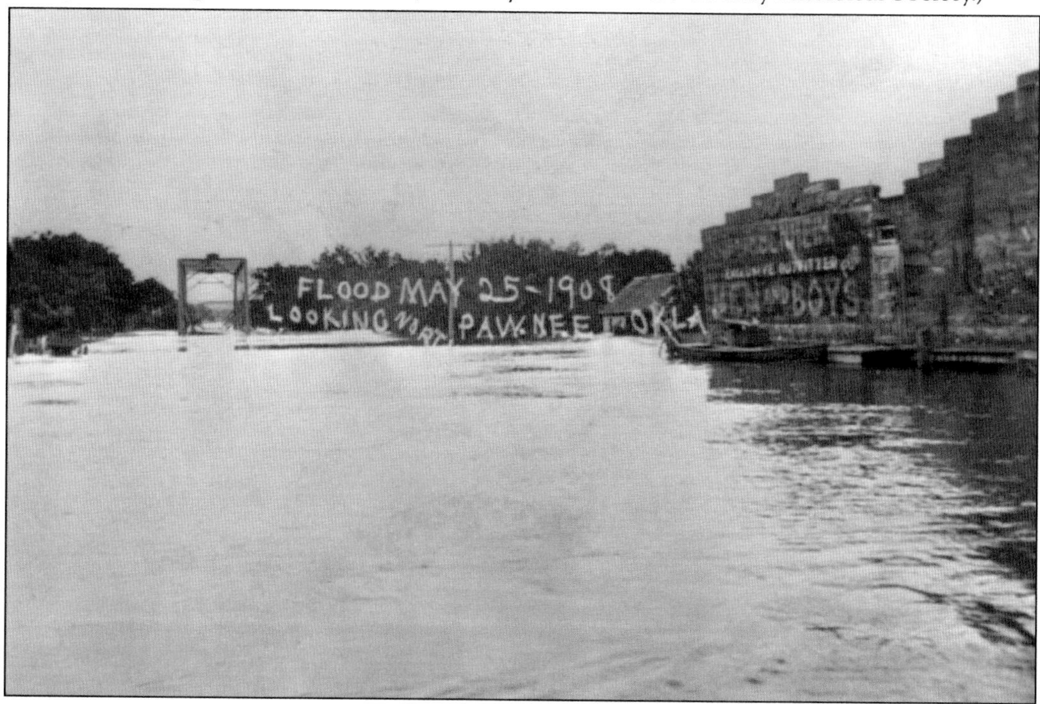

This is a photograph of the 1908 flood of Black Bear Creek that swept into the east end of Pawnee's business district. The floodwater is overflowing the bridge over Black Bear Creek in the upper left. On the right is Liebenheim's Exclusive Outfitter for Men and Boys store. Note the boat tied up in front of the store. The high water left boats as the only way many merchants could reach their establishments. (Courtesy of the Pawnee County Historical Society.)

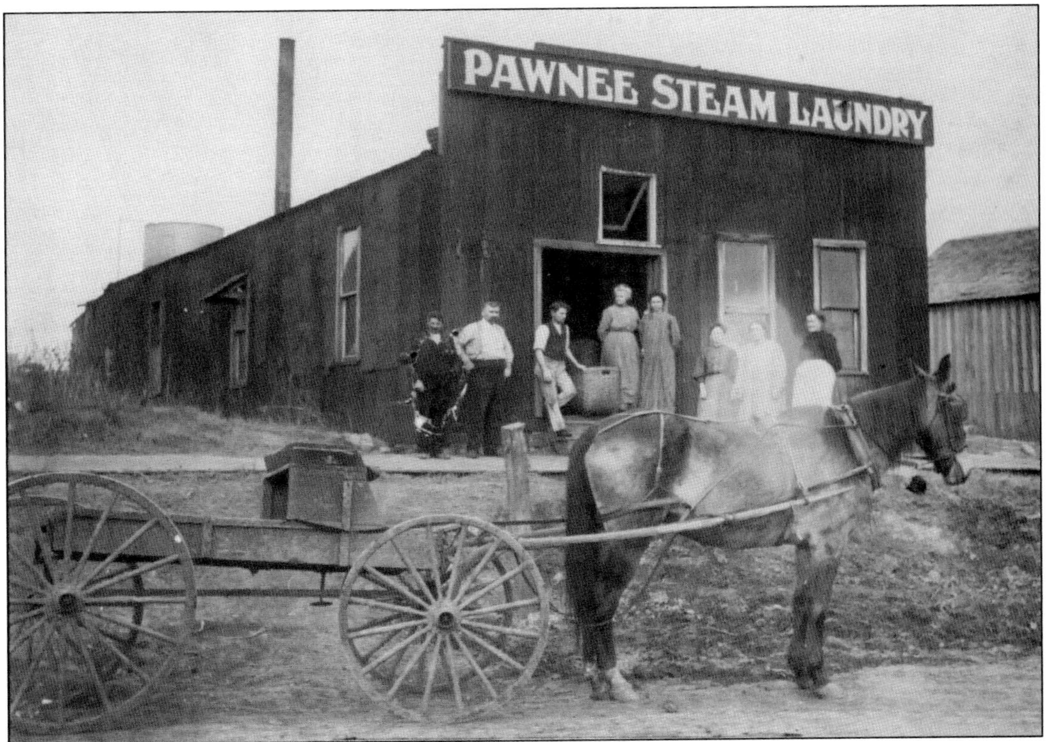

S. Lundquist, second man from the left, stands in front of the Pawnee Steam Laundry. Lundquist opened the first laundry in Pawnee. Note the woven basket in the front door. Customers would drop their clothes off in the basket to be laundered. The water tank and steam pipe for the boiler can be seen at the rear of the building. (Courtesy of the Pawnee County Historical Society.)

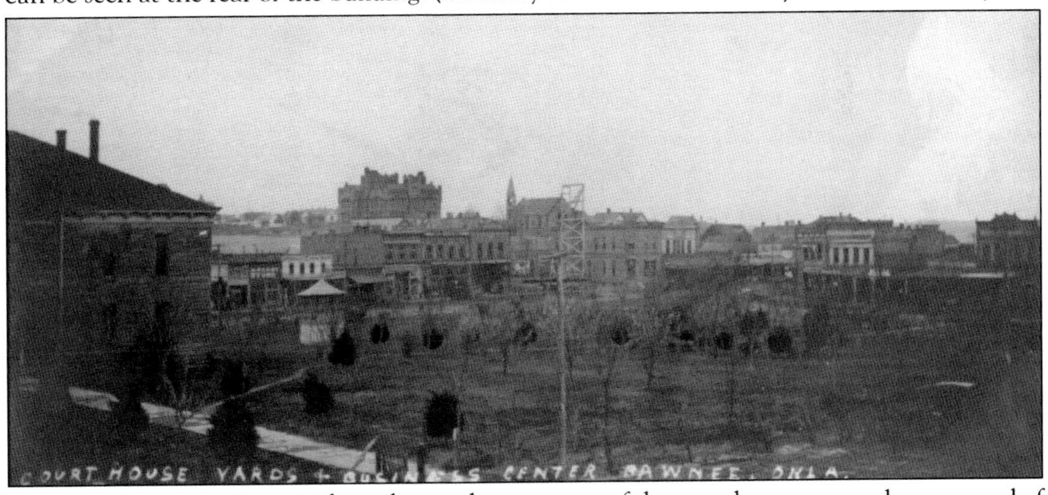

A view of downtown Pawnee from the northeast corner of the courthouse square shows several of the town's most prominent buildings. The large stone structure in the background is the Pawnee High School. The building in the right-center with the cattycorner doorway is the First National Bank of Pawnee. Across the street and to the right from the First National Bank of Pawnee is the Arkansas Valley Bank. Gordon W. "Pawnee Bill" once filled wagons with bags of silver dollars and paraded them through Pawnee to show people that the bank was sound. (Courtesy of the Pawnee County Historical Society.)

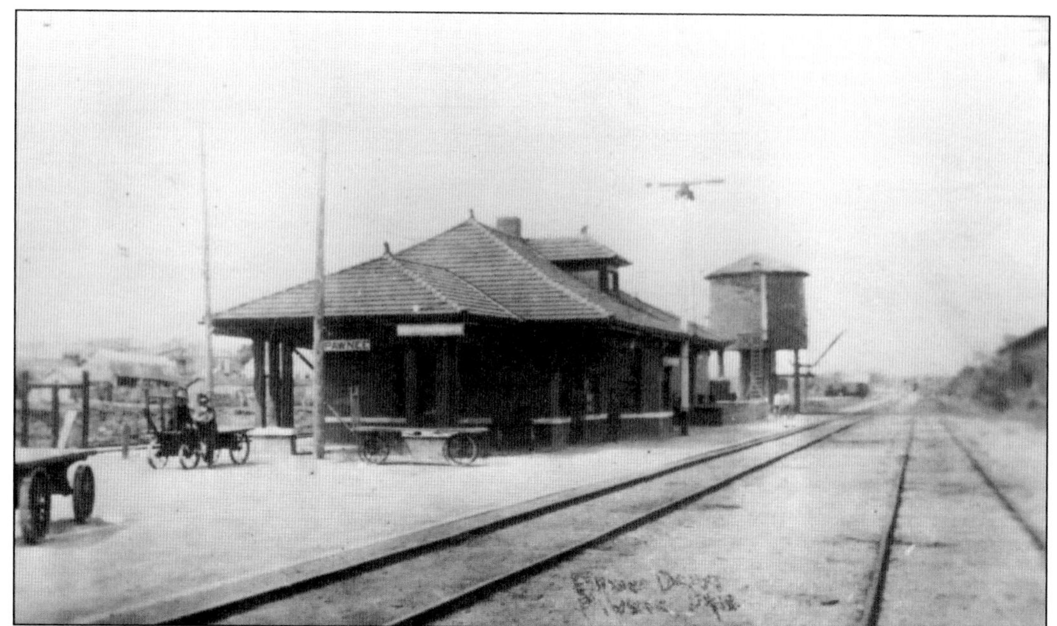

The St. Louis–San Francisco Railroad depot was located on the north side of Pawnee. The commercial success of the town was assured when it became the crossroads of the north-south Atchison, Topeka & Santa Fe Railway and the east-west St. Louis–San Francisco Railroad. Note the elevated water tank on the right of the photograph. Trains would stop beneath the spout to refill their water tender. (Courtesy of the Pawnee County Historical Society.)

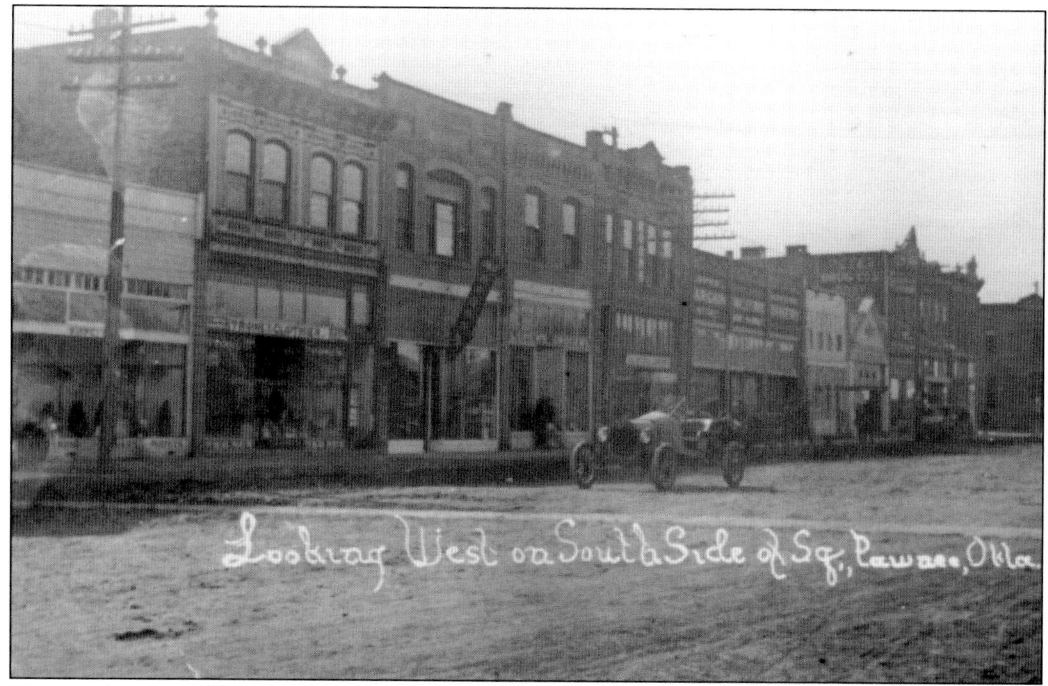

The south side of Harrison Street in Pawnee, the county seat of Pawnee County, had numerous retail businesses. While the sidewalks pictured have been paved, the streets are still dirt-lined with open ditches. (Courtesy of the Pawnee County Historical Society.)

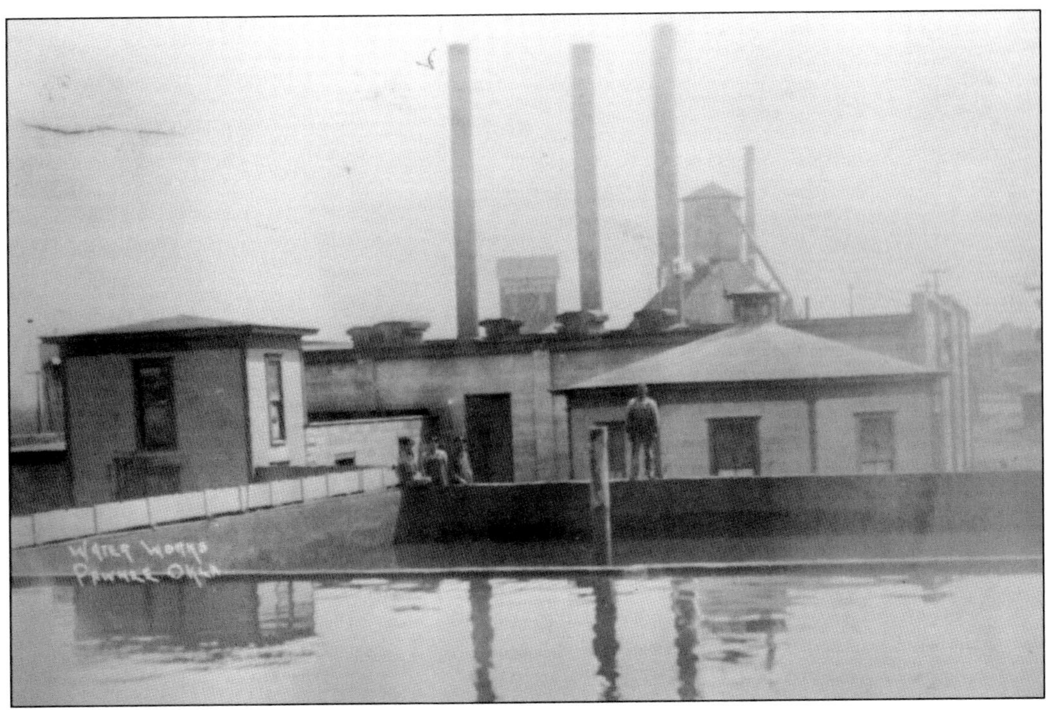

The new $45,000 waterworks built for the town of Pawnee was located on the edge of Black Bear Creek, from which water was drawn and purified for use by local residents. The waterworks eliminated the need for backyard water wells, which had been the source of much of the town's drinking water in its early years. (Courtesy of the Pawnee County Historical Society.)

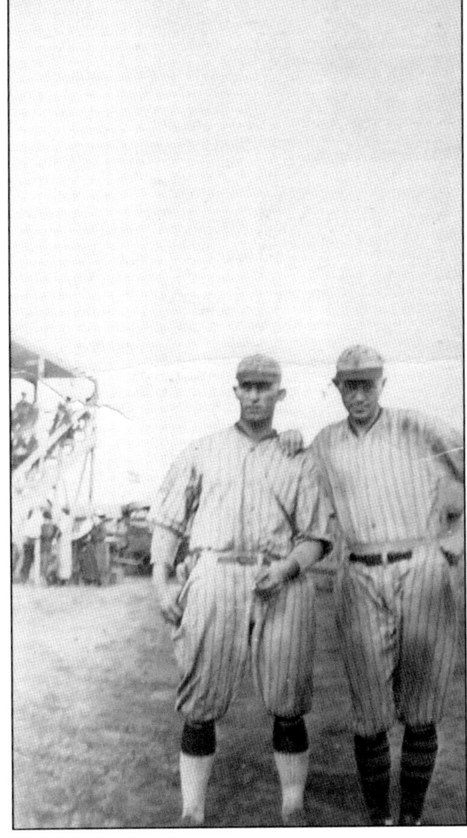

Basil "Bo" Elmore (left) and LeRoy Stewart are standing in front of the sandlot baseball wooden stadium in Pawnee in 1921. Like many towns in the area, Pawnee was home to a local sandlot baseball team that provided entertainment during the summer months. The sandlot leagues were composed of teams from other towns in the vicinity and various oil company–sponsored teams. (Courtesy of the Pawnee County Historical Society.)

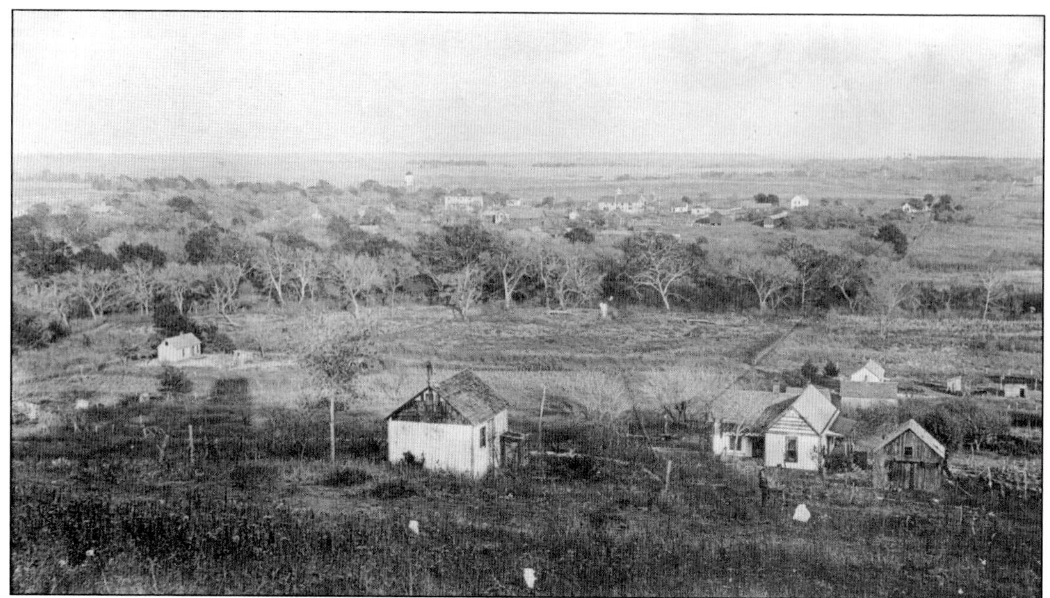

The Pawnee Indian Agency was located on the east side of Black Bear Creek from Pawnee, as seen from Standpipe Hill. The residents in the foreground are in Pawnee, then come the trees lining Black Bear Creek, with the Pawnee Agency in the background. Established in 1875, the agency gave birth to the town of Pawnee. (Courtesy of the Pawnee County Historical Society.)

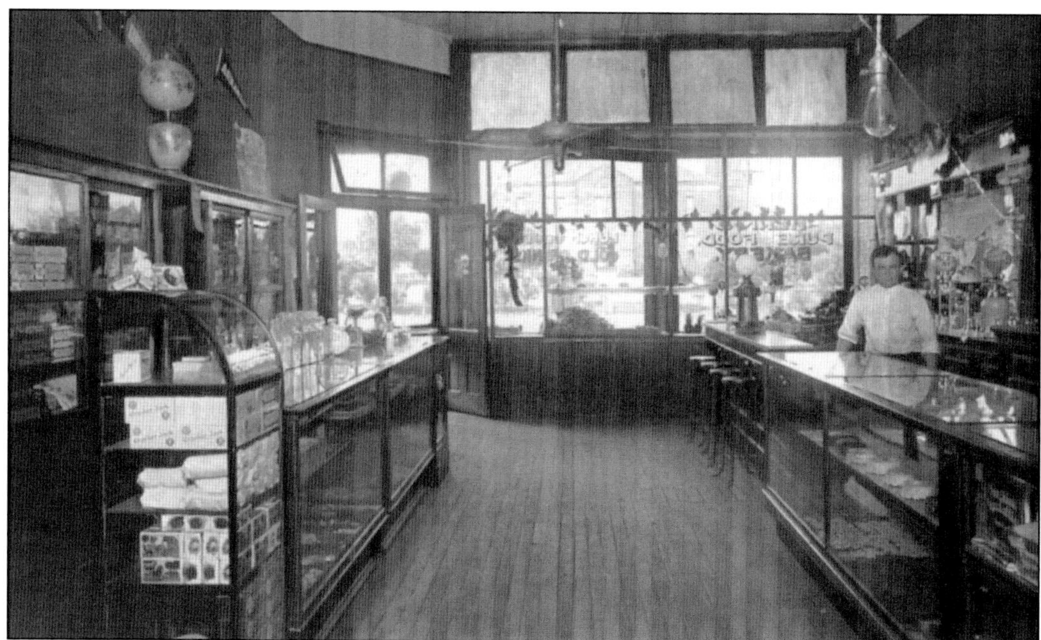

Kern's Pure Food and Bakery was operated by Leslie D. and Nellie Robbins Kern. Stanley Smith, their employee, is standing behind the counter. Pastries are displayed in the counter to Smith's left, and to his right is a soda fountain with a straw dispenser sitting on top. A bare lightbulb provides illumination for the store. Note the Texas, Oklahoma, Kansas, and Arkansas school pennants on the wall at the upper left. (Courtesy of the Pawnee County Historical Society.)

Six

Oil Boom

Natural-oil and saltwater seeps were a common occurrence along Cedar Creek, just south of Cleveland. In keeping with the prevailing geological theory of creekology, oilmen were drawn to the sandy bends in the Arkansas River near the seeps. In January 1904, W.J. Fellows examined the area and formed the Cleveland Oil, Gas & Manufacturing Company. Eventually he subleased his property to the Minnetonka Oil Company owned by George F. Getty Sr. Getty decided to drill a wildcat on the farm of William Lowery. Because Lowery was better known as "Uncle Bill," the well was dubbed the Uncle Bill No. 1.

The Uncle Bill No. 1 was spudded in on May 27, 1904. On July 2, the well struck natural gas and flowed between 10 and 20 million cubic feet per day. After the well had been bailed and the tools were being lowered into the hole, someone noticed that a film of oil covered the cable. Shortly afterward, Mrs. E.G. Todd, who was holding her hand over the hole to feel the flow of natural gas, was sprayed with crude oil. As the crew hurriedly pulled the tools from the oil, the Uncle Bill No. 1 came in as a 10-barrel-per-day oil well.

Hopeful of increasing the Uncle Bill's production, J.C. Moore, a "shooter" with the Kansas Torpedo Company, was contracted to shoot the well. Moore arrived from Bartlesville on July 23, 1904, and spent almost half a day filling his torpedo with 40 quarts of nitroglycerine, lowering it into the well, and attaching the go-devil to the cable. When Moore dropped the go-devil down the hole and it struck the torpedo, the explosive charge detonated with a muffled roar. An onlooker described the scene when he said, "The shot tore the casing . . . and blew part of the packer in the bottom clean to the top." Production from the Uncle Bill No. 1 immediately jumped to almost 250 barrels daily and then stabilized at 50 barrels per day. The Pawnee County oil boom was on.

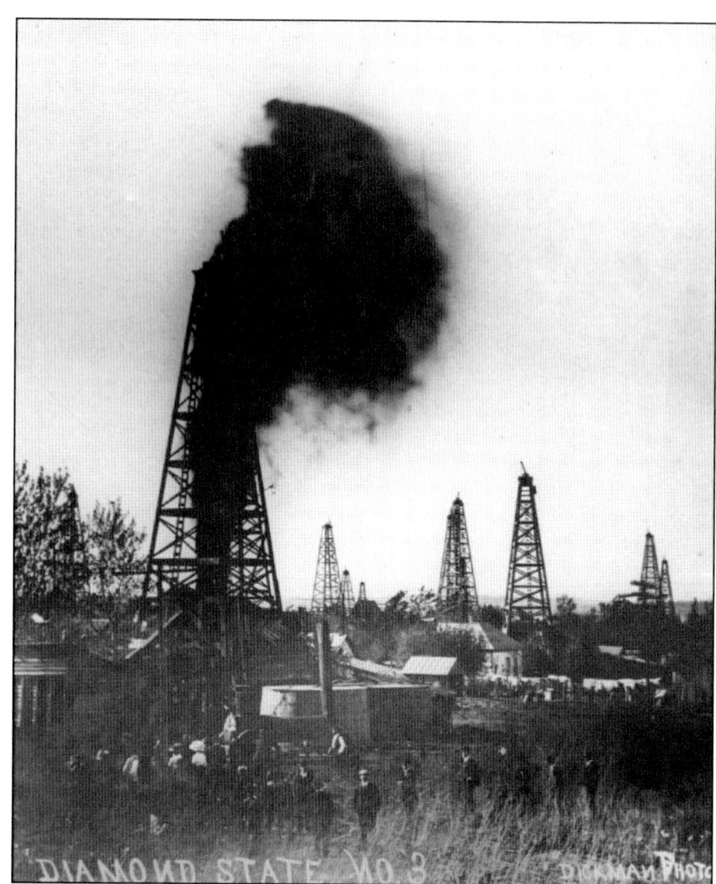

The Diamond State Oil Company's No. 3 well, located between the town of Cleveland and the Arkansas River, blew in as a gusher. A crowd of onlookers has gathered to see the well completed. Notice the laundry hanging on the nearby clothesline that probably will be soaked with oil. The spewing oil would coat nearby homes, making them firetraps. (Author's collection.)

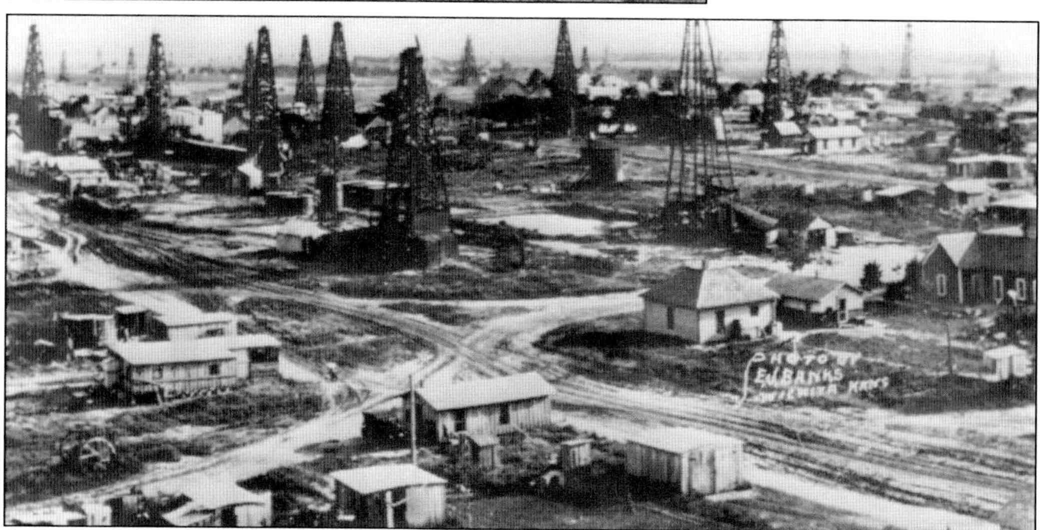

Note the open earthen oil-storage tank in the middle of this photograph of the Quay Oil Field. Such earthen tanks lost much oil to seepage and evaporation. The shotgun houses in the left foreground provided cheap housing for workers. Notice the outhouses behind the homes. Oil company officials lived in the more substantial houses scattered in the photograph. (Courtesy of the Pawnee County Historical Society.)

Two 55,000-barrel oil storage tanks are on fire in the Cleveland Oil Field. Electrical storms often ignited the steel tanks. When this happened, all the oilfielders could do was to keep the fire from spreading and let the fire burn itself out. This particular fire burned for four days. (Courtesy of Triangle Heritage Association.)

The main street of the town of Watchorn was the center of activity in the Watchorn Oil Field. The field was located in what was the Otoe-Missouri Reservation along the Pawnee County–Payne County line in 1915. Notice the tents and false-front structures hurriedly constructed to handle the influx of oilmen rushing to the latest strike. (Courtesy of H.P. Laird.)

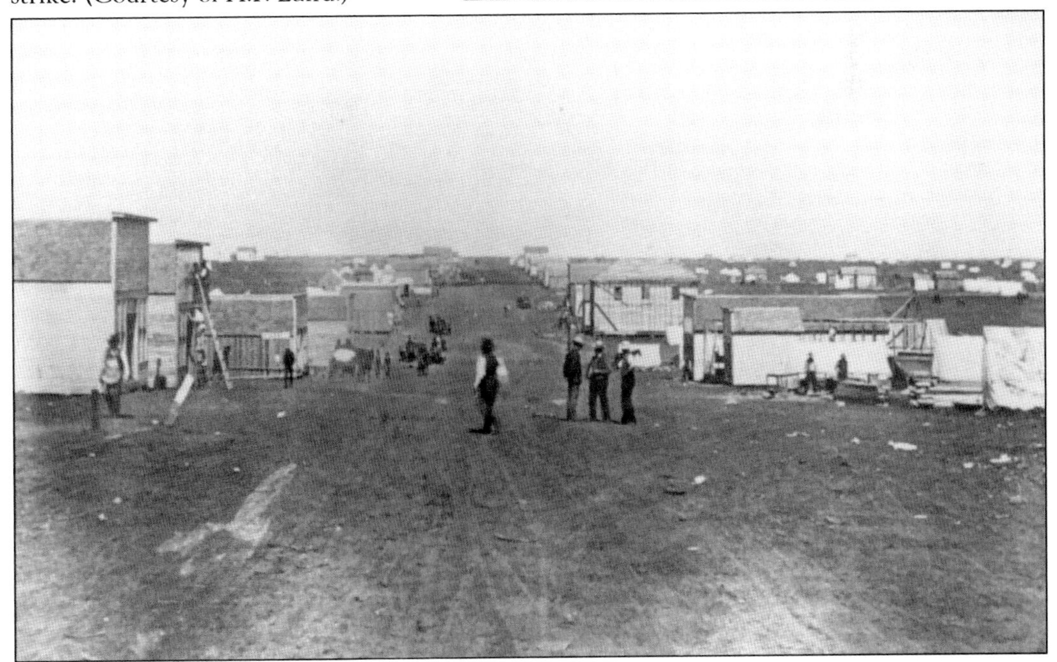

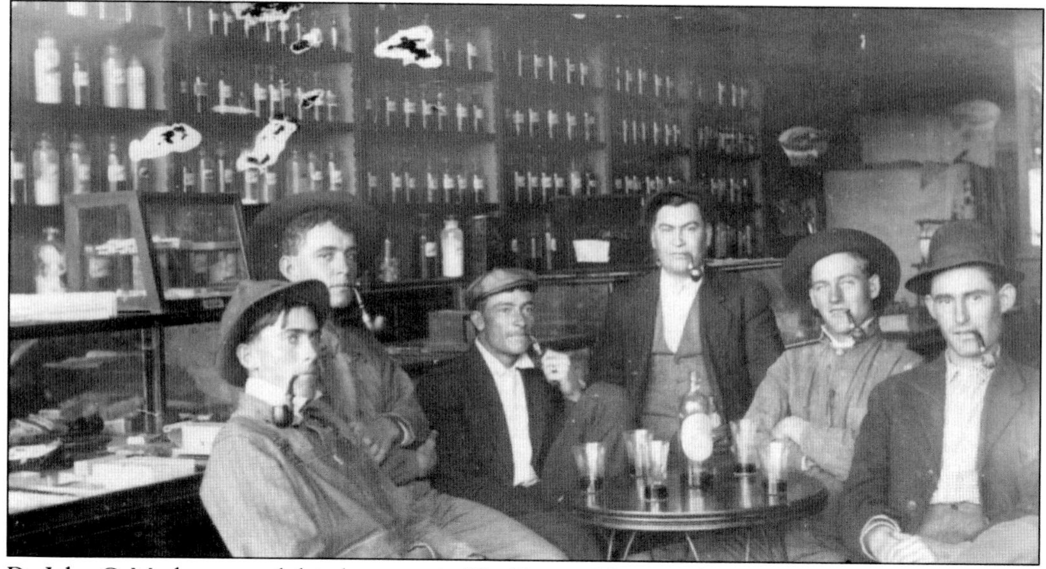

Dr. John C. Marlow owned this drugstore in Blackburn. After statehood and Prohibition, drugstores were one of the few places oilfielders could by liquor, which was sold for medicinal purposes. Note the bottles of different medicines lining the shelf in the background. Each of the customers is enjoying a pipe with his refreshment. (Courtesy of the Pawnee County Historical Society.)

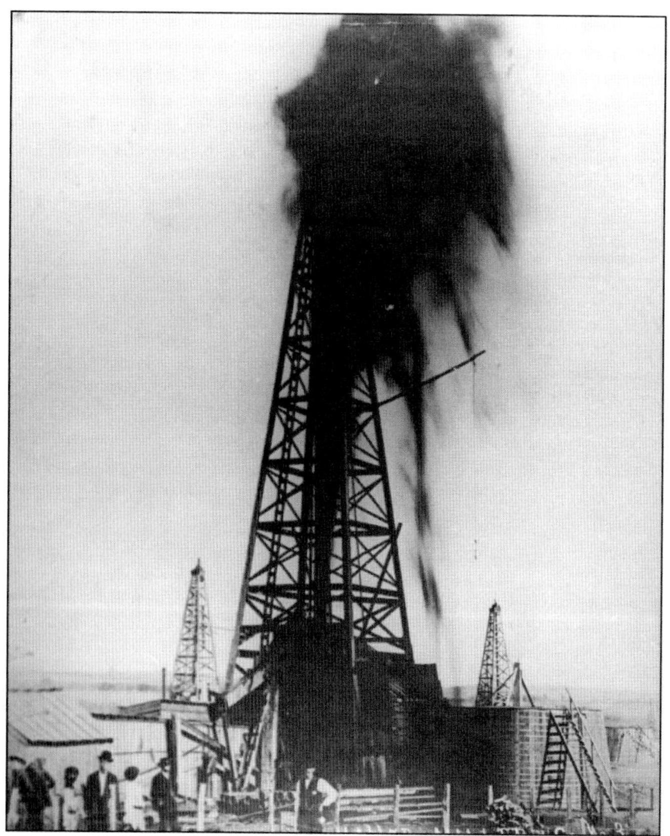

The Mayfield Oil Company No. 1 well was in the Cleveland Oil Field. No means of storing production can be seen. Hence, the oil is being allowed to run in rivulets across the countryside. Notice the workers sitting and standing on the rig's braces. To the right are crude houses used by the workers. (Courtesy of Triangle Heritage Association.)

The Pawnee's National Hotel was a popular place to stay for oil company executives. Shown in this view looking out the front entrance is the hotel's lobby. In the upper left of the photograph is a birdcage, and in the left foreground are several writing tables for guests. The front doors have screens on them so that they can be left open to let in the breeze but keep out bugs. (Courtesy of the Pawnee County Historical Society.)

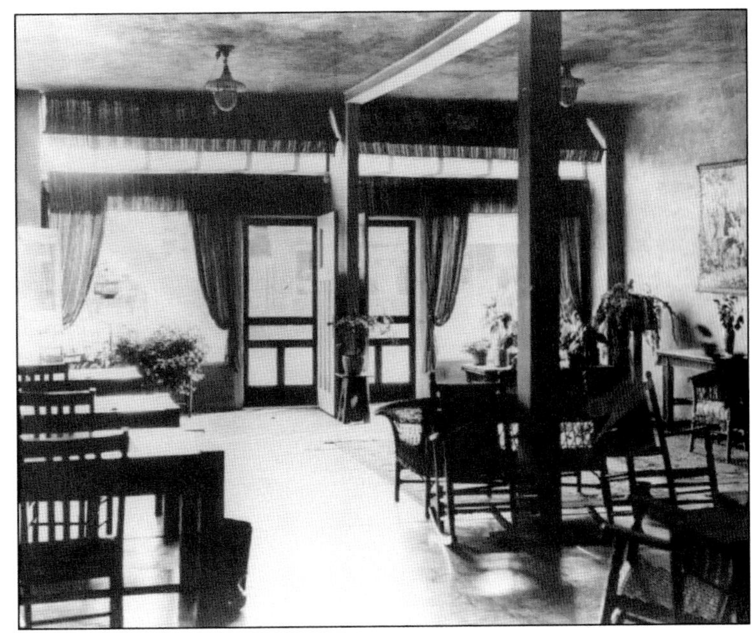

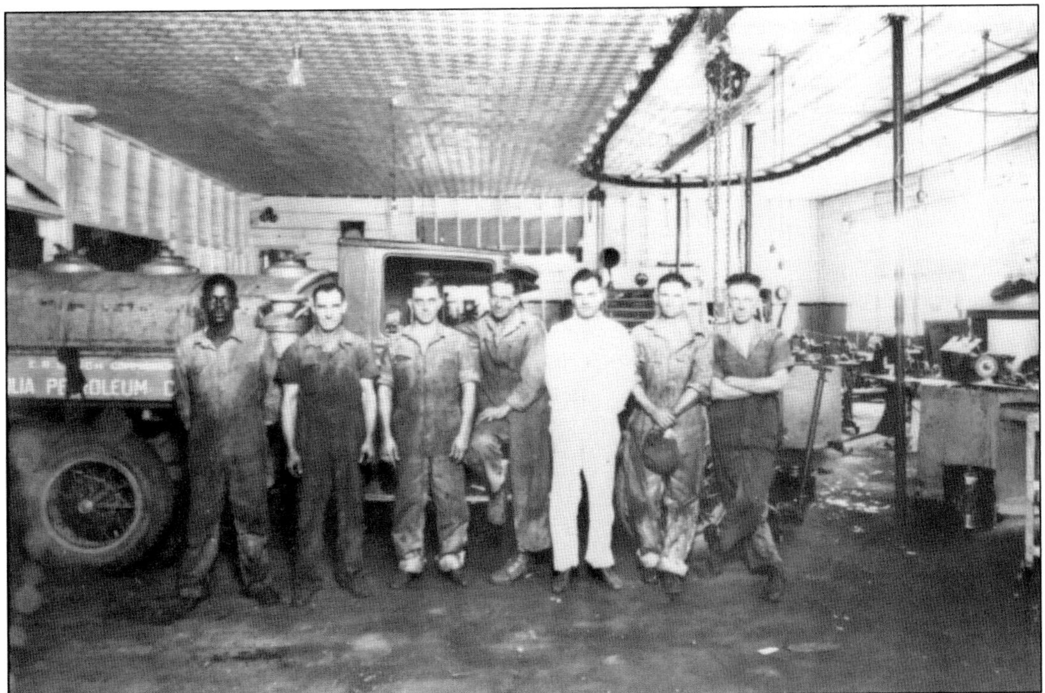

This is the Magnolia Pipeline Company's garage in Pawnee County. The mechanics are, from left to right, Noah ?, Hally Gilland, Leo Simmons, Carl Uhl, Ray Justes, John H. Turner, and John Bishop. Justes must be the shop manager; he is the only one in a clean uniform. (Courtesy of the Pawnee County Historical Society.)

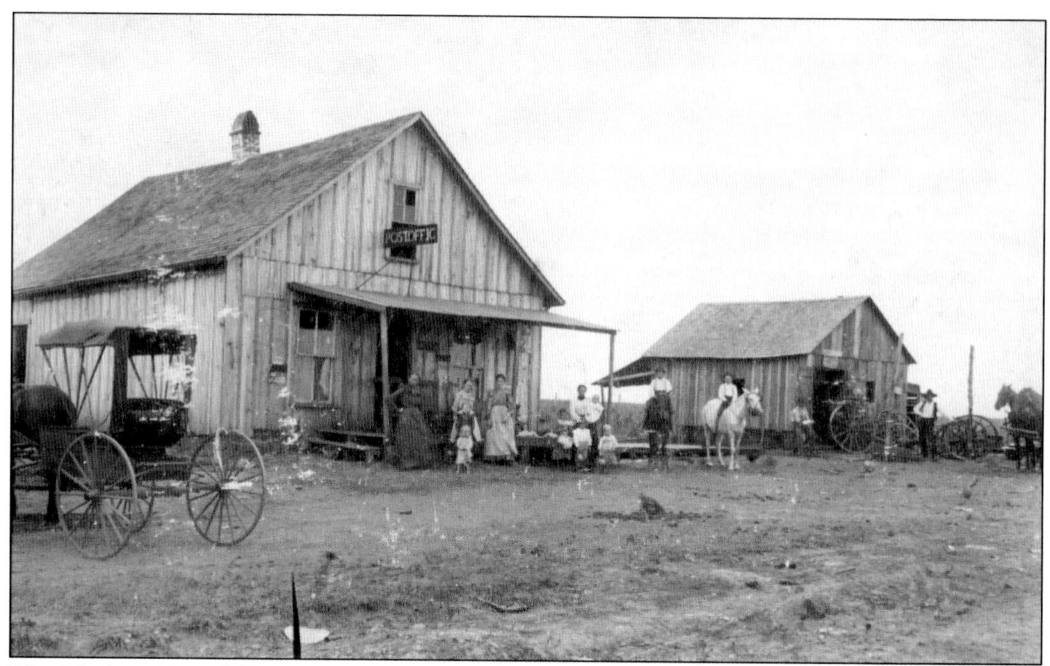

The Masham Post Office was just to the south of the discovery well of the Masham Oil Field. It was also called the Donahue Field, for J.L. Donahue, who drilled the discovery well. Note the chicken scratching in the dirt in front of the post office. (Courtesy of the Pawnee County Historical Society.)

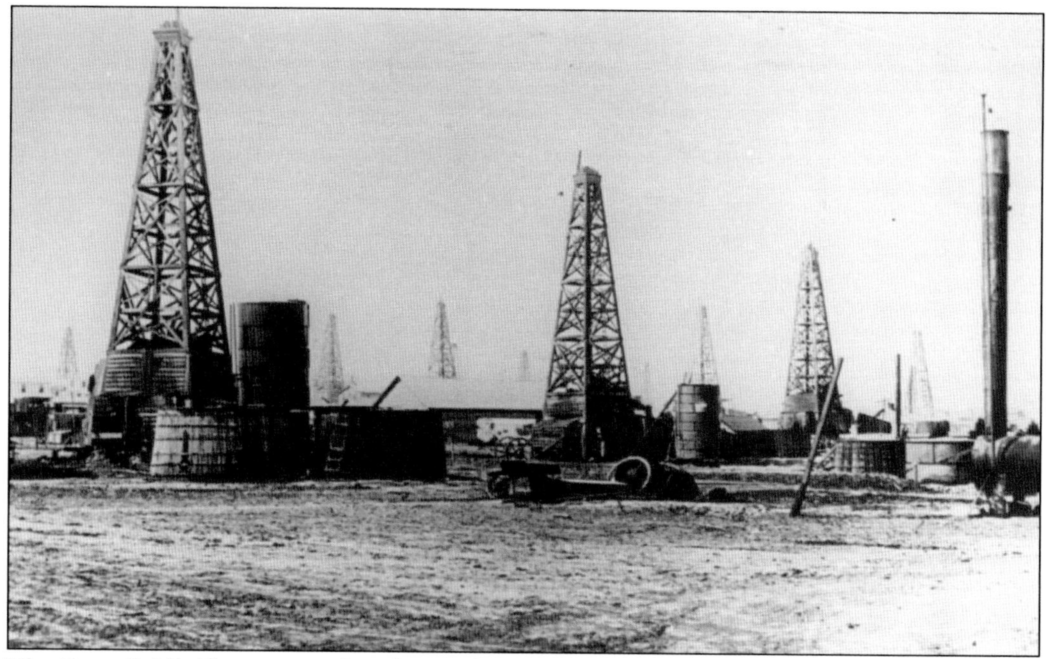

The Quay Oil Field was opened to the southeast of Jennings, along the Pawnee County–Creek County line, in 1914 and ranked second only to the Cleveland Field in the production of crude oil. This photograph, taken in 1914, illustrates the rapid development of the field, with closely spaced wells and inadequate storage facilities. (Author's collection.)

Shooting a well with nitroglycerin in the Cleveland Oil Field was a dangerous occupation. The shooter would load several tin torpedoes with nitroglycerin, attach them to a cable, and then lower them to the desired depth in the well's hole. He would then attach a go-devil, which would trigger the explosion, to the cable and drop it in the hole. When the go-devil struck the torpedo, it triggered an explosion that ostensibly would increase a well's production. Nitroglycerin was so dangerous that nitroglycerin magazines were not allowed in the town. (Courtesy of Triangle Heritage Association.)

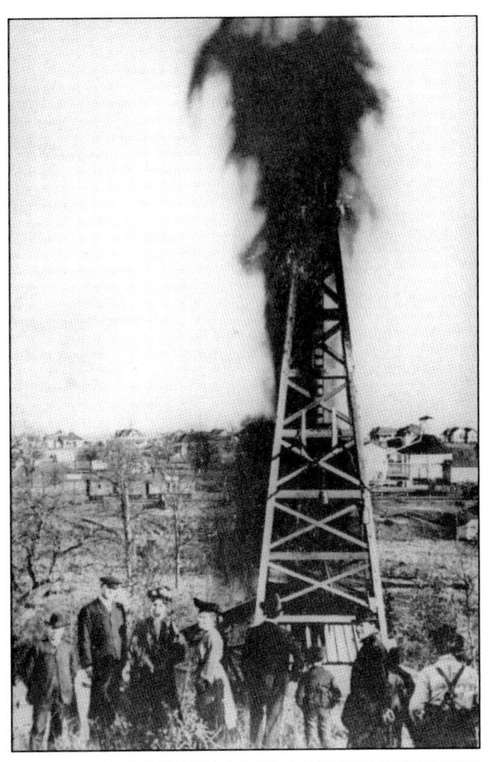

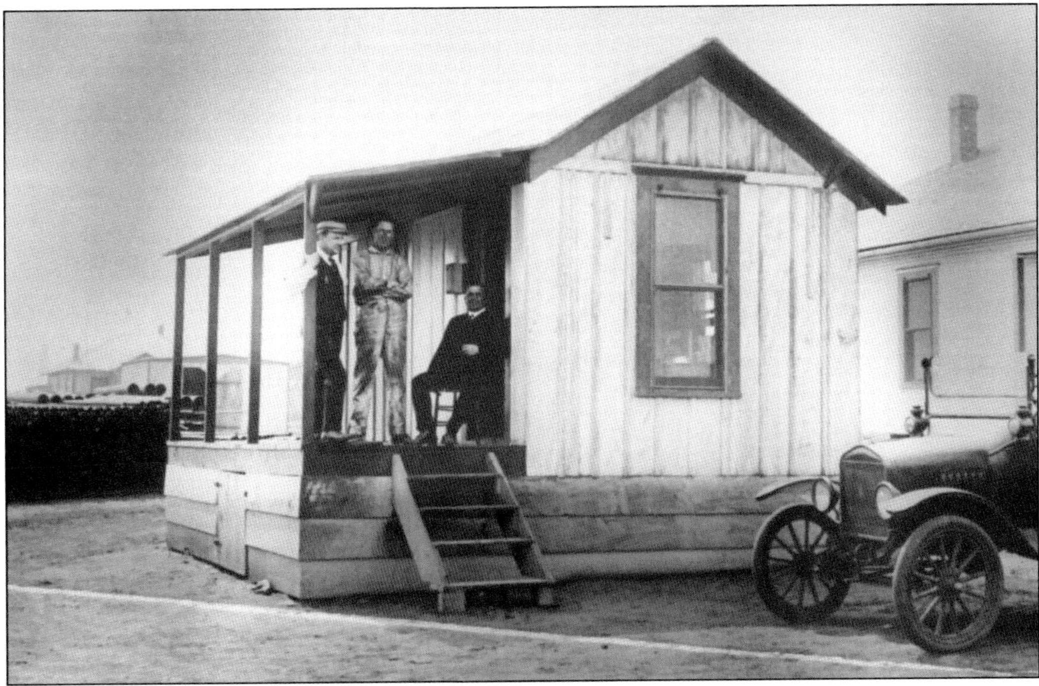

An early-day oil company office in the Quay Oil Field was a primitive board-and-batten construction of 1-by-12 lumber nailed to a wooden frame with smaller boards covering the cracks between the larger boards. The field superintendent, dressed in a suit, is conferring with one of the company's workers, whose clothes are covered with oil. (Author's collection.)

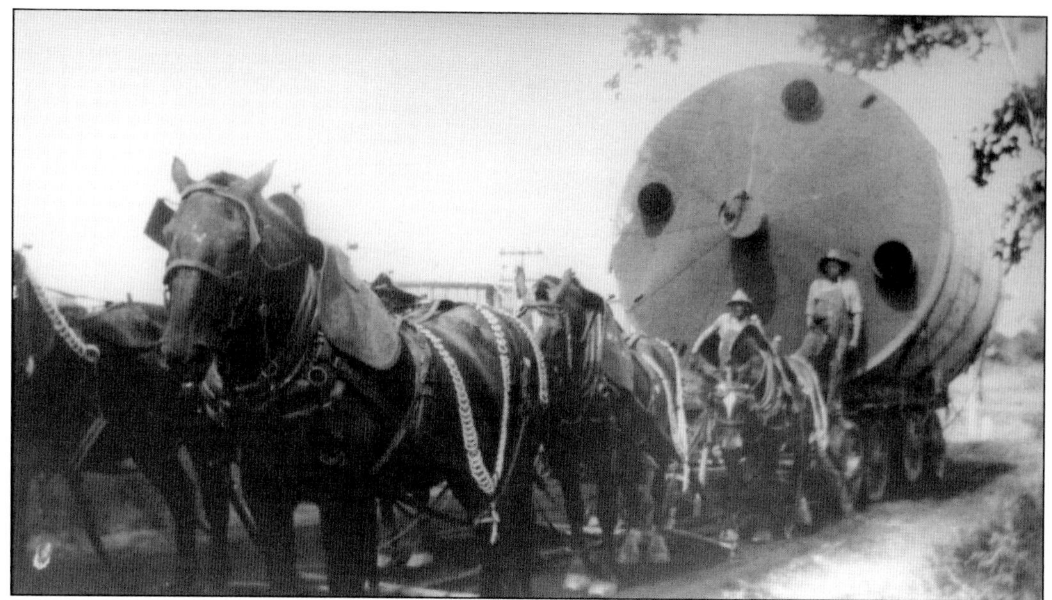

A six-horse team is pulling an eight-wheeled wagon hauling a metal oil-storage tank in the Cleveland Oil Field. The metal tanks were an improvement over the wooden tanks that leaked so badly; however, the metal tanks often developed leaks around the bolts that held the metal plating together. (Courtesy of Triangle Heritage Association.)

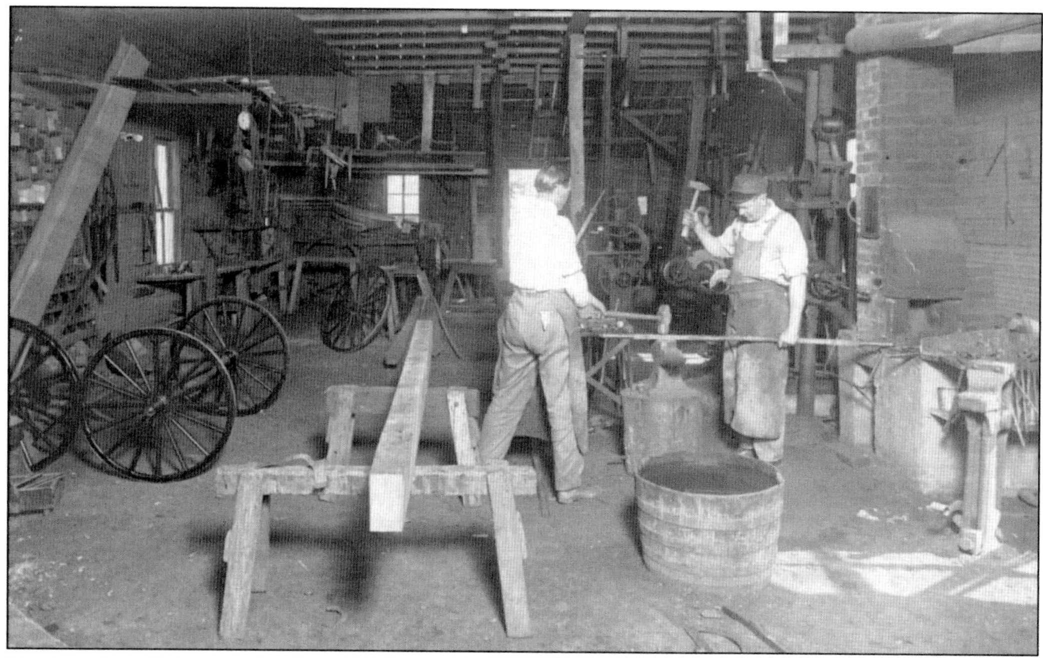

During the oil boom, the local Ralston blacksmith shop was one of the community's busiest establishments. These two men are preparing an iron rod to fit around the wooden wheels on the left of the photograph. Once the rod is heated, it would be placed on the wheel, and as it cooled it would shrink to insure a snug fit. (Courtesy of the Pawnee County Historical Society.)

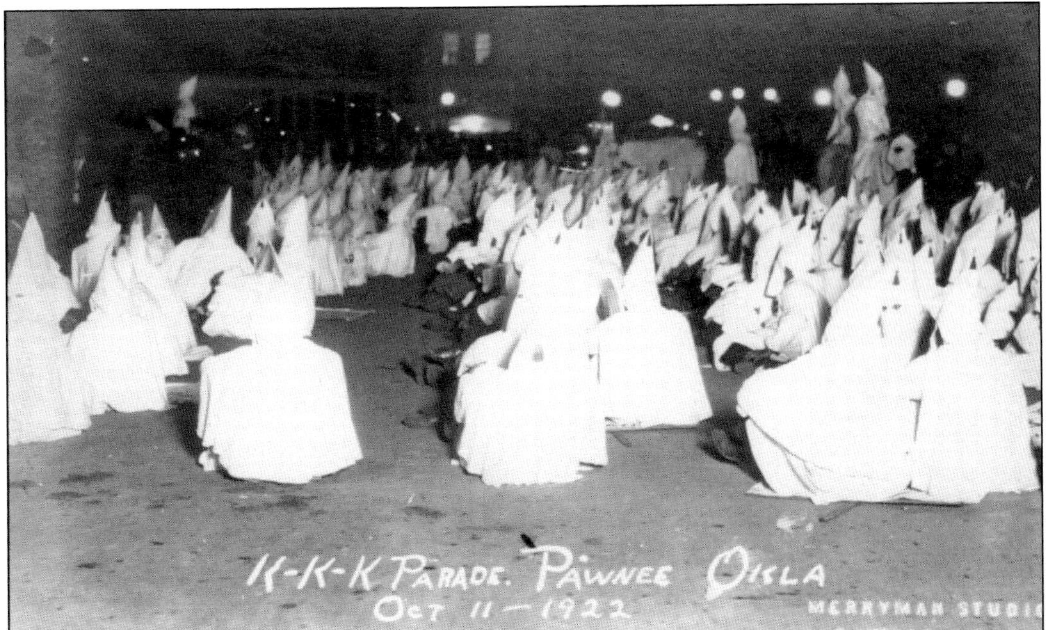

A Ku Klux Klan gathering is pictured in Pawnee on October 11, 1922. The KKK often was the leader of the moral outrage against the vice and violence in the oil boomtowns. On August 7, 1922, the Klansmen paraded through the streets of Jennings carrying banners reading "We Stand For a Clean Town," "Loafers Work Or Leave Town," "Gamblers Leave Town," and "Bootleggers—We See All—We Know All." (Courtesy of the Pawnee County Historical Society.)

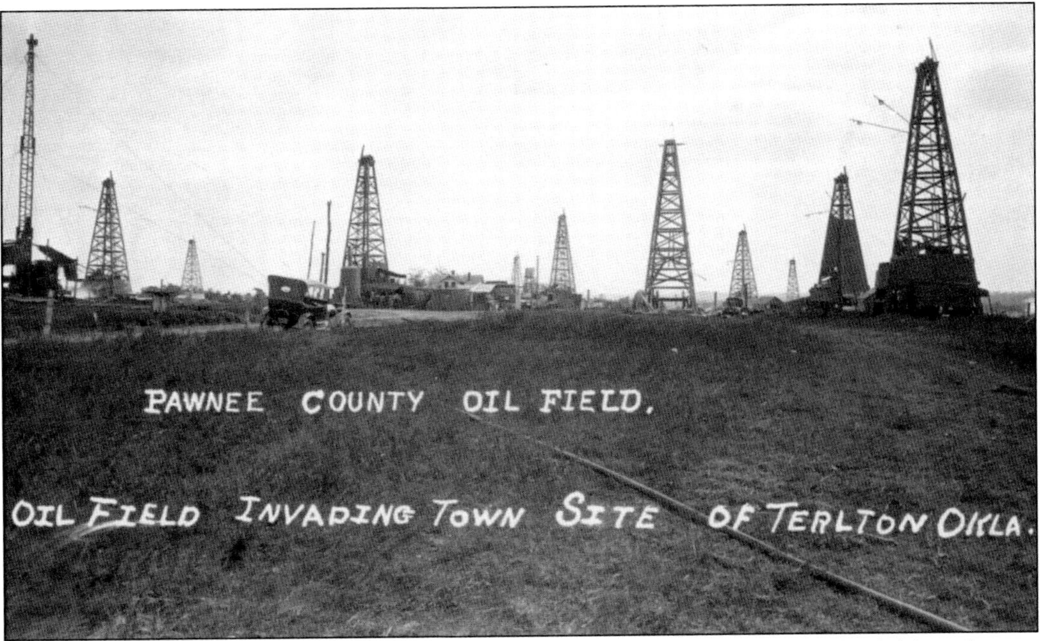

In the foreground of this photograph of the Terlton Oil Field, pipelines from the field's gathering system are carrying oil to a storage tank. The two men in the center of the photograph are using teams of horses to grade a roadway. Notice how close to the house on the right that an oil derrick has been built. (Courtesy of the Pawnee County Historical Society.)

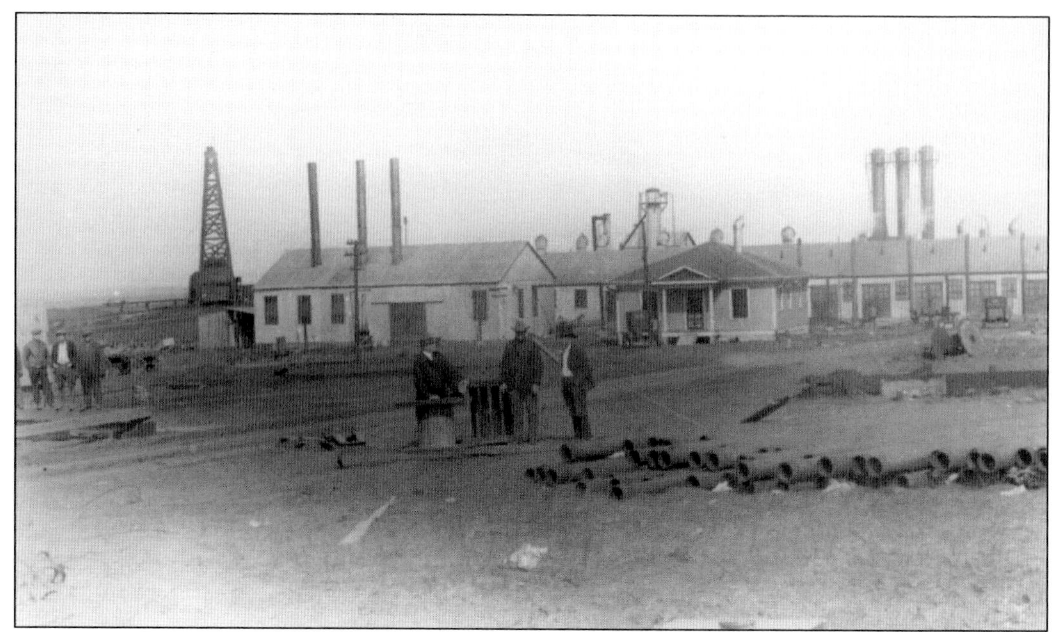

This is a natural-gas processing plant in the Watchorn Oil Field. Some Watchorn wells flowed as much as 35 million cubic feet of natural gas daily. Much of the early gas production was viewed as worthless until D.W. Franchot brought the casing-head natural gas industry to Oklahoma. Afterward, the natural gas produced by a well was condensed to form natural gasoline. (Courtesy of H.P. Laird.)

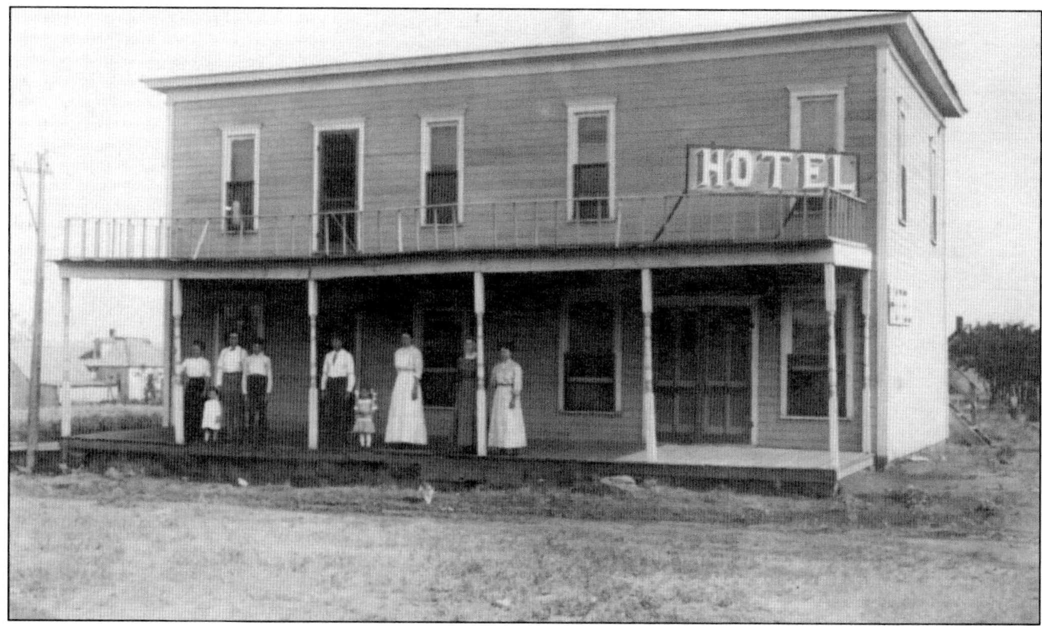

The Skedee Hotel was typical of the oil boomtown catering to oilmen. The front boasted a covered wooden walkway; however, the sidewalks are dirt paths. Note the steps in the back of the building allowing access to the upstairs rooms. They were sometimes used by oilfielders to smuggle chippies, as prostitutes were called, into their rooms. (Courtesy of the Pawnee County Historical Society.)

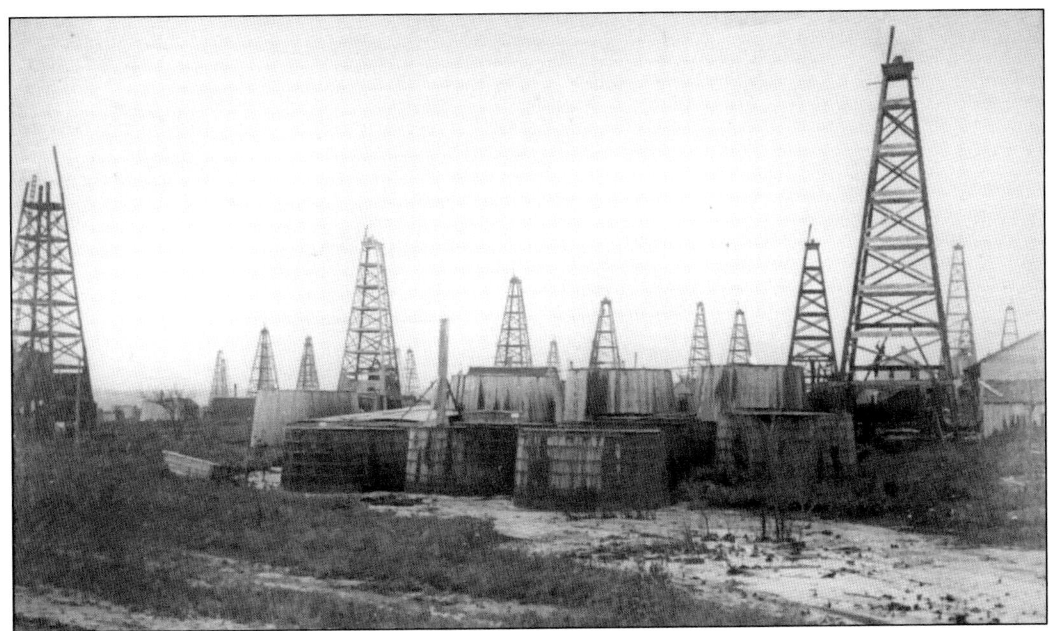

Wooden storage tanks were used to contain production when the Cleveland Oil Field was discovered. These primitive holding tanks were hurriedly constructed with wooden planks held together by bands and caulked with whatever was handy, including horse manure. They all leaked. Note the oil in the forefront of the photograph. On the wooden drilling rig in the right foreground, a workman can be seen climbing with a hammer to make repairs. (Author's collection.)

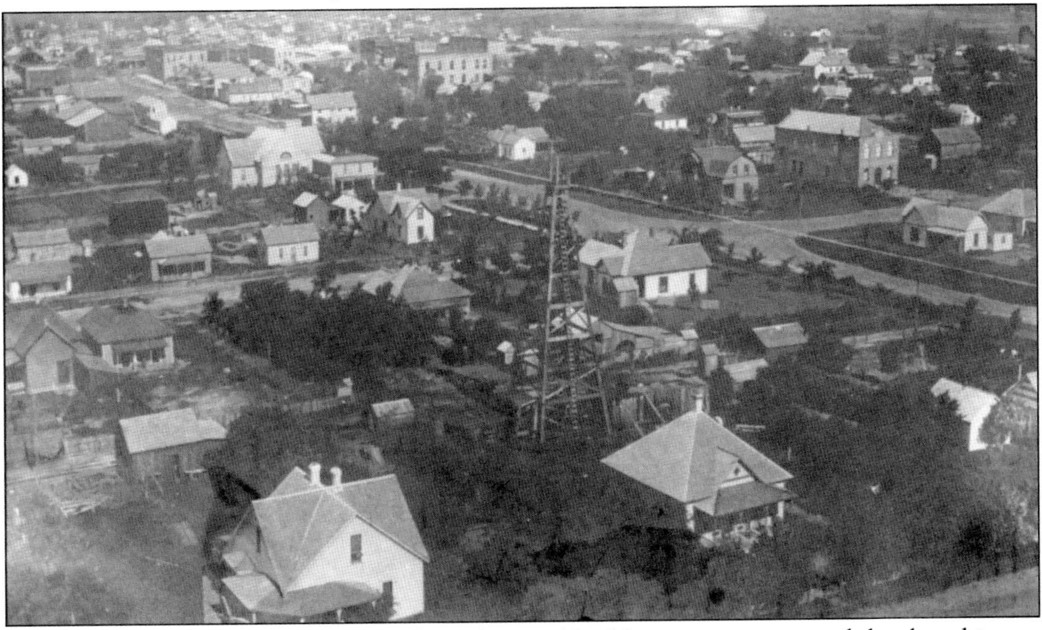

Although Cleveland quickly passed through its wild oil-boomtown stage and developed into a modern community, this photograph with a view looking west toward the main street still shows drilling rigs within the town proper. In the upper right of the photograph is the intersection of East Cherokee and South Vine Streets. The large stone structure near the intersection is the Masonic lodge. To the left of the lodge is the author's childhood home. (Author's collection.)

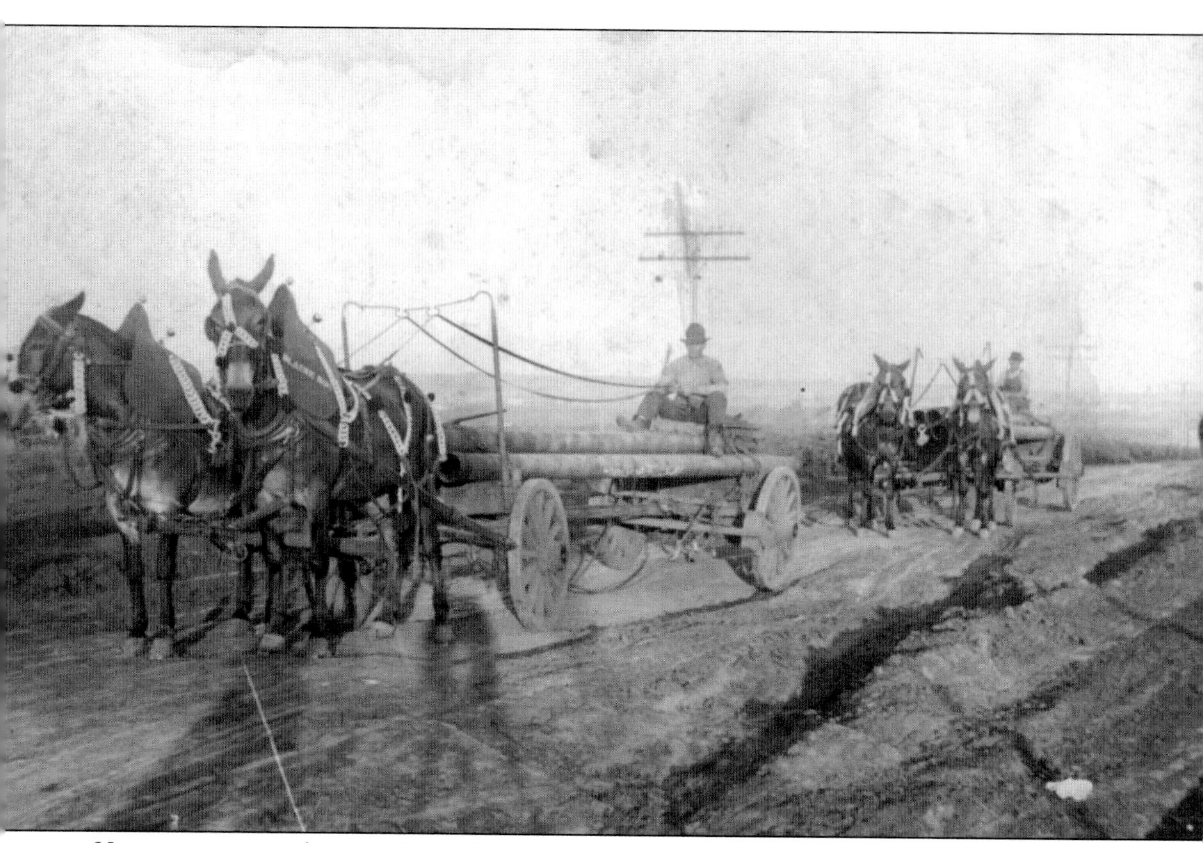

Here is a teamster driving a horse-drawn wagon loaded with casing in the Cleveland Oil Field. The heavy iron-rimmed wheels of the wagons transformed the field's primitive dirt roads into dust. When the rains came, the roads soon became axle-deep in mud that only horses or mules could navigate. (Courtesy of the Pawnee County Historical Society.)

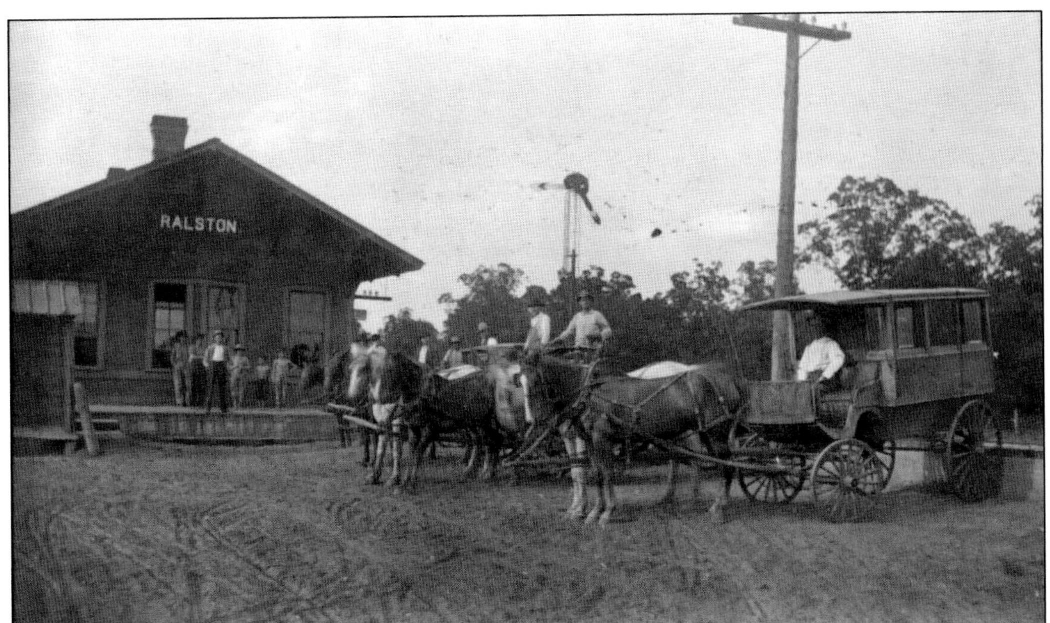

Pictured here is the St. Louis–San Francisco Railway depot in Ralston. The railroad gave Ralston an advantage over other Pawnee oil-boom towns because it provided a readily available means for shipping crude. Note the three hacks on the right of the photograph waiting to take arriving visitors to their destinations. (Courtesy of the Pawnee County Historical Society.)

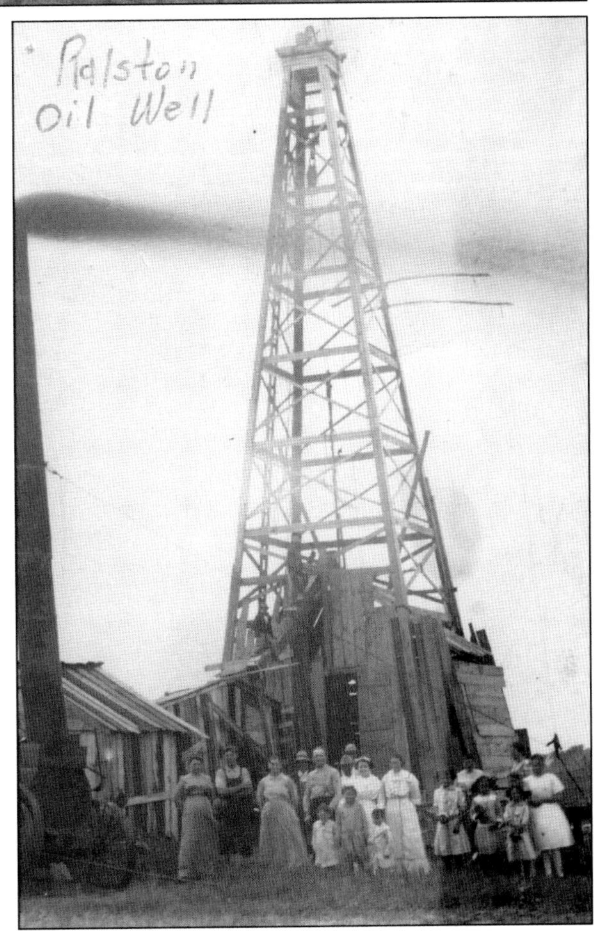

As early as 1902, local residents of Ralston raised $10,000 to drill for oil around their community; however, it was not until 1910, when J.M. Critchlow and his partners completed a wildcat well, that the Ralston Oil Field was located on the Pawnee County–Osage County border. A market for the crude was guaranteed when the Gulf Oil Company completed its pipeline between Eldorado, Kansas, through Ralston, to Beaumont, Texas. (Courtesy of the Pawnee County Historical Society.)

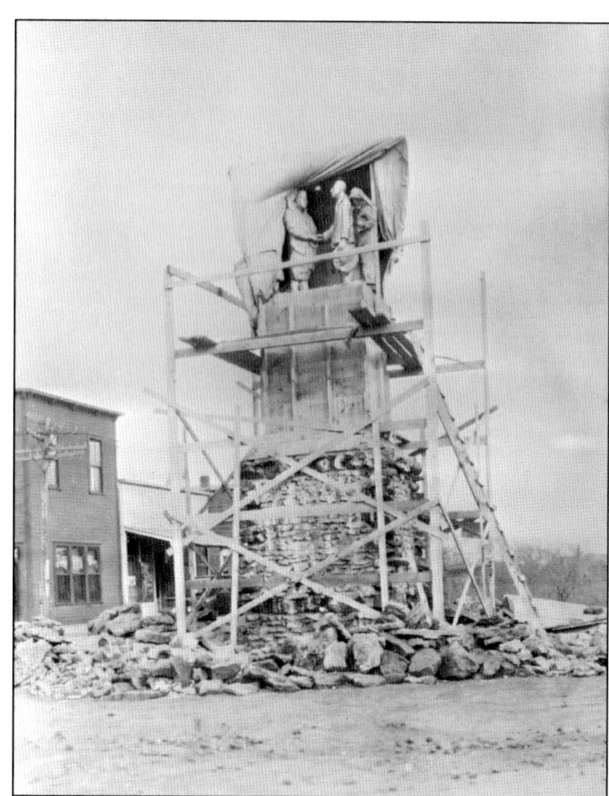

Margette Baker is seen working on the *Bond of Friendship* statue of E.E. Walters and Chief Baconrind in downtown Skedee. Walters was the auctioneer who sold millions of dollars of oil leases for the Osage tribe. The statue was commissioned by Walters to show his friendship for the Osage. In return, he was given a large diamond ring. (Author's collection.)

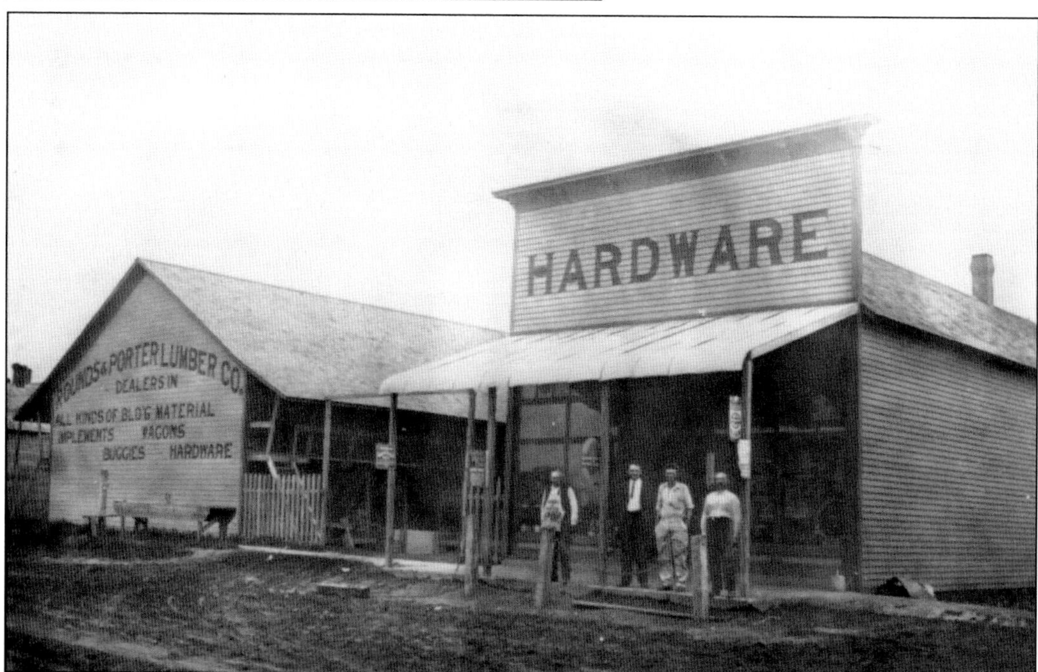

The Rounds & Porter Lumber Company in Pawnee was a major source of timber for oilmen building the thousands of drilling rigs in Pawnee County during the oil-boom era. (Courtesy of the Pawnee County Historical Society.)

The Maher-Miller Oil Company No. 3 well in the Cleveland Oil Field blowing in was an awesome sight. Many early-day oilmen believed that if one allowed a new well to blow wild for a time, it would clean the well and increase production. Notice the barbed-wire fence surrounding the well site to keep stray livestock away. (Author's collection.)

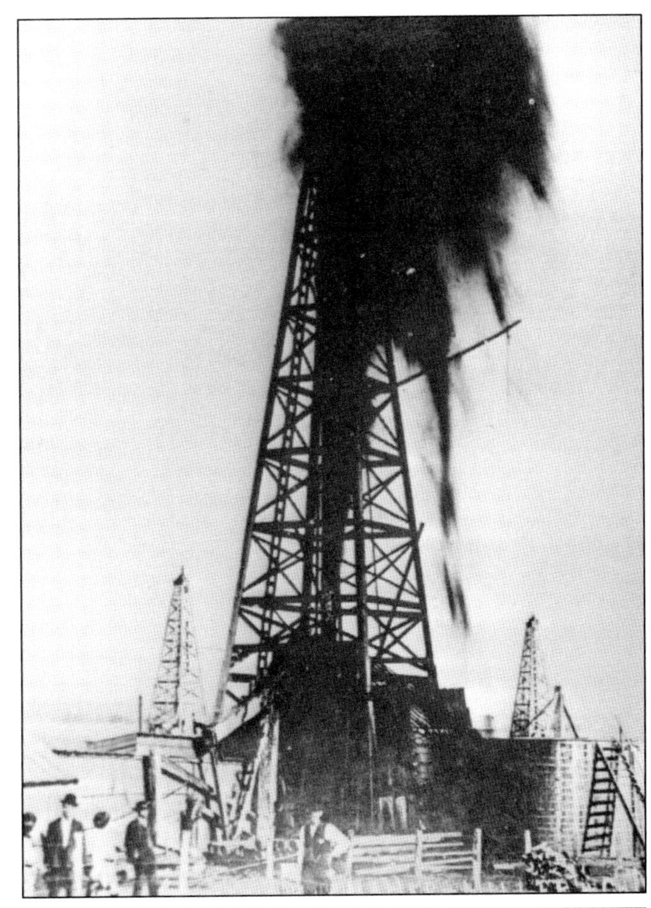

Patrons entered the Cleveland Boiler Shop establishment by crossing the boards over a ditch beside the dirt street. The boilers were used to supply power to the many oil wells in the fields surrounding Cleveland. Finished boilers are stacked to the right of the door. Boilers under construction are to the left of the door. (Courtesy of Robert Jordan.)

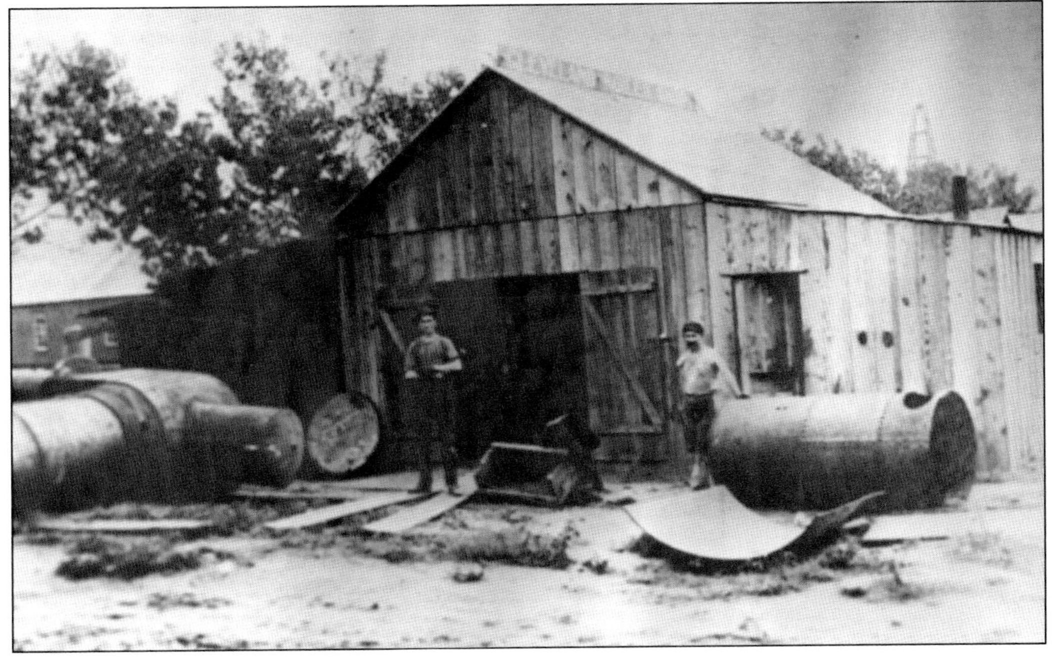

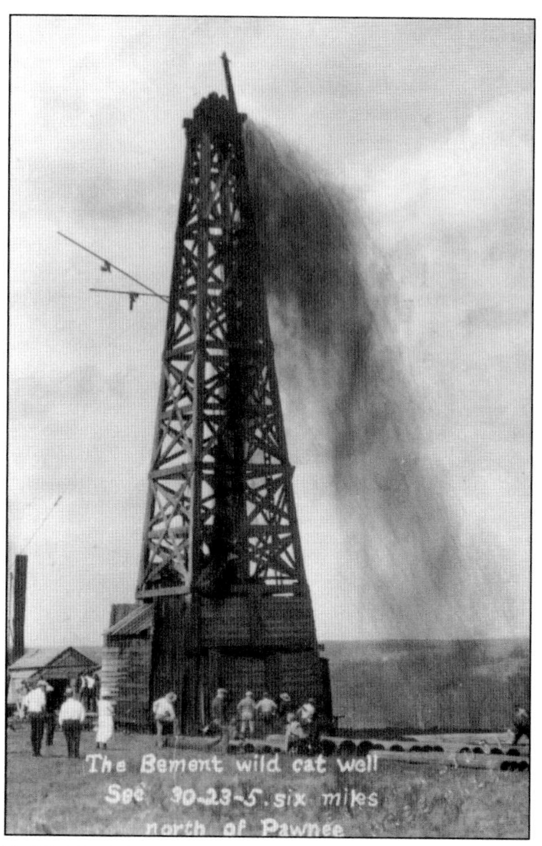

The Bement No. 1 was a wildcat well drilled six miles north of Pawnee in the post oak–covered hills near the Masham store. Eventually, the area was developed as the Masham Field. Once the gusher was brought under control, the pipe in front of the well would be used as casing. (Courtesy of Triangle Heritage Historical Museum.)

The Uncle Bill Lowery, in the upper right of the photograph, was the discovery well of the Cleveland Field. Because it was a wildcat, inadequate storage tanks were constructed when it was drilled. As a result, much of the oil was allowed to flow down Cedar Creek. To prevent it from harming their crops, farmers often set the escaping oil on fire. (Courtesy of Robert Jordan.)

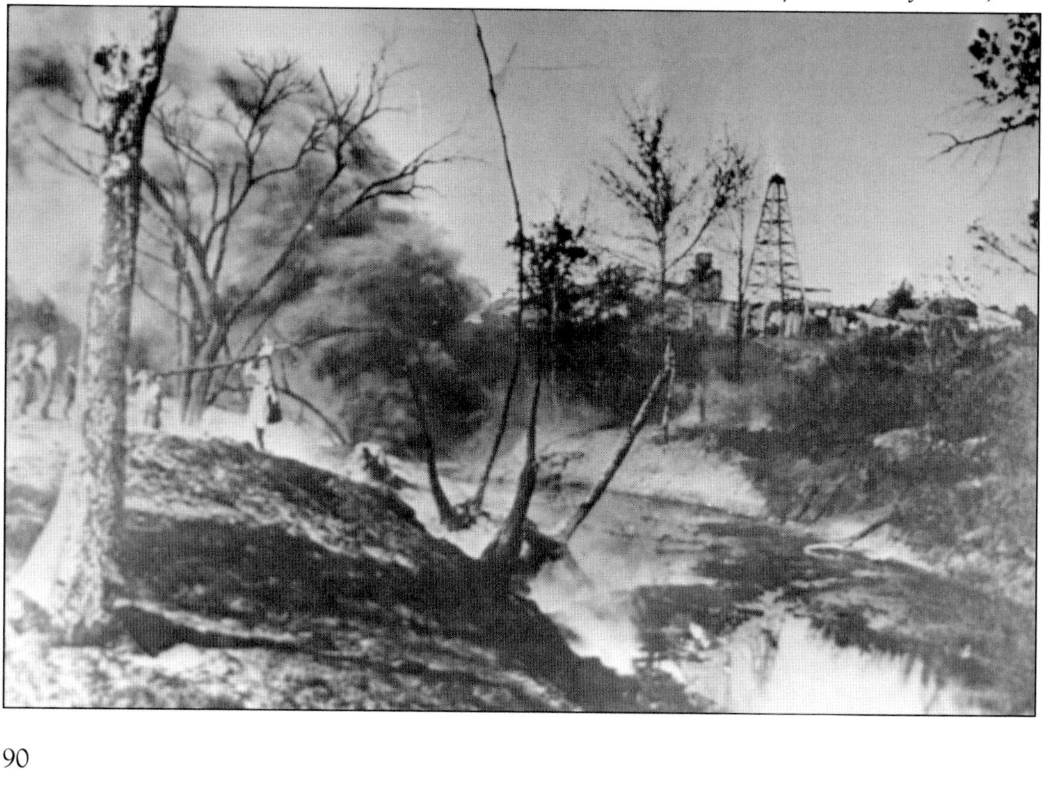

Seven

CLEVELAND

A myriad of honest merchants, gamblers, roustabouts, hijackers, millionaires, prostitutes, conmen, bootleggers, farmers, and lawmen rubbed elbows on the muddy streets of Cleveland. They came for one thing—black gold. Many sought their wealth honestly. Others preyed on the workers and merchants in search of ill-gotten gain.

Thousands of people hurried to the new find. Housing was quickly overtaxed. Many found shelter in private homes, but these were quickly filled, as were attics, haylofts, and chicken coops. Often, several occupants shared the same bed in shifts. Generally, the hotels offered "small rooms, hard beds and neither heat nor stands for pitchers of water." It was not uncommon for three cots to be placed in one room.

Toilet facilities consisted of a wash pan, placed on the lean-to's front porch along with a community towel, a bar of soap, and a dipper. A two-hole outhouse was in the backyard. Nonetheless, hustlers easily collected from $2 per eight-hour shift to $30 per week for such accommodations. Many workers were forced to sleep on rooftops, under pool tables, in theater seats, or on derrick floors. When the weather was warm, it was not uncommon for the wooden sidewalks to be covered with sleeping workers.

Wild women and whiskey were prominent. At the height of the boom, Cleveland boasted 150 to 200 prostitutes plying their trade in the two-block section of Main Street that also held most of the city's saloons. The saloons operated on the first floor and the prostitutes on the second floor.

Cleveland once boasted 13 saloons and two distilleries inside the city limits. Most of the whiskey was manufactured locally and contained chewing tobacco or creosote to give the mixture color and sulfuric acid to give the drink a kick. The ingredients were mixed together with 120-proof alcohol and allowed to age while waiting behind the bar to be served.

Eventually, wells encroached inside the town of Cleveland. The natural gas spewing from gushers coated the community's collection of wooden structures. It was a disaster waiting to happen, and early-day Cleveland burned several times.

Eventually, Cleveland threw off its boomtown upbringing and developed into the modern economic center of eastern Pawnee County.

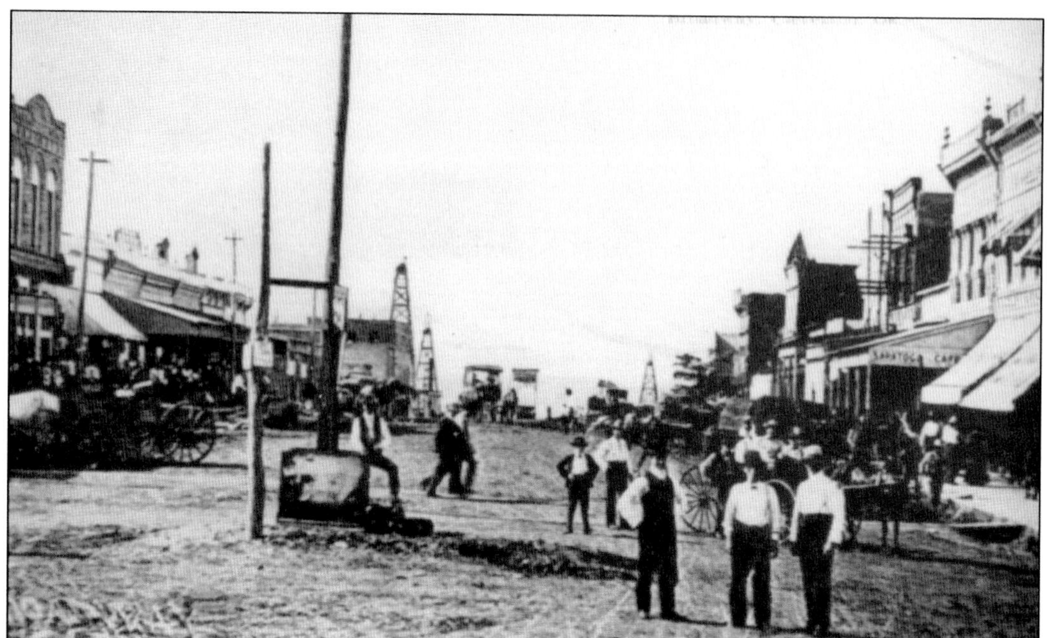

In 1912, Cleveland's main street was a busy place. In center of the street in the foreground is the town flagpole, and in the center of the street in the background is the town well. On the right is the Saratoga Café. Concrete sidewalks have been built, but the street remains dirt. Bordering the street are open ditches with boards laid across them for pedestrians. (Courtesy of Evelyn "Zeke" Cheek.)

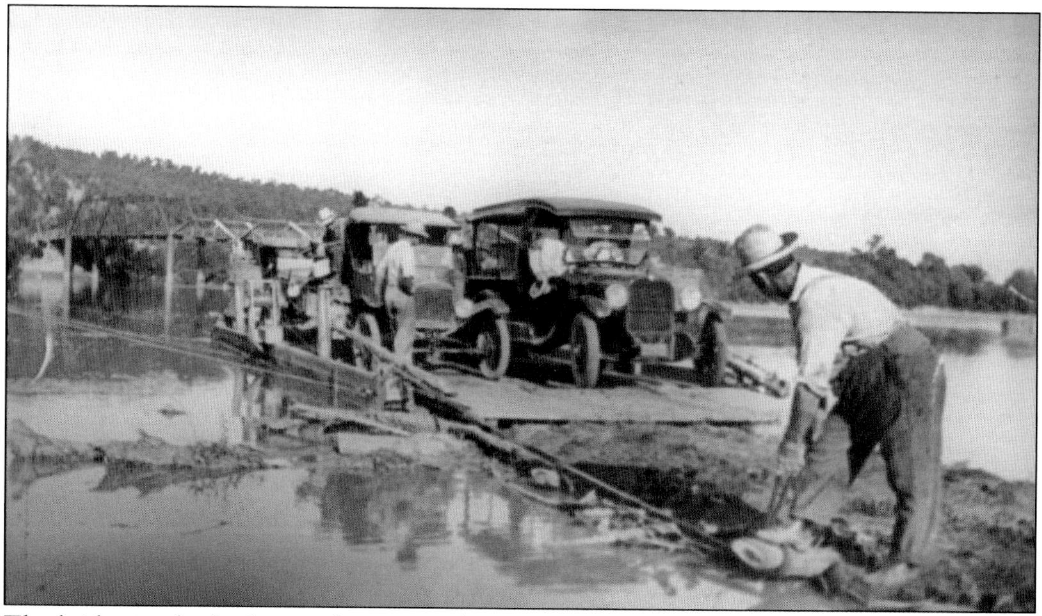

The bridge in the background is across the Arkansas River east of Cleveland and was later destroyed in the flood of 1924. Afterward, the only way to avoid a lengthy detour was to use the temporary ferry north of the bridge. Notice the vehicle on the right. The passenger is looking out to the rear as the driver backs onto the ferry. Clayton Lucas is the man on the right holding the ropes anchoring the ferry. (Courtesy of Triangle Heritage Association.)

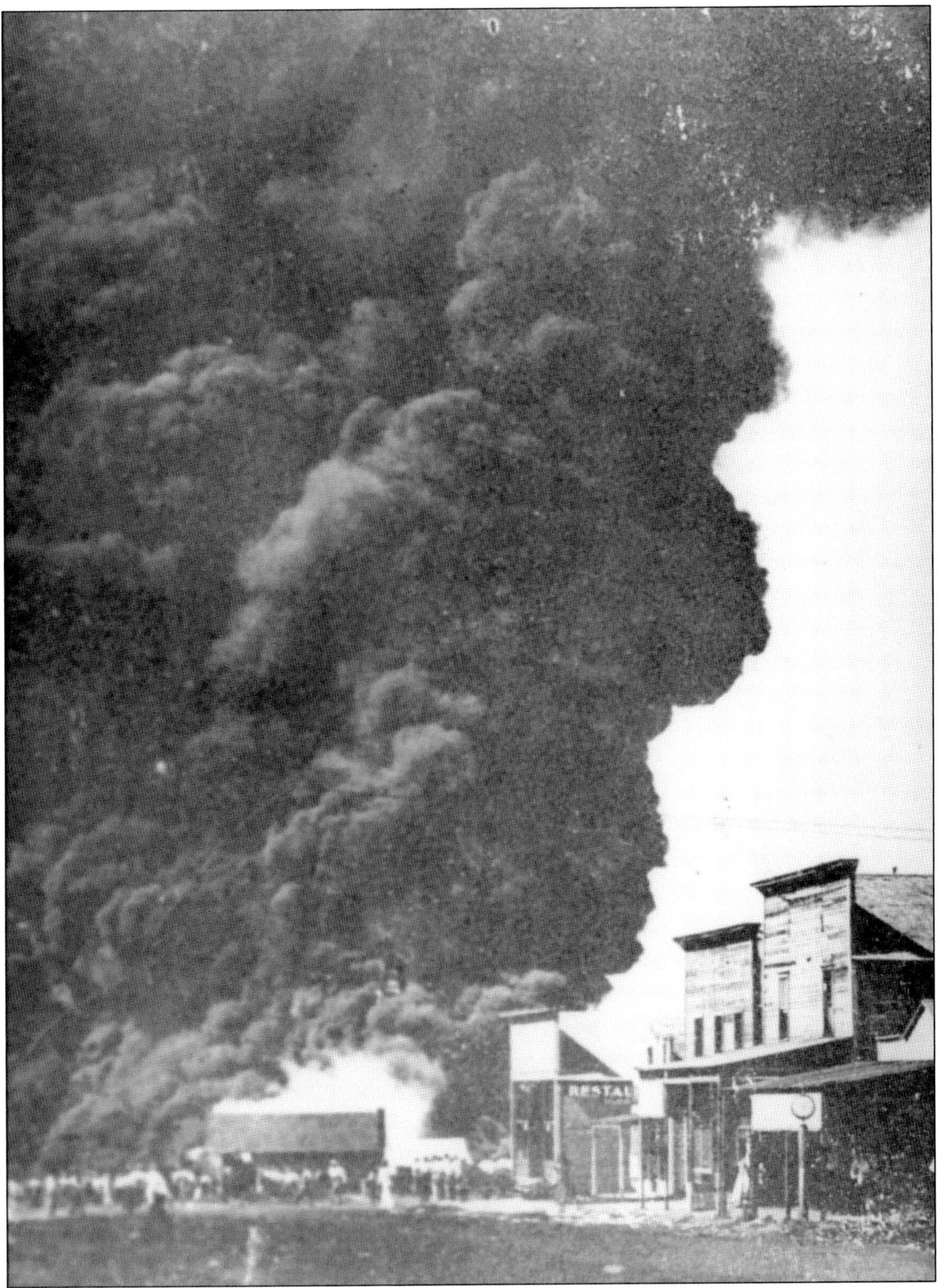

Because of the high natural-gas pressure in the Cleveland Oil Field, many wells blew in as gushers soaking the unpainted wooden buildings with coats of oil. Fires were common and often spread into town. This is an oil-field fire on the south end of Broadway, just reaching the business section. (Author's collection.)

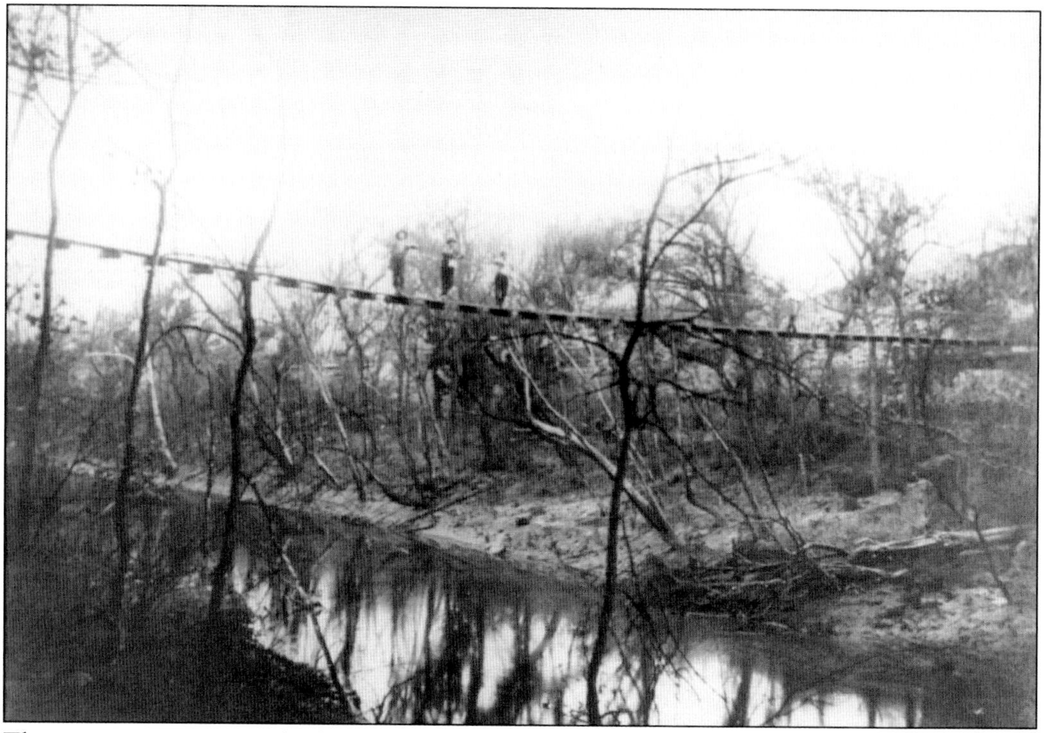

The swinging suspension bridge over Cedar Creek connected Cleveland to the drilling activity south of town. The creek was often covered with escaping oil from the drilling rigs. Note all the dead vegetation along the creek's banks. To keep the oil from reaching their land, local farmers would set the floating oil on fire. (Author's collection.)

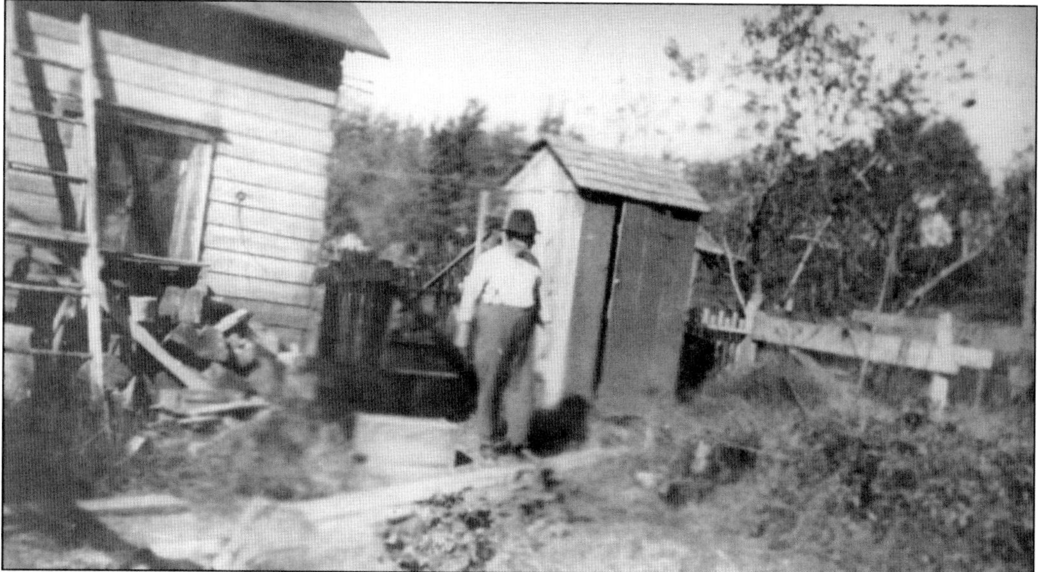

Sanitary conditions in Cleveland were primitive at best at the onset of the oil boom. Lacking a sewer system, most residents relied on a two-hole outhouse such as the one seen here. Note that wooden boards have been laid on the ground to keep the homeowner out of the mud on trips to the outhouse. (Author's collection.)

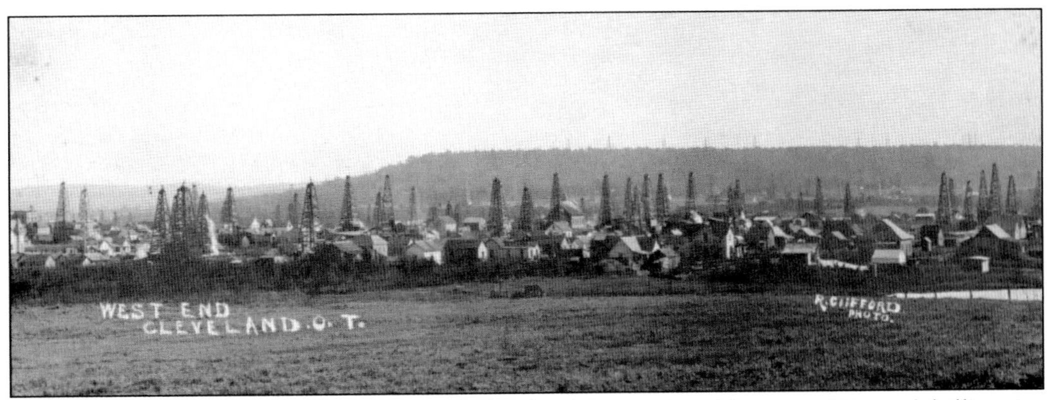

Pictured here is the west end of the town of Cleveland during the oil boom. Additional drilling rigs can be seen on the hilltop across the Arkansas River. They are a part of the Osage City Oil Field, one of the many offshoots of the 1904 Cleveland discovery. An open-pit earthen oil-storage pit is at the lower right of the photograph. (Courtesy of the Pawnee County Historical Society.)

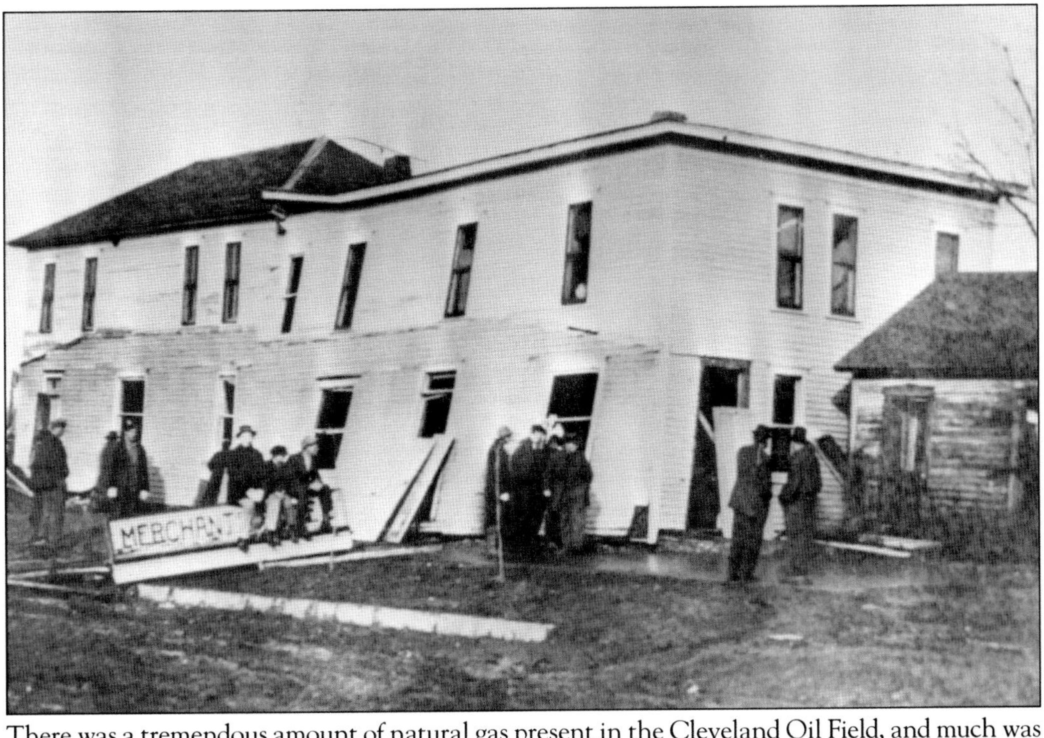

There was a tremendous amount of natural gas present in the Cleveland Oil Field, and much was simply vented into the atmosphere, where it often accumulated in low places beneath buildings. This photograph shows the remains of Cleveland's Merchants Hotel after a natural-gas explosion on January 20, 1916. (Courtesy of Triangle Heritage Association.)

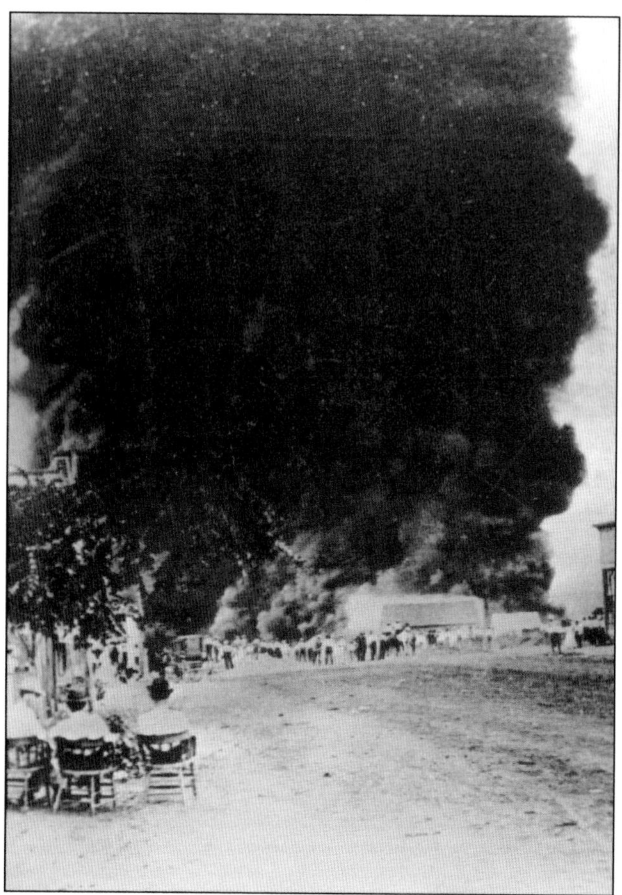

As this oil-field fire spread into the business district, several patrons of Cleveland's Dunlop Hotel moved chairs out into the street to watch the conflagration. Others are rushing down the street to get a better look as the flames spread. (Courtesy of Robert Jordan.)

By 1919, most of the oil-boomtown wooden structures on Cleveland's main street have been replaced by more substantial and fire-resistant brick and stone structures. Nonetheless, a few oil derricks can still be seen. In the center of the intersection is the town's flagpole. (Courtesy of Evelyn "Zeke" Cheek.)

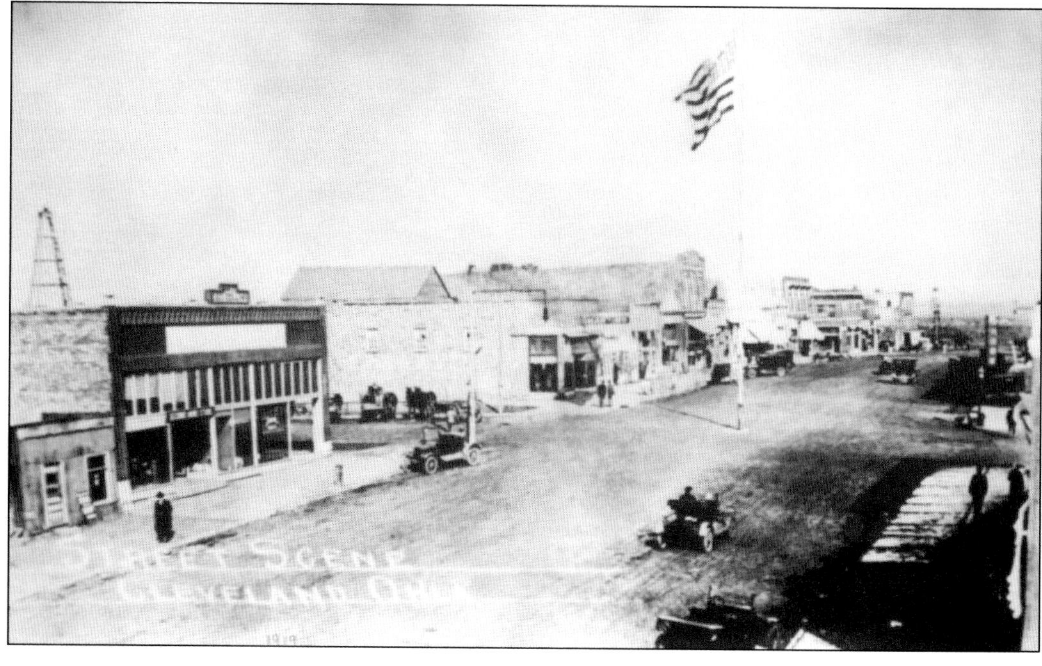

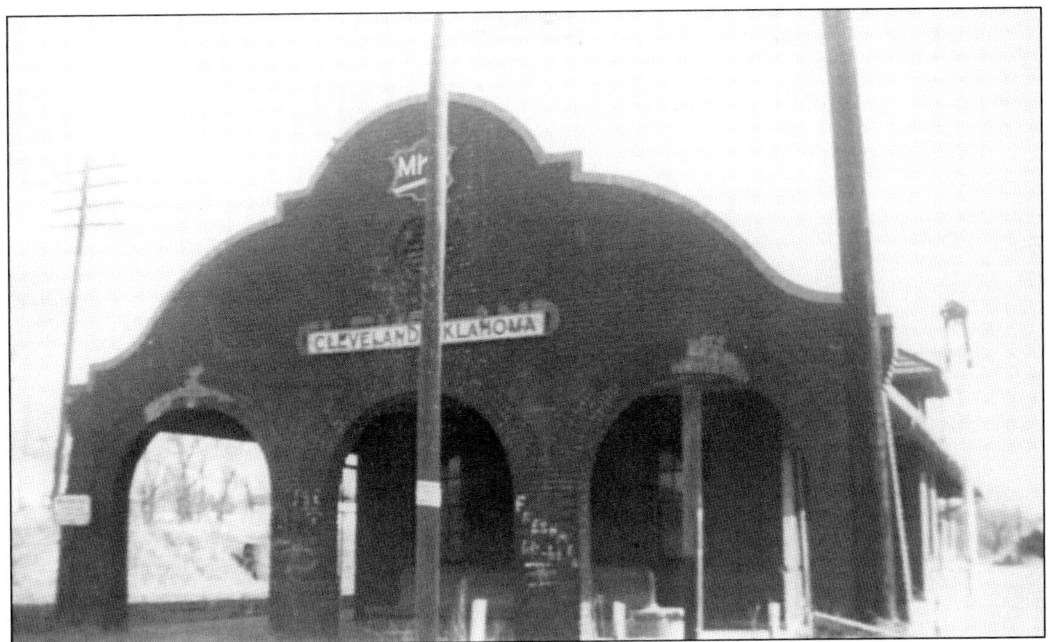

The Missouri-Kansas-Texas Railroad depot was on the eastern side of Cleveland. The M-K-T intersected the Oil Belt Terminal Railroad at Jennings, southwest of Cleveland. The Oil Belt Terminal Railroad connected the oil fields of Cleveland and Payne Counties to the refineries in Tulsa. (Courtesy of the Osage County Historical Society.)

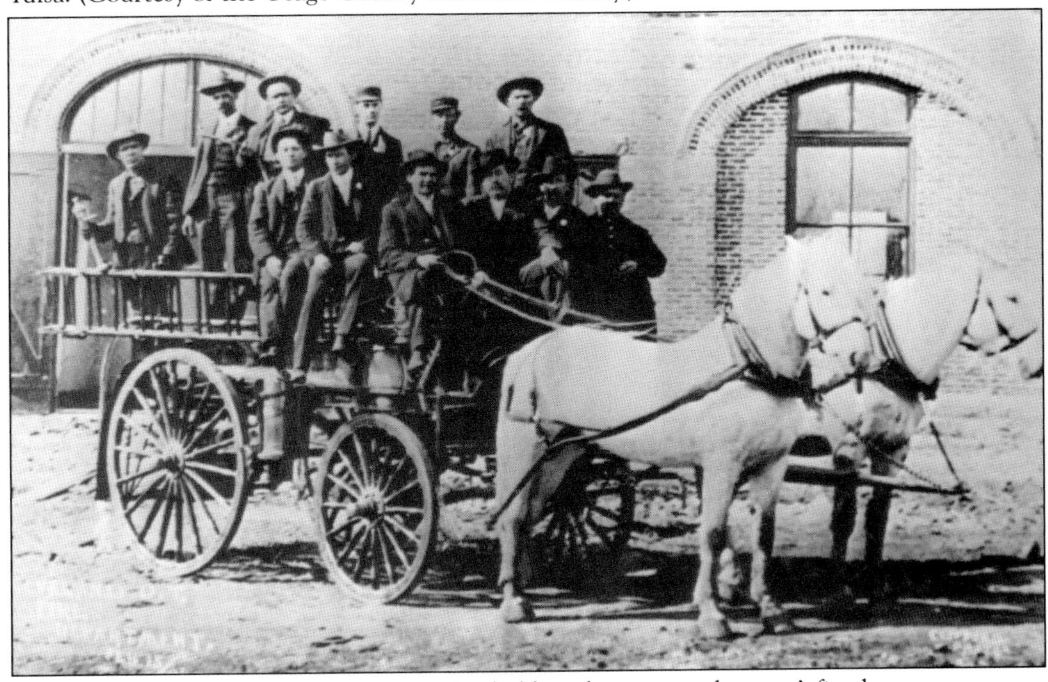

George Lanning, Cleveland's town marshal, is holding the reins on the town's fire department wagon in 1906. Lanning was charged with keeping the peace among Cleveland's more rowdy elements during the oil boom and with protecting the community's oil-soaked buildings from catching fire. The man on the rear of the wagon is holding a fire-hose nozzle. (Courtesy of Robert Jordan.)

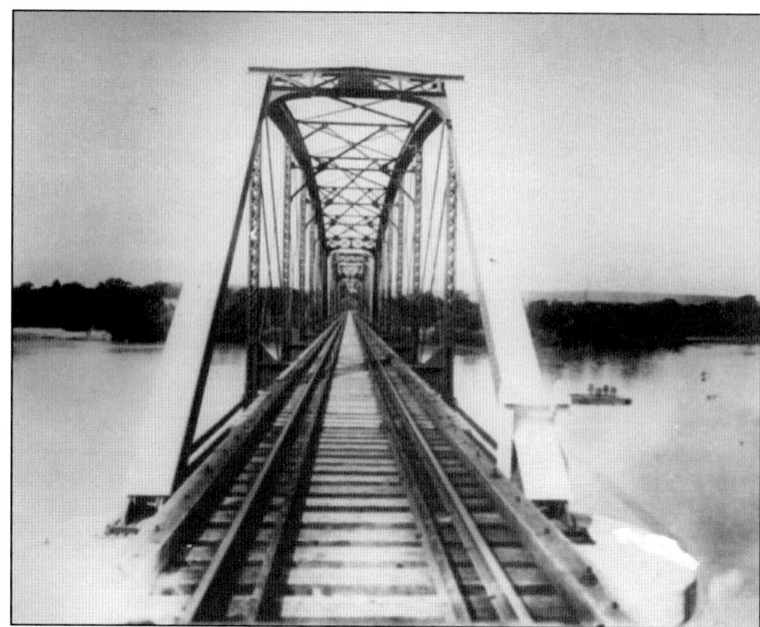

The Missouri-Kansas-Texas, or M-K-T, Railroad bridge crossed the Arkansas River east of Cleveland. The M-K-T built south from the Oklahoma-Kansas border and reached the Arkansas River in 1903. This modern steel bridge carried the rails across the river into Pawnee County. The Arkansas Valley & Western Railway's tracks, which ran from Enid to Sapulpa, joined the M-K-T at Jennings. (Author's collection.)

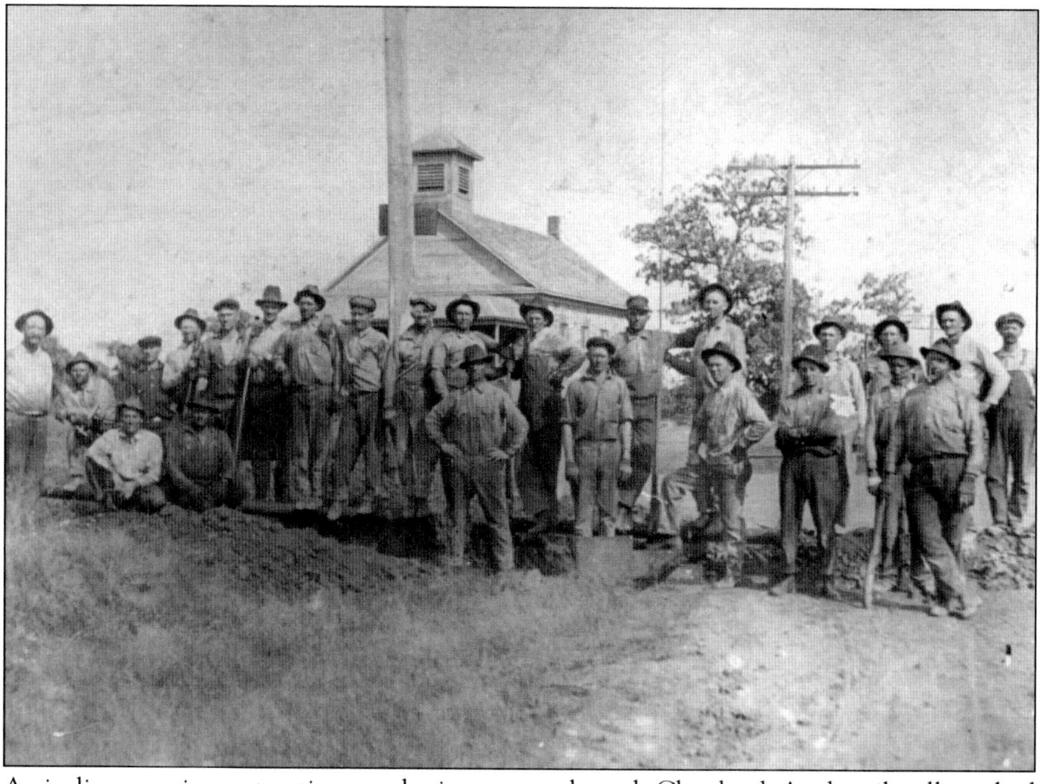

A pipeline crew is constructing a gathering system through Cleveland. As the oil wells pushed into the community, a proper and extensive pipeline gathering system was necessary to carry the oil to storage tanks. This crew is digging a shallow ditch to carry a pipeline beneath one of Cleveland's dirt streets. Because it was a shallow pipeline, most of the work was done by men using shovels. (Author's collection.)

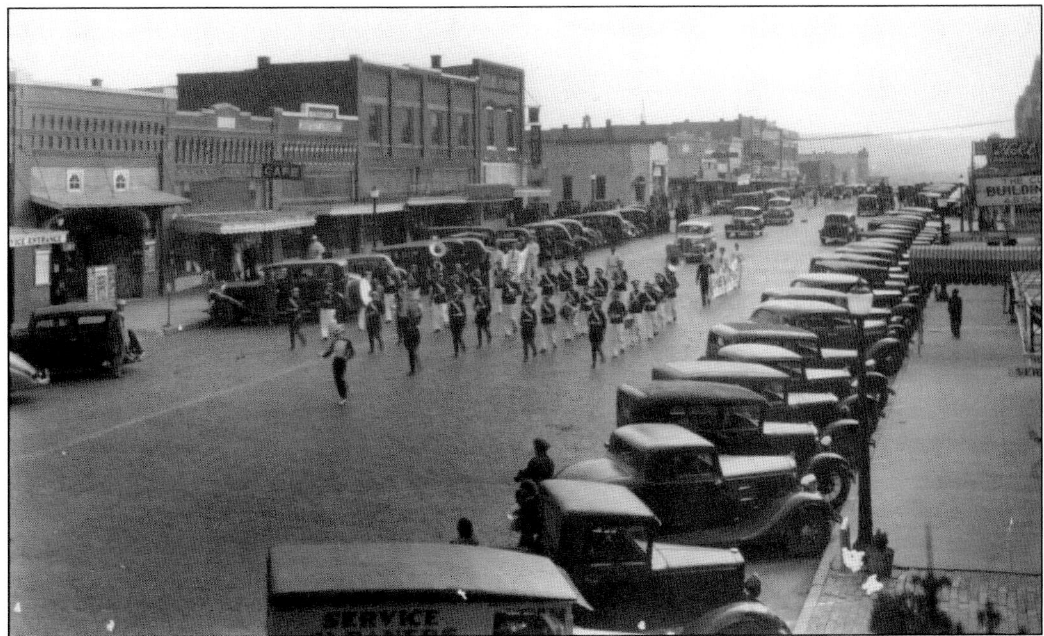

The Cleveland High School Band is leading a parade down Cleveland's main street in the late 1930s. The street has been paved with bricks, and the sidewalks are a mixture of brick and concrete. On the right side are the Cleveland Building Association, Moore's Grocery and Meat, a bar advertising Budweiser beer, and Holt's Jewelry and Optical. On the left are Crady's Grocery and Market and the Case Hardware Store. (Courtesy of Evelyn "Zeke" Cheek.)

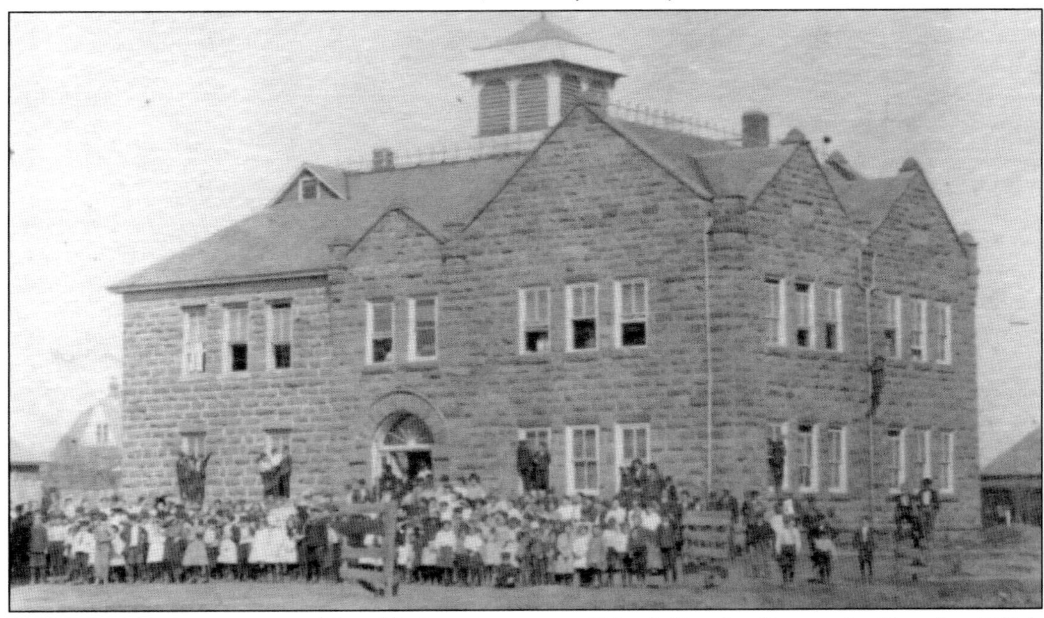

Located at the intersection of East Wichita Avenue and North Dunlap Street, the Cleveland High School building was constructed in 1909 and was in use until 1993, when it was demolished. A later addition was built on the north side of the school. It contained a gymnasium on the east side and an auditorium on the west side. In 1930, a grade school was constructed to the southeast of the high school. (Courtesy of Evelyn "Zeke" Cheek.)

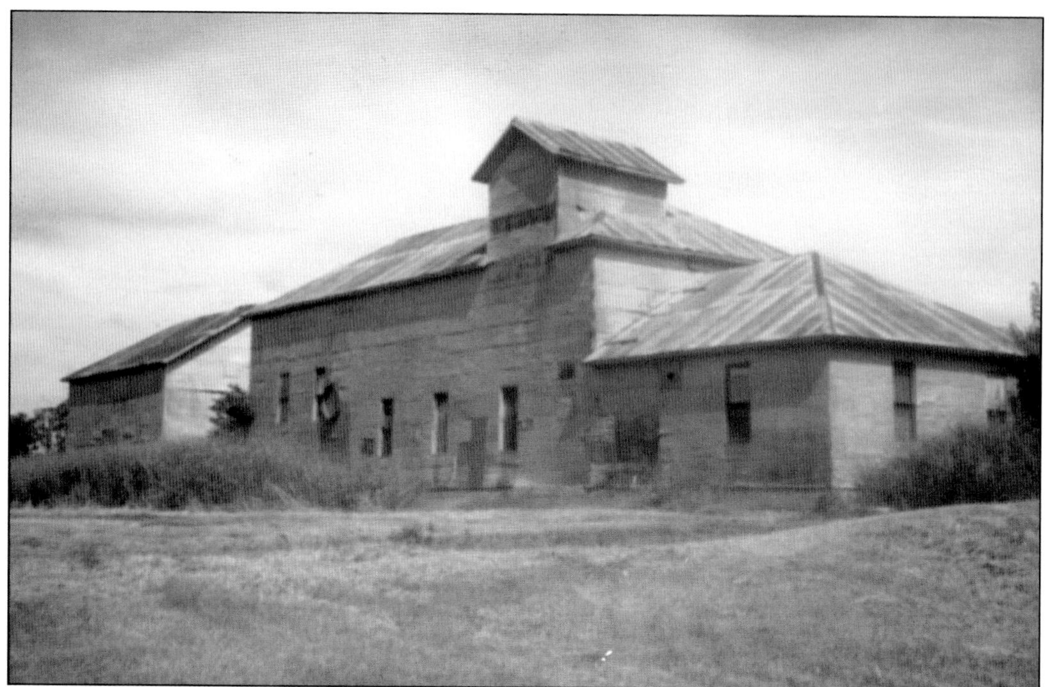

The old tin cotton gin was on the southeast side of Cleveland and served the area's farmers for many years. Cleveland was the commercial center for most of eastern Pawnee County and the shipping point for the area's agribusiness. Prior to the Great Depression, cotton was king in Oklahoma and the major cash crop for Pawnee County farmers. (Courtesy of Evelyn "Zeke" Cheek.)

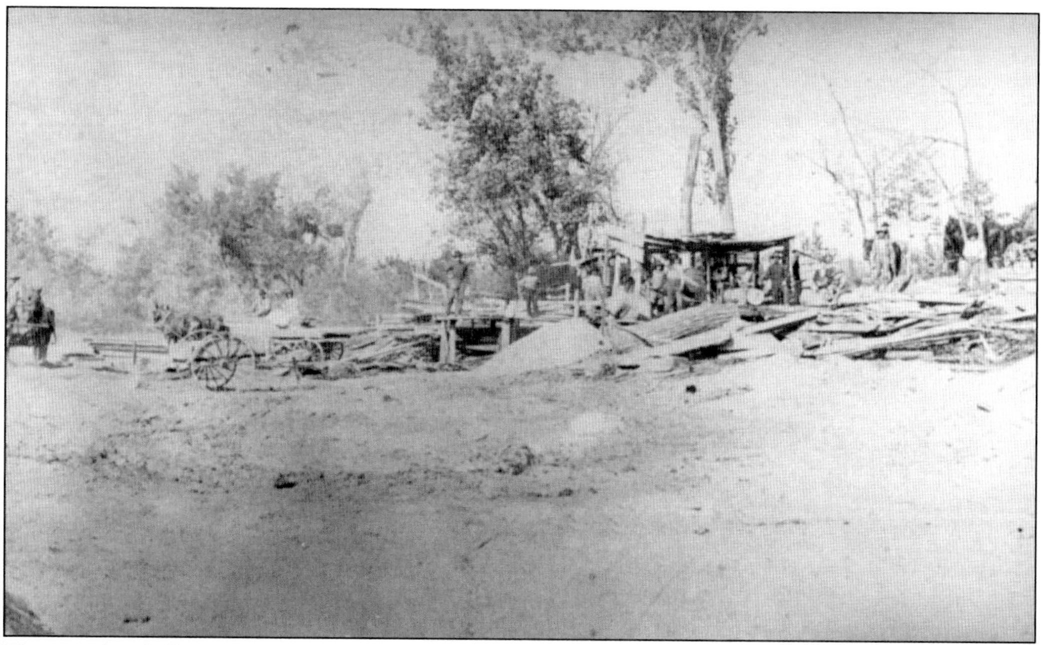

The wooden drilling rigs and hastily constructed buildings in the Cleveland Oil Field demanded large amounts of lumber. This is a steam-powered sawmill cutting derrick timbers. To the left of the sawmill is a loading platform where wagons were filled with the cut timber. (Author's collection.)

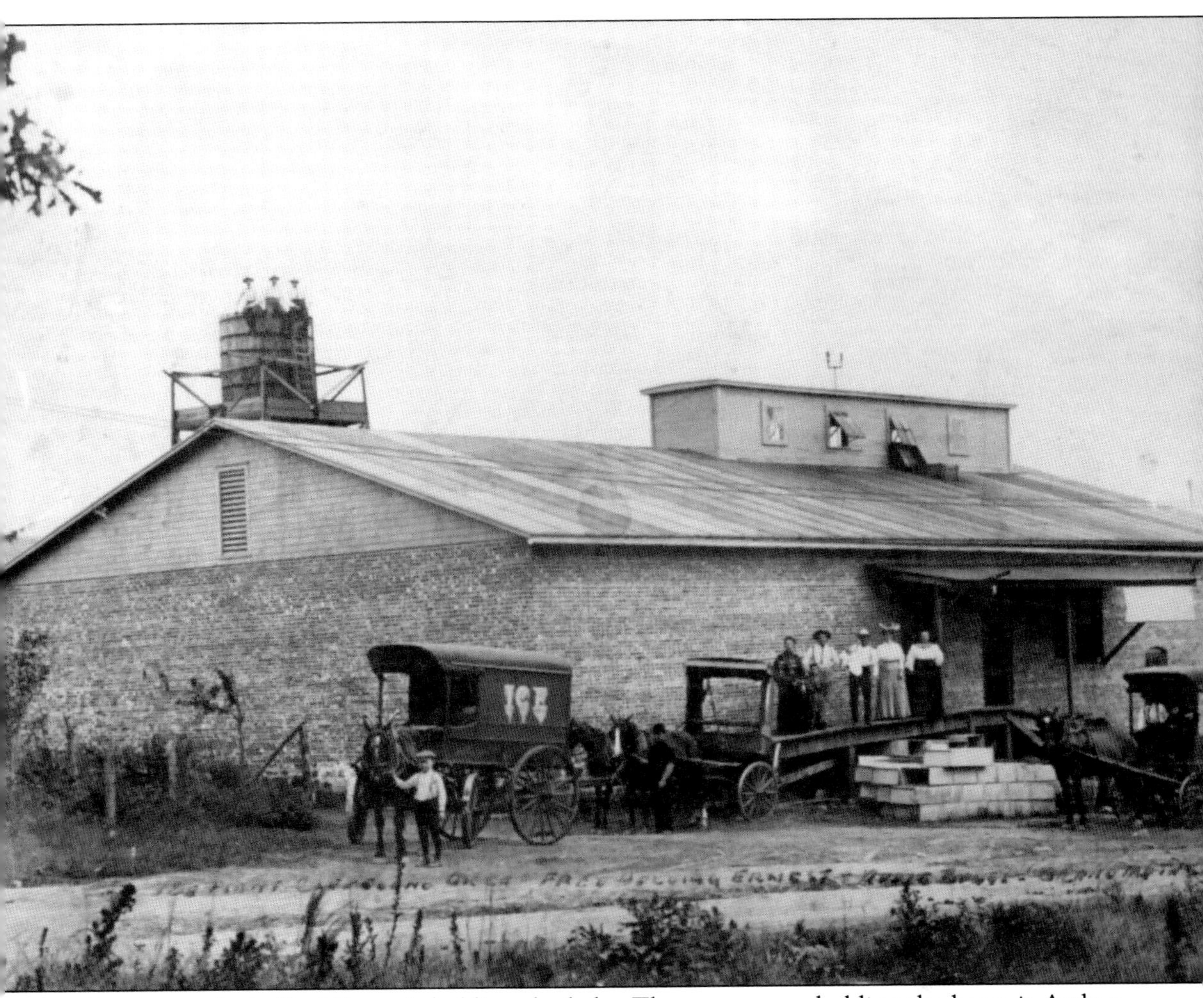

On the ice dock, Fred Boggs is holding the baby. The young man holding the horse is Arthur Lucas. Note the three ice wagons in front of the plant. The wagon in the center is waiting at the bottom of the loading dock down which the frozen ice was slid. Three men are sitting on top of the ice plant's water tank. (Courtesy of Evelyn "Zeke" Cheek.)

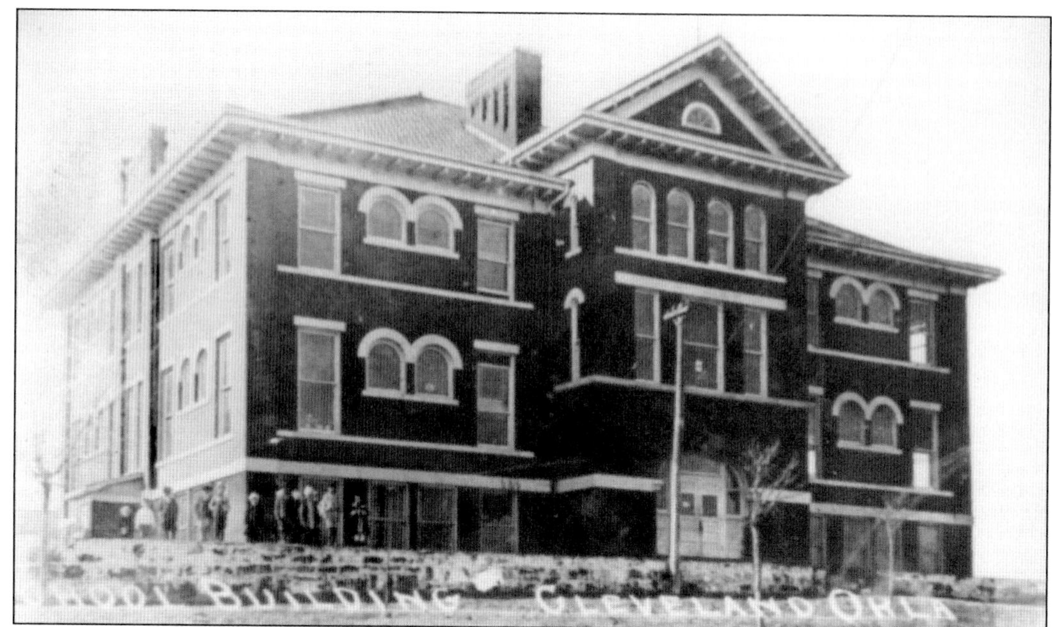

Built in 1910 at a cost of $18,000, this three-story native-stone structure replaced Cleveland's original two-room school. While most of the students are gathered in front of the building or standing on the windowsills, one young man on the right has climbed up on the school's downspouts for the photograph. (Courtesy of the Pawnee County Historical Society.)

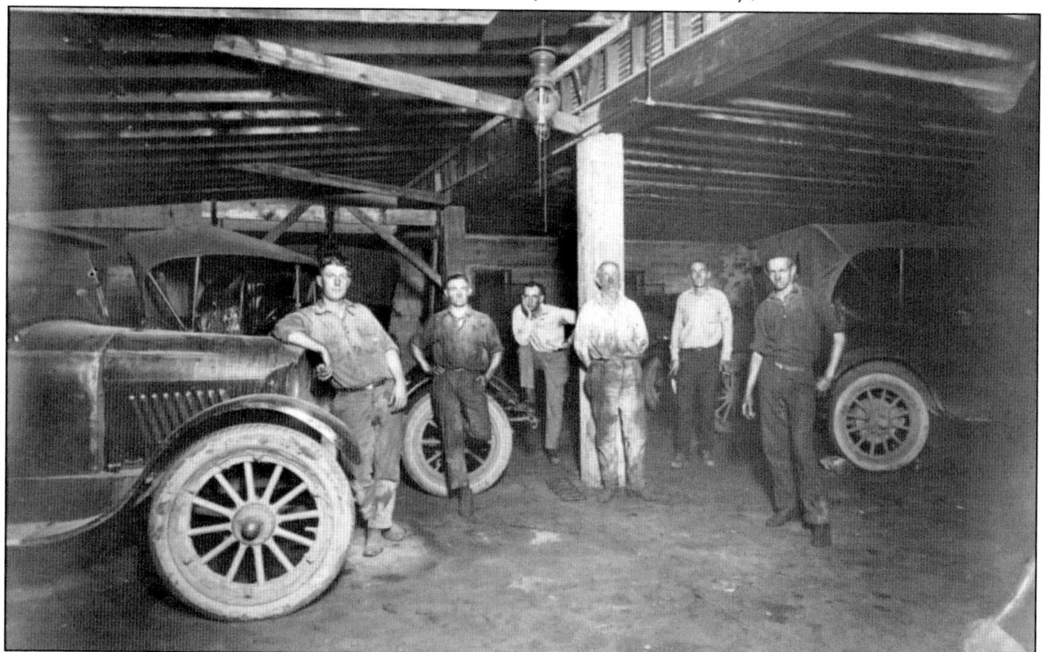

Bill Crook's Motor Inn Garage was in the 300 block of South Broadway in Cleveland. The man in the center with his foot on a car's bumper must be the manager. He is the only one not covered in grease from working on automobiles. The automobile on the right has a chock block against its rear wheel to keep it from rolling backward when it is raised by a winch. (Courtesy of Evelyn "Zeke" Cheek.)

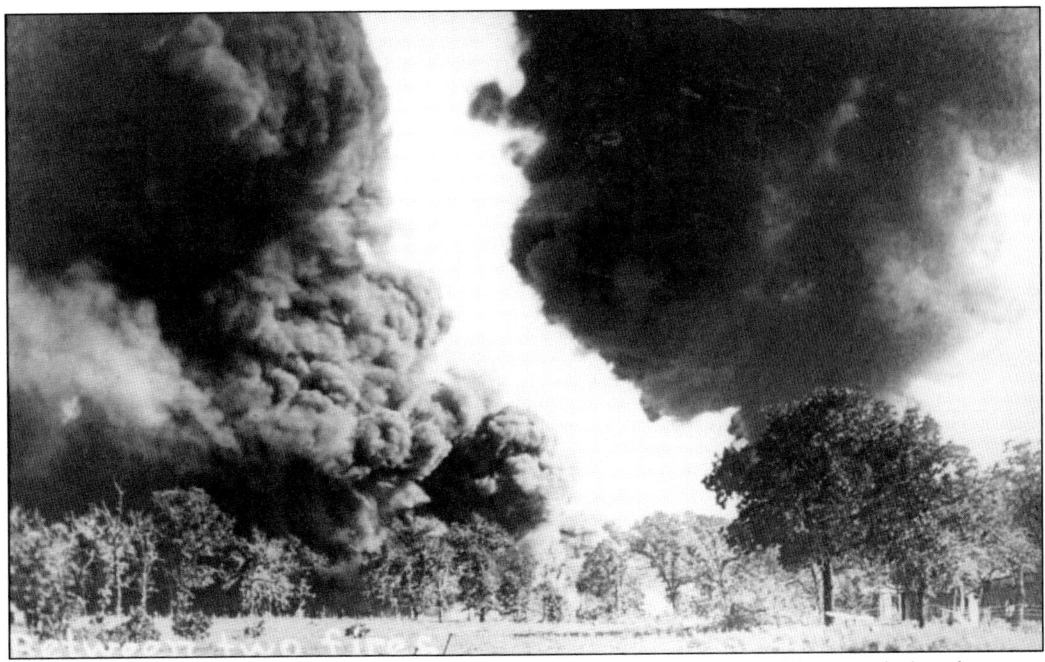

Fires were the bane of the early Cleveland Oil Field, as production quickly overwhelmed storage facilities. The overflowing tanks often caught fire. Here, two nearby tanks are burning simultaneously. When one tank caught on fire, the rats that had nested underneath would often race to another nearby tank or home, spreading the flames. (Courtesy of Triangle Heritage Association.)

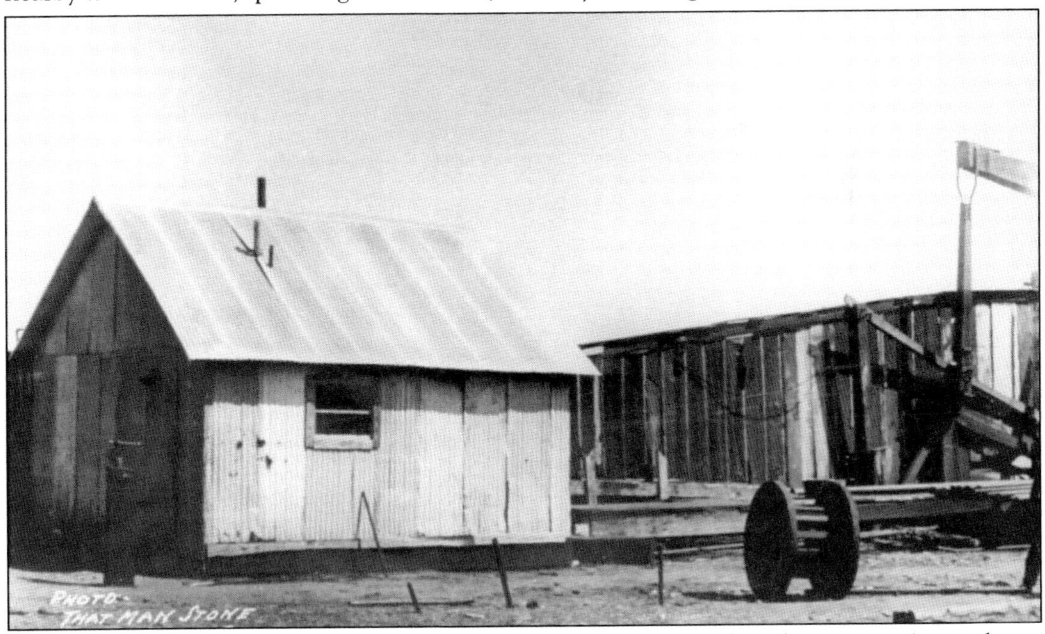

The New England Oil Company's toolhouse was north of Cleveland on the company's river lease. Built of sheet metal nailed to a wooden frame, such buildings were typical of early Cleveland. The metal has been cut to form a window that is framed by rough boards. In front and to the left of the building is a vise bolted to a timber set in the ground. The spool wheel in the right foreground once held cable that was used to suspend the bit in the well's hole. (Author's collection.)

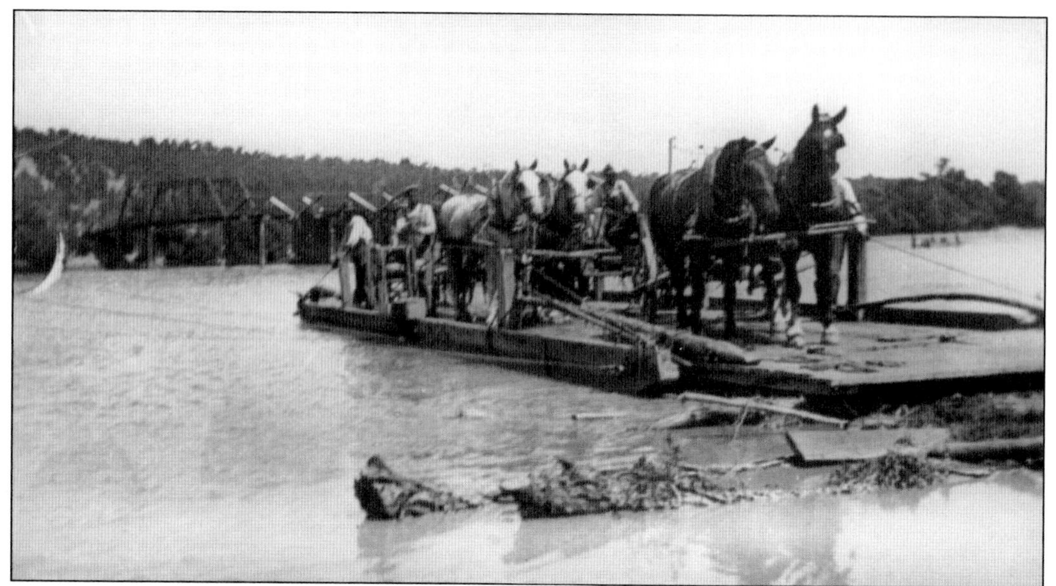

Teamsters and their horse-drawn wagons are crossing the Arkansas River east of Cleveland after the 1924 flood. Most oil-field equipment was hauled to Cleveland by railroad and then moved by horse and wagon over the hilly, scrub oak–covered terrain that was all but impassable by motor vehicles. (Courtesy of Triangle Heritage Association.)

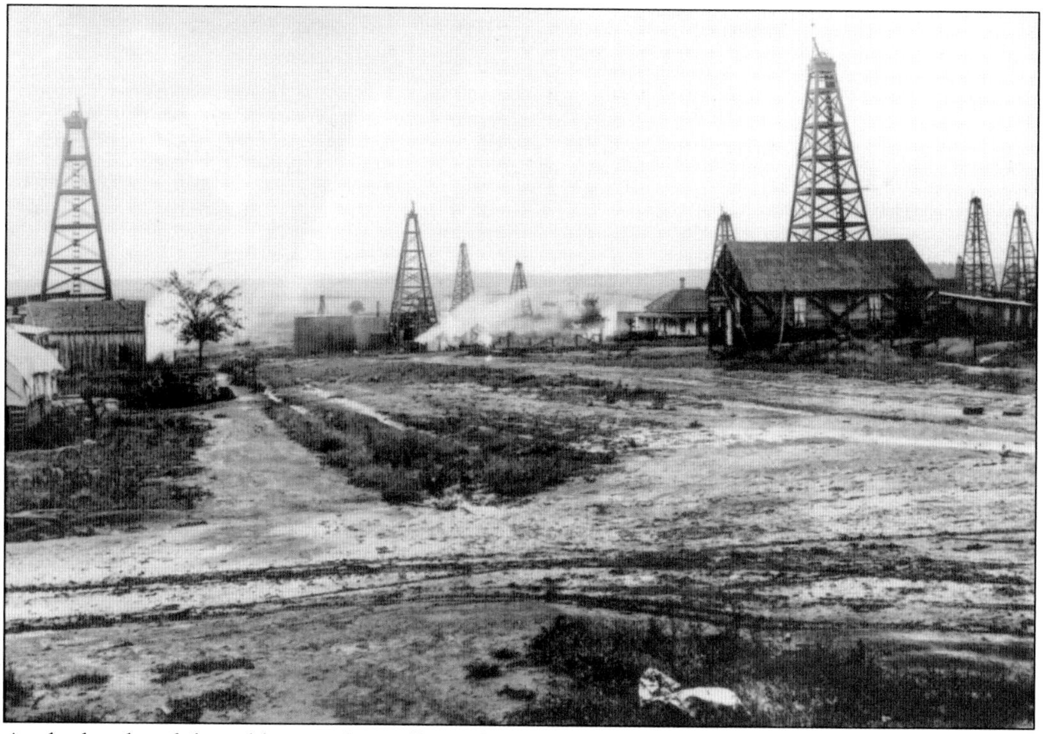

At the height of the oil boom, the wells in the Cleveland Oil Field encroached inside the town of Cleveland, and numerous wells were drilled among the town's collection of wooden boomtown buildings. Note the Presbyterian chapel, located at the corner of Delaware and Vine Streets, on the right side of the photograph. (Courtesy of the Oklahoma History Center.)

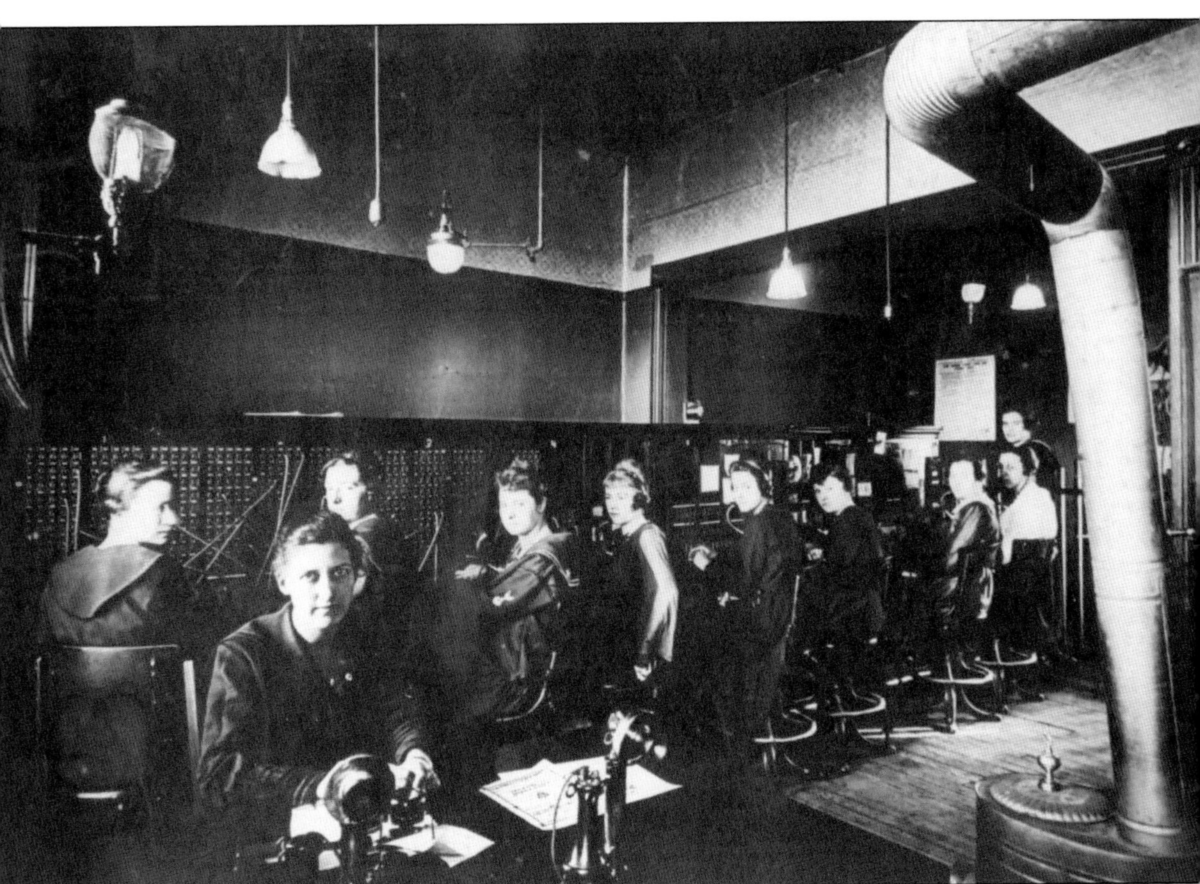

The Cleveland telephone switchboard operators in 1916 are, from left to right, Hazel Foley, Gladys Pursley, Maude Lee, Lola House, Elizabeth Griffith, Lavera Widener, Lorna Taylor, Blanche Foley, Sadie Squires, and Virginia Maxwell. To make a telephone call, a customer would pick up the phone, it would connect to the switchboard, the customer would give the number he or she wanted to talk with, and operators would plug in a cable to make the connection. (Courtesy of Evelyn "Zeke" Cheek.)

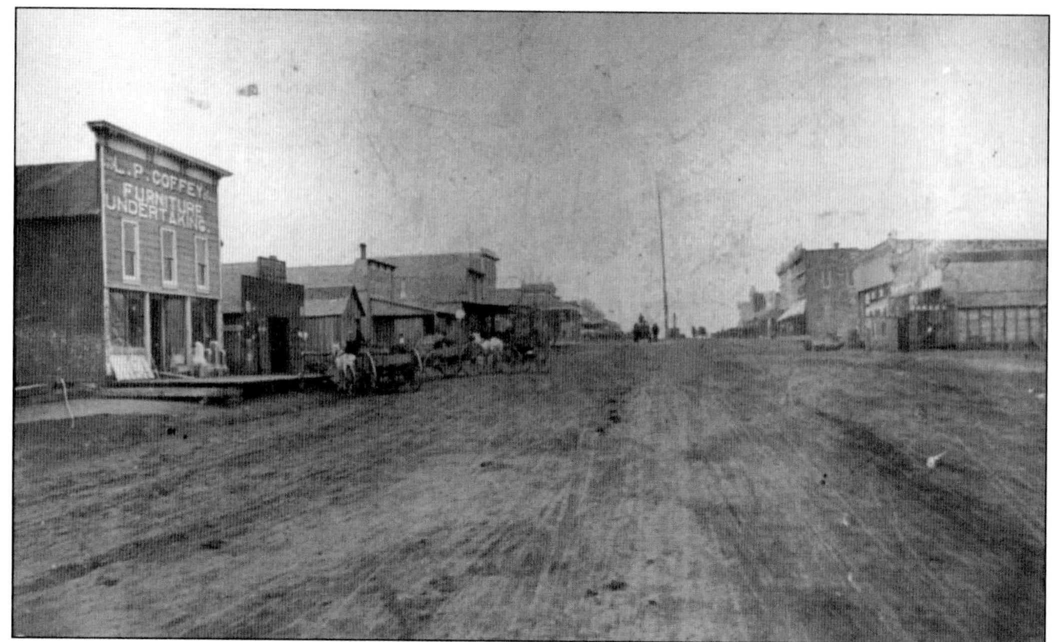

This is Cleveland's main street prior to the oil boom. The town's flagpole and well can be seen in the center of the street. The small building on the far right of the photograph is a bakery. On the left is the L.P. Coffey Furniture and Undertaking business. Note the horses and buggies tied to the hitching rails. (Author's collection.)

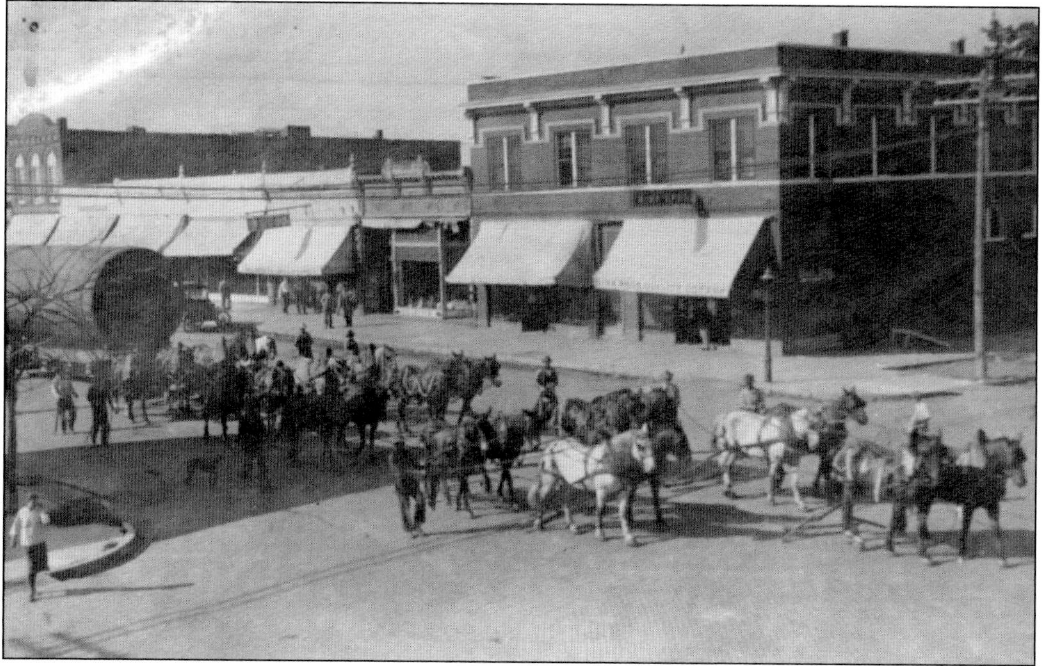

In this photograph, numerous teams of horses are being used to pull a large oil-storage tank down the main street of Cleveland. Each team is being controlled by its own teamster. Because Cleveland was located in the middle of an oil field, local residents were often witnesses to such scenes. (Courtesy of Evelyn "Zeke" Cheek.)

Eight

Gordon W. "Pawnee Bill" Lillie

Endemic to the Wild West, of which Pawnee County was a part, was Gordon W. "Pawnee Bill" Lillie, who made his Wild West show an international attraction. He was born on February 14, 1860, at Bloomingdale, Illinois. As a youth, Lillie visited Oldtown, a nearby Indian settlement. Numerous Indians passed through Oldtown. One was an English-speaking Pawnee named Blue Hawk, who became Lillie's boyhood friend. Blue Hawk lived on the Pawnee Reservation along Black Bear Creek in present-day Pawnee County. When they parted, Lillie promised Blue Hawk he would visit him along Black Bear Creek.

Later, Lillie's family moved to Wellington, Kansas, where once again he encountered the Pawnee camped along the Ninnescah River. In 1875, he headed for Wichita, Kansas, where he hoped to join a cattle drive. Instead, he became involved in a confrontation with "Trigger" Jim Braden, whom he killed in a gunfight. Although he was acquitted, Lillie left Wichita and journeyed south and visited Blue Hawk.

While working as a teacher, secretary, and interpreter at the Pawnee Agency, Lillie was given the name Ku-luks-Kitty-butks by the Pawnee. Non-Indians called him "Pawnee Bill." On August 31, 1886, he married Mary "May" Manning.

Lillie toured with Buffalo Bill's Wild West Show from 1883 until 1888, when he formed his own show—Pawnee Bill Wild West Show, later known as Pawnee Bill's Wild West and Great Far East Show. In 1908, Pawnee Bill and Buffalo Bill became partners in Buffalo Bill's Wild West and Pawnee Bill's Far East Show.

In May 1902, Lillie purchased 2,000 acres surrounding Blue Hawk Peak and just south of Black Bear Creek. It was here in 1909 that Pawnee Bill and May built their home. In 1930, he opened the Old Town and Indian Trading Post two miles southwest of Pawnee on the edge of Black Bear Creek along US-64

Gordon W. "Pawnee Bill" Lillie died on February 3, 1942. His wife, May, had died on September 15, 1936. Their home on Blue Hawk Peak is maintained as a state park.

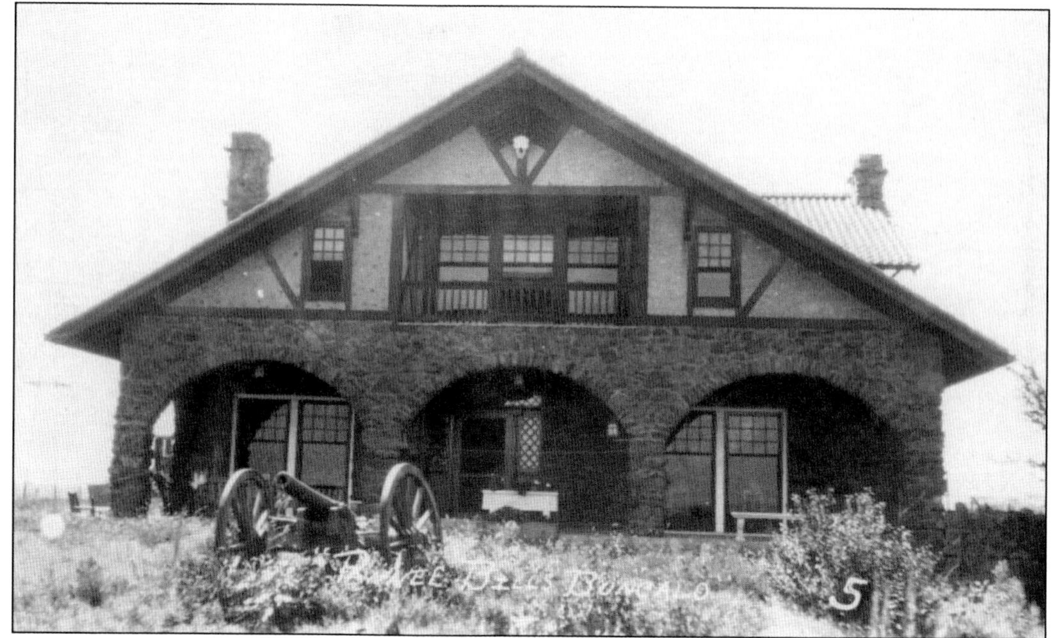

A Civil War–era cannon sits in front of Gordon and May Lillie's home on Blue Hawk Peak. Construction of the home began in 1909, and on December 10, 1910, a housewarming party was held. The entertainment was a buffalo barbecue and a Pawnee dance and council. Note the cow skull attached to the building at the peak of the roof. (Courtesy of the Pawnee County Historical Society.)

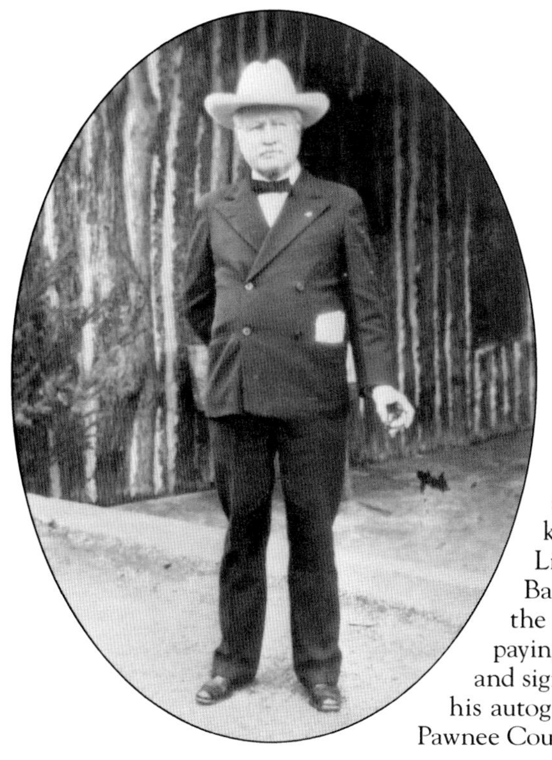

Gordon W. "Pawnee Bill" Lillie, standing in front of the log walls surrounding Old Town and Indian Trading Post east of Pawnee, was known as Ku-luks-Kitty-butks by the Pawnee. Lillie also owned the Arkansas Valley National Bank in Pawnee and carried unsigned sheets of the bank's national banknotes with him. When paying bills, Lillie would pull out the unsigned sheets and sign them, knowing that they would be kept for his autograph and never be cashed. (Courtesy of the Pawnee County Historical Society.)

Jose Barrera, or "Mexican Joe," performed tricks with a lariat for Pawnee Bill's Wild West Show for years. Later, when Lillie retired to his 2,000-acre buffalo ranch on Blue Hawk Peak, Barrera remained with him as the ranch's foreman. (Courtesy of the Pawnee County Historical Society.)

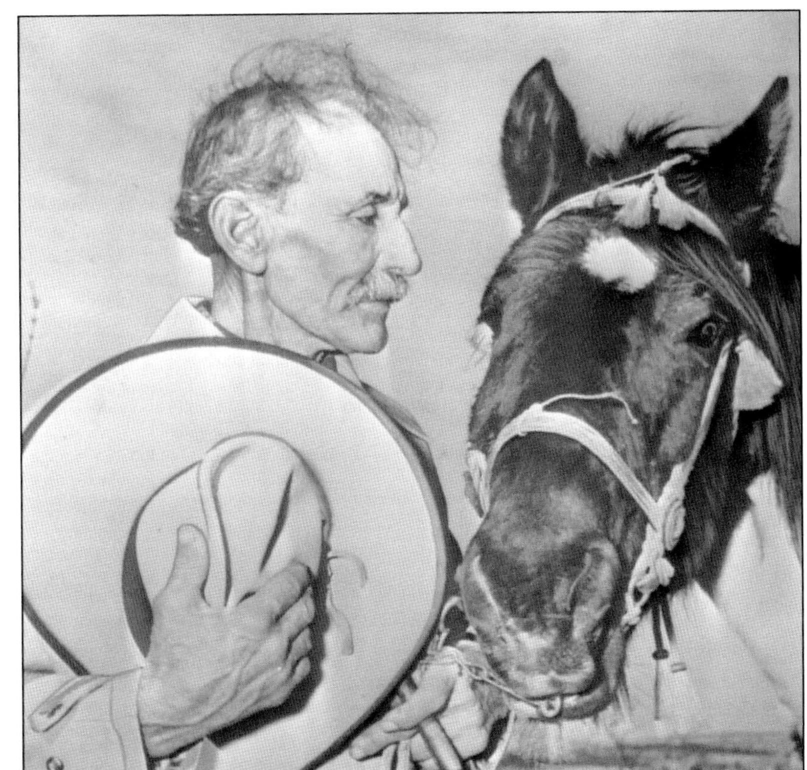

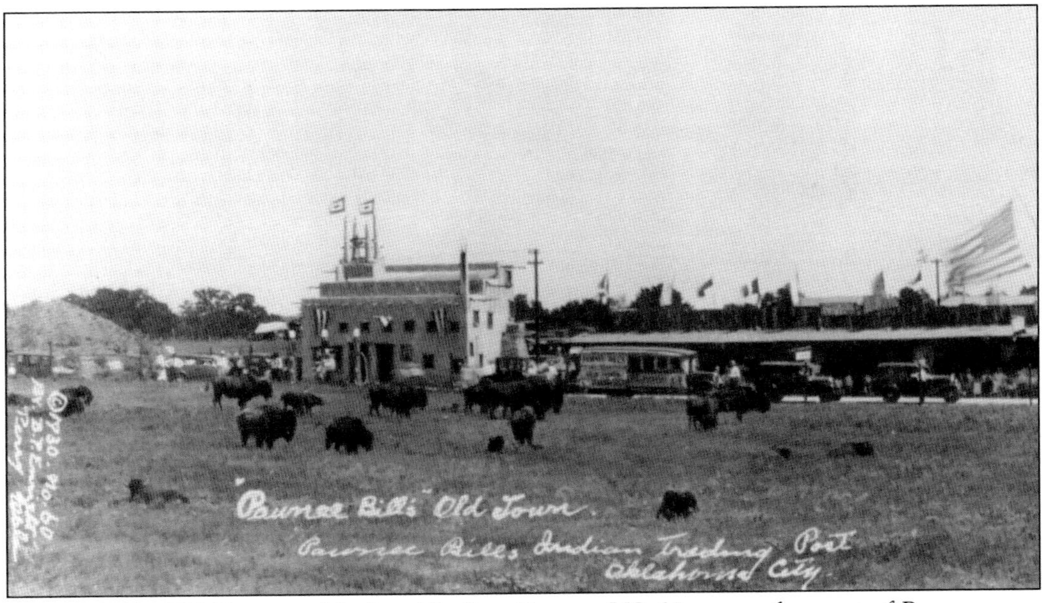

Pawnee Bill's Old Town and Indian Trading Post on US 64, two miles west of Pawnee, was opened on May 1, 1930. Note the buffalo grazing in the foreground; they were Pawnee Bill's passion. On the left of the photograph is one of the several Pawnee earth lodges on the east side of the site. The trading post, on the right, was built of 16-foot-tall split logs. The 2-John Bar, dotted with bullet holes, was located in the rear of the building. (Courtesy of the Pawnee County Historical Society.)

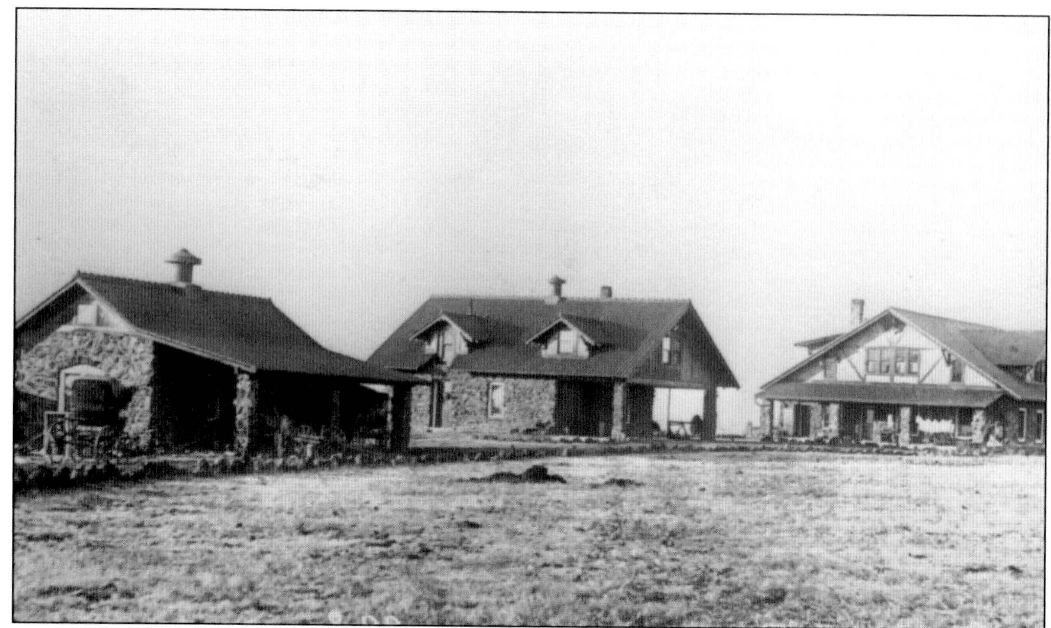

The Lillie homesite on Blue Hawk Peak includes the house and several other buildings. There is a stagecoach beneath the roof of the front porch of the building to the left and a buggy just the left of the building. Today, the center building serves as a home for the park ranger at Pawnee Bill Ranch State Park. (Courtesy of the Pawnee County Historical Society.)

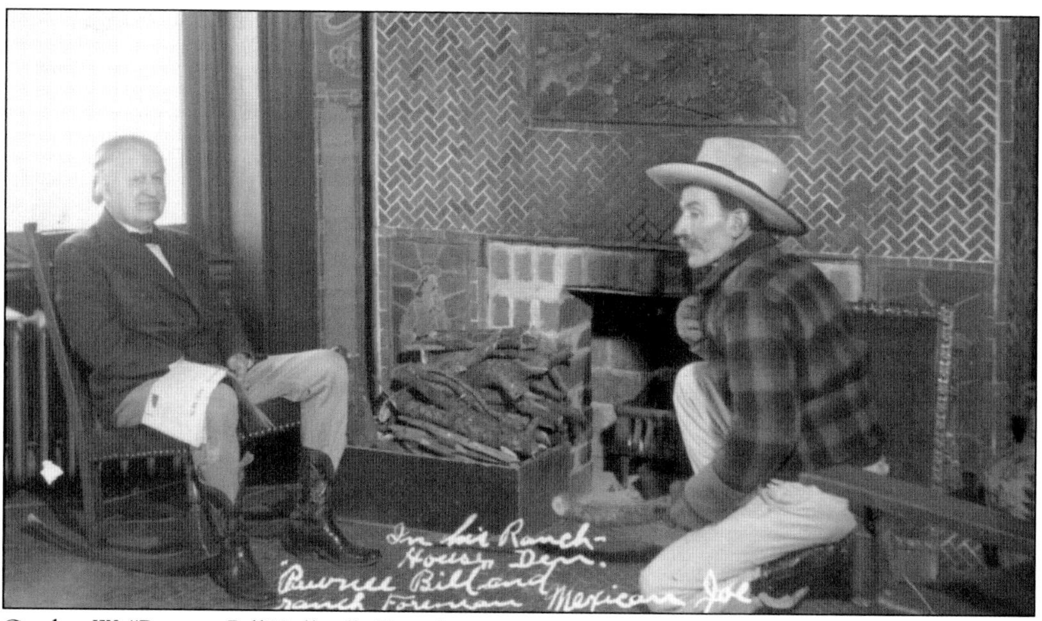

Gordon W. "Pawnee Bill" Lillie (left) and Mexican Joe, whose actual name was Jose Barrera, are sitting in front of the fireplace inside Lillie's home on Blue Hawk Peak. Notice the stone-carved mantel piece depicting a mounted Indian overlooking a buffalo herd. (Courtesy of the Pawnee County Historical Society.)

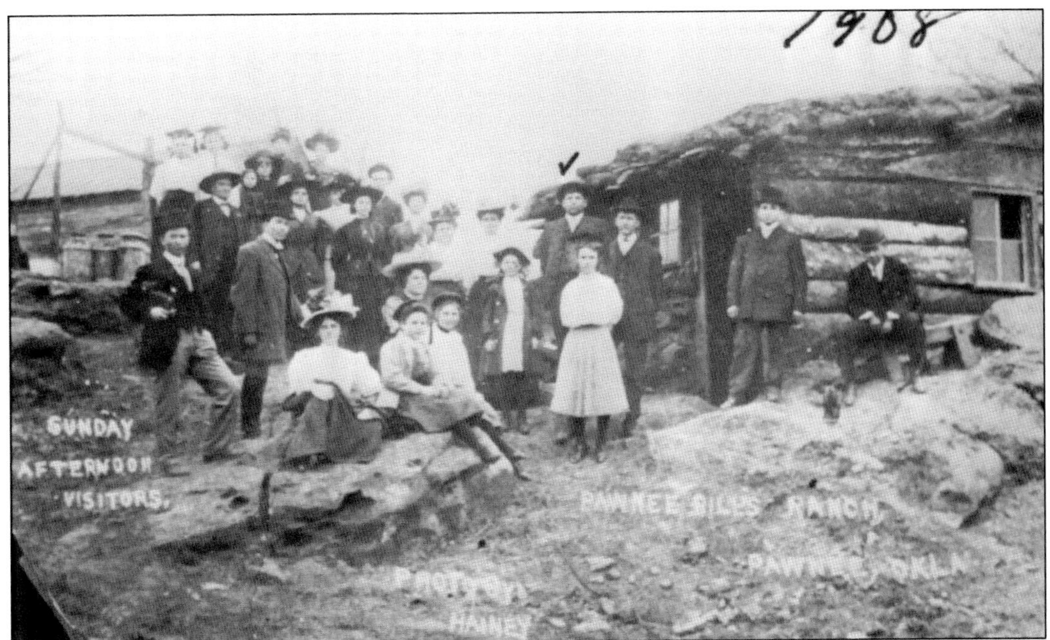

Pawnee Bill's original log cabin was built on a rock outcrop on Blue Hawk Peak west of Pawnee. Constructed of logs cut nearby and covered with a roof made of logs and sod, this was the beginning of Gordon and May Lillie's dream home. Note the two figures in the left background who are wearing their high school graduation robes and caps. (Courtesy of the Pawnee County Historical Society.)

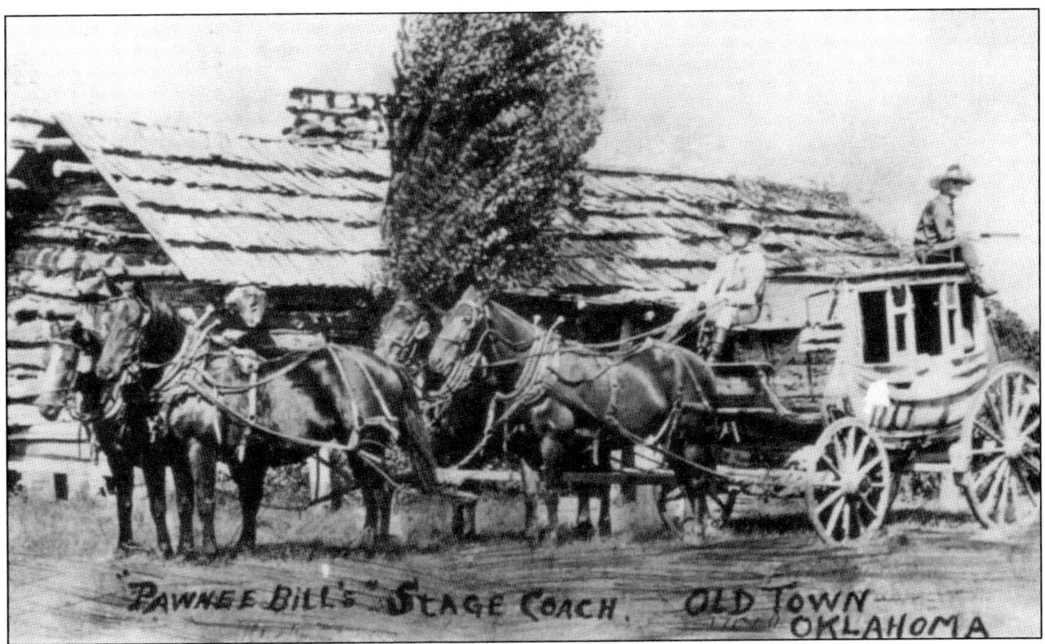

Old Town's stagecoach with its four-horse team was used to reenact robberies, first with Pawnee Bill's Wild West Show and then for the tourists visiting Old Town. On top of the stage are the driver and guard. (Courtesy of the Pawnee County Historical Society.)

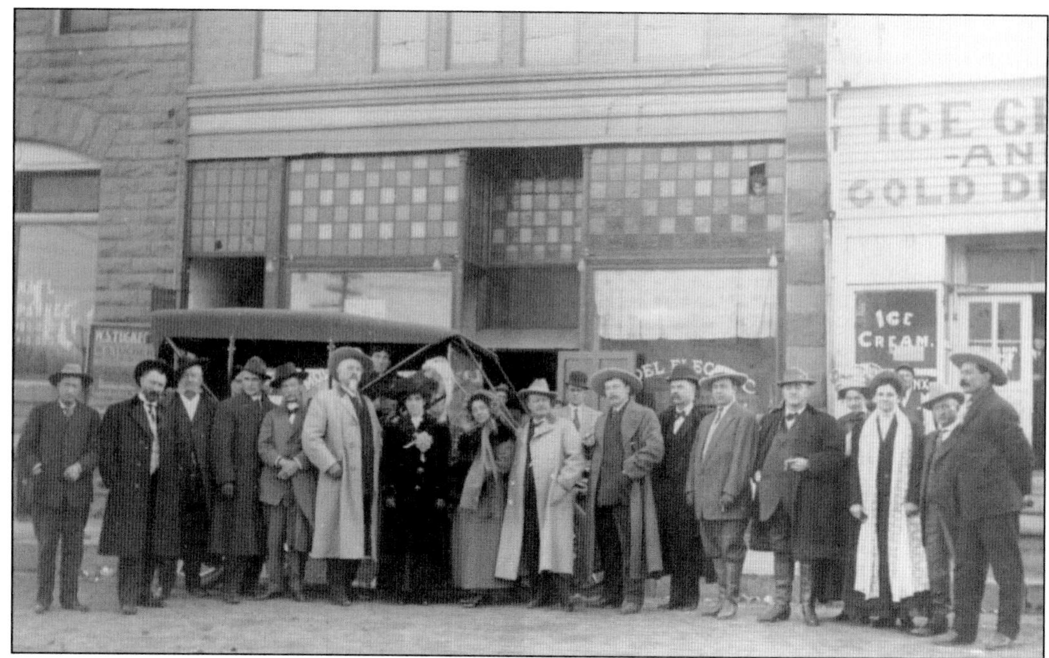

In this photograph, William F. "Buffalo Bill" Cody stands sixth from the left, and Pawnee Bill Lillie is tenth from the right. Lillie started his showman career with Buffalo Bill's Wild West Show. Later, the two men joined to form Buffalo Bill's Wild West and Pawnee Bill's Far East Show. (Courtesy of the Pawnee County Historical Society.)

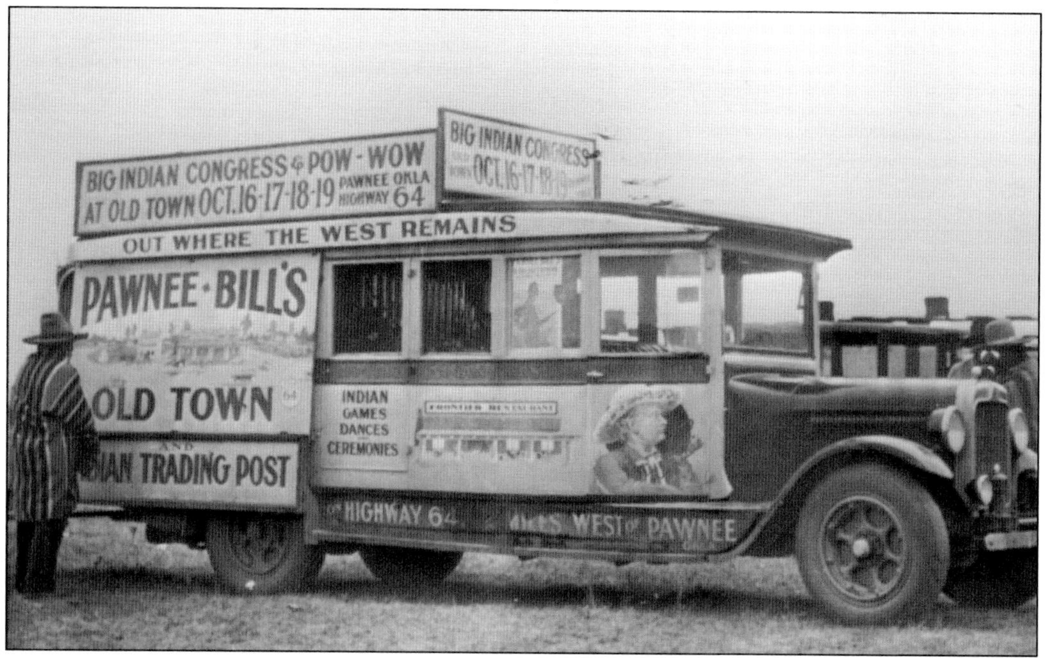

The bus that serviced visitors to Old Town was a mobile advertisement of "Out Where The West Remains." Some of the Indians who entertained visitors are standing around the bus. Many of the original Pawnee Bill's Wild West Show members remained to work at Old Town when the show closed. (Courtesy of the Pawnee County Historical Society.)

This is a photograph of May Manning Lillie (left) and Pawnee Bill's sister Lena Lillie Green. Lena followed Pawnee Bill to the Pawnee Agency, where she attended the Indian school and later worked as a matron for the agency school. (Courtesy of the Pawnee County Historical Society.)

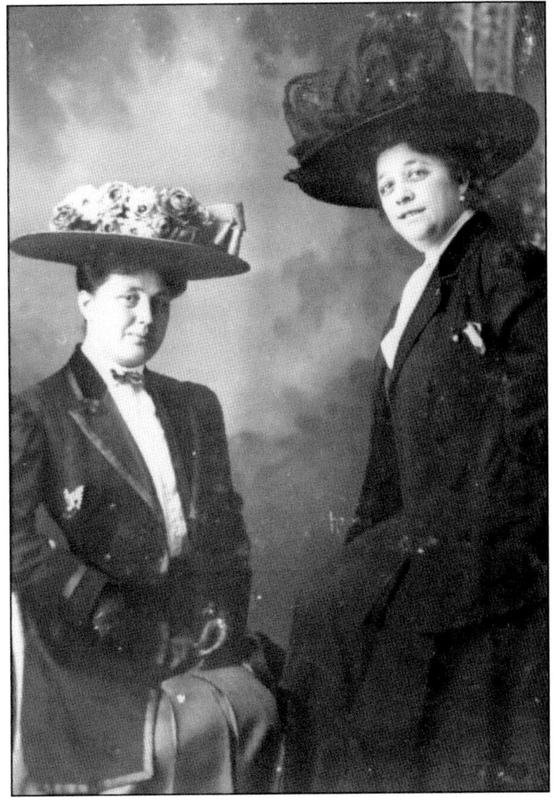

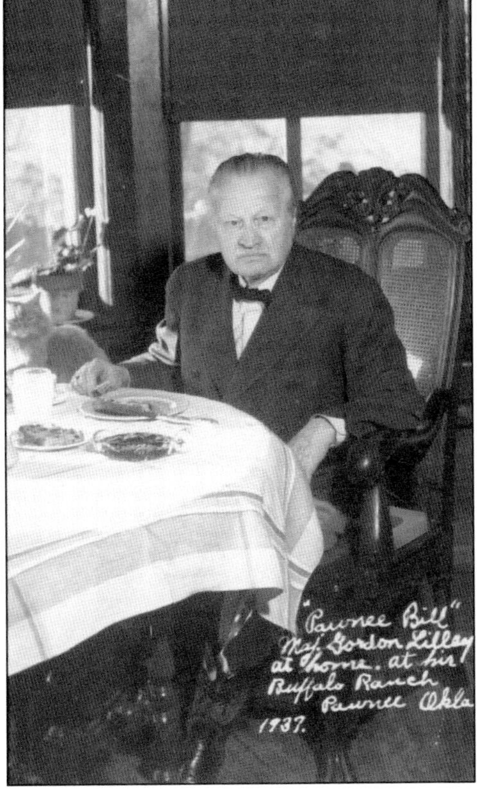

Gordon W. Lillie is enjoying a meal at his home in 1937. Kenneth Good Eagle served Lillie as his driver and helped care for him as his health failed. Good Eagle lived in a room over Lillie's bedroom. Whenever Lillie needed help, he would bang on his bedroom's ceiling with a broom, and Good Eagle would come down. (Courtesy of the Pawnee County Historical Society.)

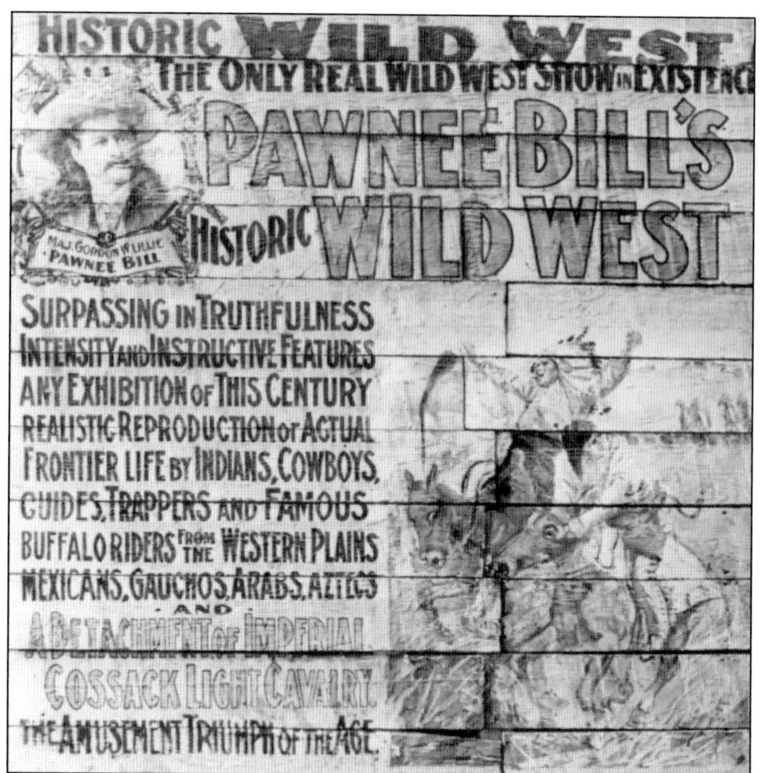

A broadside advertised Pawnee Bill's Historic Wild West Show, featuring life on the frontier as portrayed by Indians and cowboys. There also were performers riding wild buffalo and examples of Mexican vaqueros, South American gauchos, Arabs from the Middle East, and a Russian Imperial Cossack cavalry. (Courtesy of the Pawnee County Historical Society.)

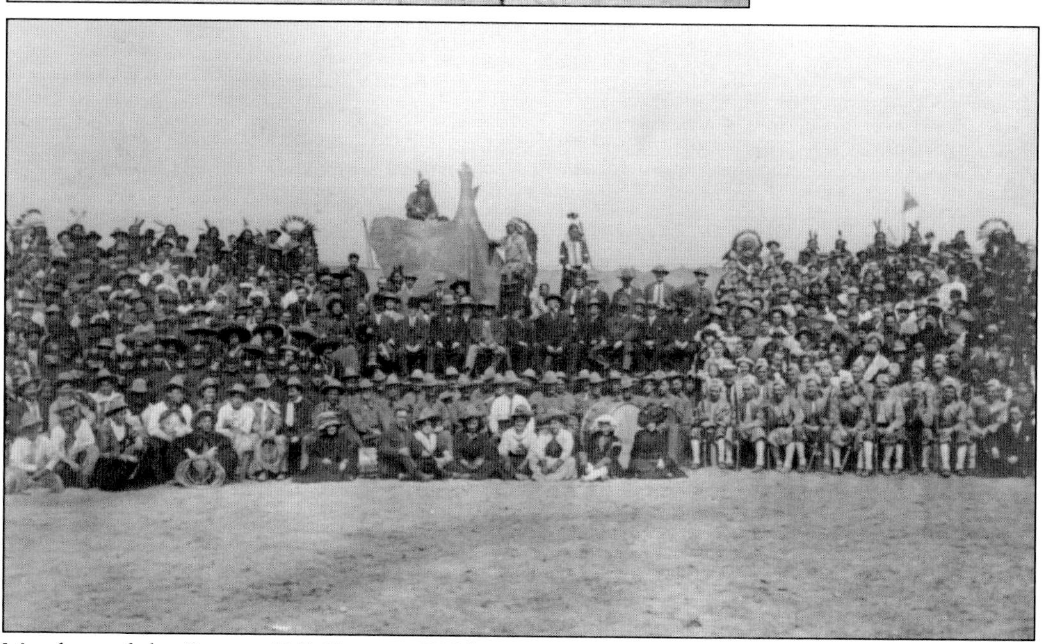

Members of the Pawnee Bill Historic Wild West, Indian Museum Encampment, and Pawnee Bill's Wild West and Great Far Eastern Show pose before a performance. His troupe performed in Spain, Italy, Austria, Hungary, Germany, South Africa, England, Mexico, and Canada and included performers from America, South Africa, Abyssinia, Russia, and Australia. (Courtesy of the Pawnee County Historical Society.)

Maj. Gordon W. "Pawnee Bill" Lillie is pictured wearing his buffalo-hide coat. He often used the honorific title in reference to his service as a government scout and interpreter with the Pawnee Indian Agency School, where he served as a teacher. It was while he was at the agency that he acquired the moniker Pawnee Bill. (Courtesy of the Pawnee County Historical Society.)

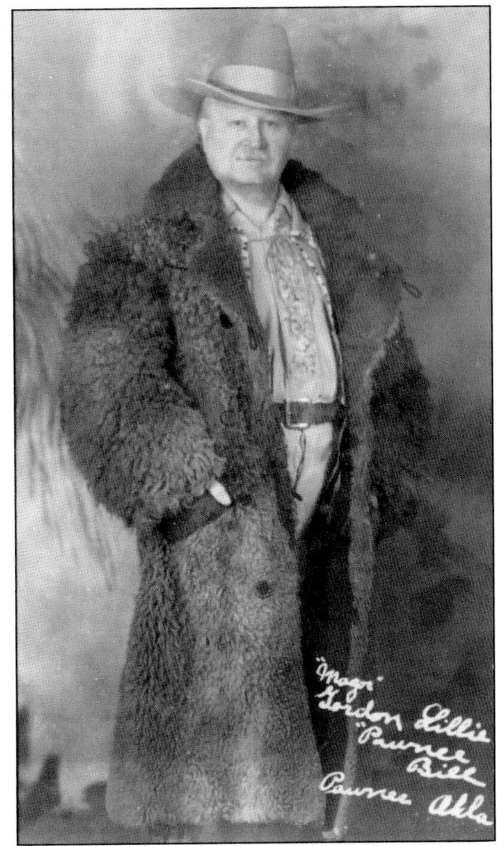

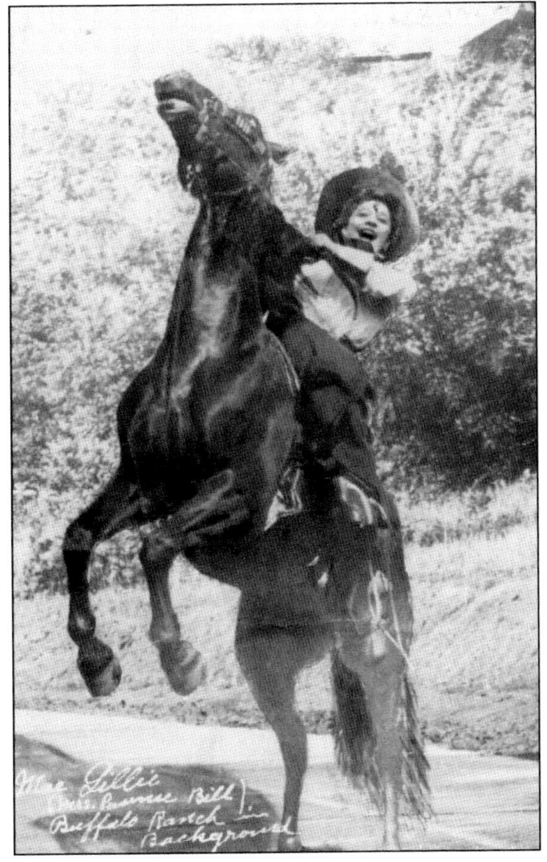

Pawnee Bill's wife, May Lillie, performed with her horse in her husband's Wild West show. Although she was known as May, her actual name was Mary. In the background is the barn at Lillie's buffalo ranch east of Pawnee. Billed as the "rifle queen," May also performed as an expert marksman with Pawnee Bill's Wild West Show. (Courtesy of the Pawnee County Historical Society.)

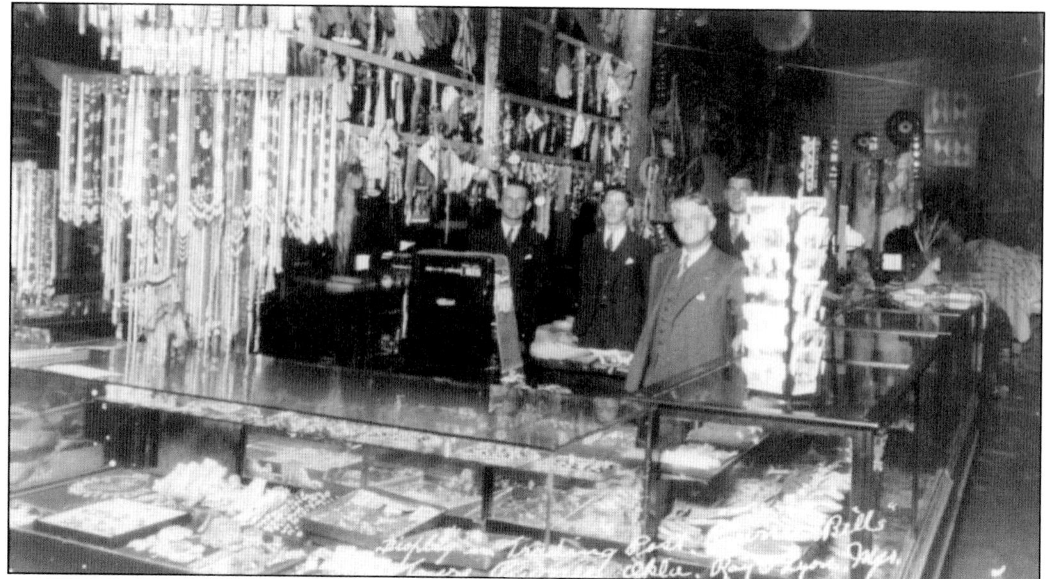

Pictured here is the Indian jewelry sales counter in Pawnee Bill's Trading Post, which was managed by Roy Lyons. When Lyons moved his store to the trading post, he was the largest dealer in eagle feathers in America. To insure the authenticity of the material, Lyons contracted with local Indians to produce his merchandise. (Courtesy of the Pawnee County Historical Society.)

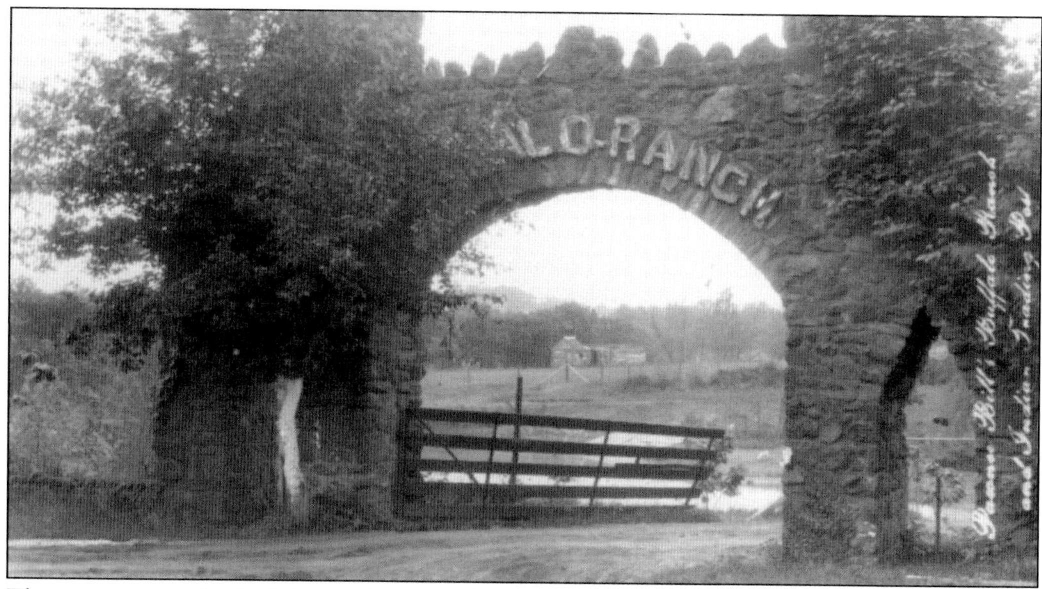

The entryway to the buffalo ranch just to the south and east of Blue Hawk Peak is impressive. Pawnee Bill rid his herd of unwanted bulls in an annual buffalo hunt. The meat from the buffalo was distributed to restaurants nationwide. In 1906, Lillie had the third-largest buffalo herd in America. One prized bull was valued at $5,000. (Courtesy of the Pawnee County Historical Society.)

Nine

Modern Era

The city of Pawnee is the oldest town in and the county seat of Pawnee County. Much of its Wild West legacy remains in the form of the Pawnee Bill Ranch, once the showplace of the world-renowned Wild West show entertainer, Gordon W. "Pawnee Bill" Lillie. The fully furnished 14-room home, which was completed in 1910, is maintained as a state park. Every year, in June, the Pawnee Bill Ranch recreates Pawnee Bill's Original Wild West Show and barbecue.

Pawnee also hosts the Pawnee Bill Memorial Rodeo, judged the best small-town rodeo in America. Every Fourth of July, the Pawnee Nation hosts its annual Veterans Powwow honoring tribal members who have served in the nation's military.

Pawnee is also the home of Chester Gould, who created the *Dick Tracy* comic strip, which made its debut on October 4, 1931. Distributed by the *Chicago Tribune* and the New York News Syndicate, the comic strip's characters are based on actual people Gould grew up with in Pawnee. Cleveland is the home of Jack Bender, the creator of the *Alley Oop* comic strip, and Billy Vessels, the 1952 Heisman Trophy winner.

Named for Pres. Grover Cleveland, Cleveland dominated the economy of eastern Pawnee County. Bordering Cleveland is Keystone Lake, built and operated by the US Army Corps of Engineers. At normal elevation, Keystone Lake covers about 23,600 acres and has 350 miles of shoreline.

On the western edge of Keystone Lake is Bear's Glen, made famous by Washington Irving in his 1835 book *A Tour on the Prairies*. Nearby is Pawnee County's newest community, Westport, founded after the building of Keystone Lake.

The Hallett Motor Speedway at Hallett attracts both modern and vintage racing cars from around the nation during racing season.

South of Cleveland, just east of the intersection of OK 48 and US 412, is a geological formation studied worldwide: Matched to southern England through the study of ancient pollen fossils found only in the two areas, it found its way to Pawnee County through continental drift.

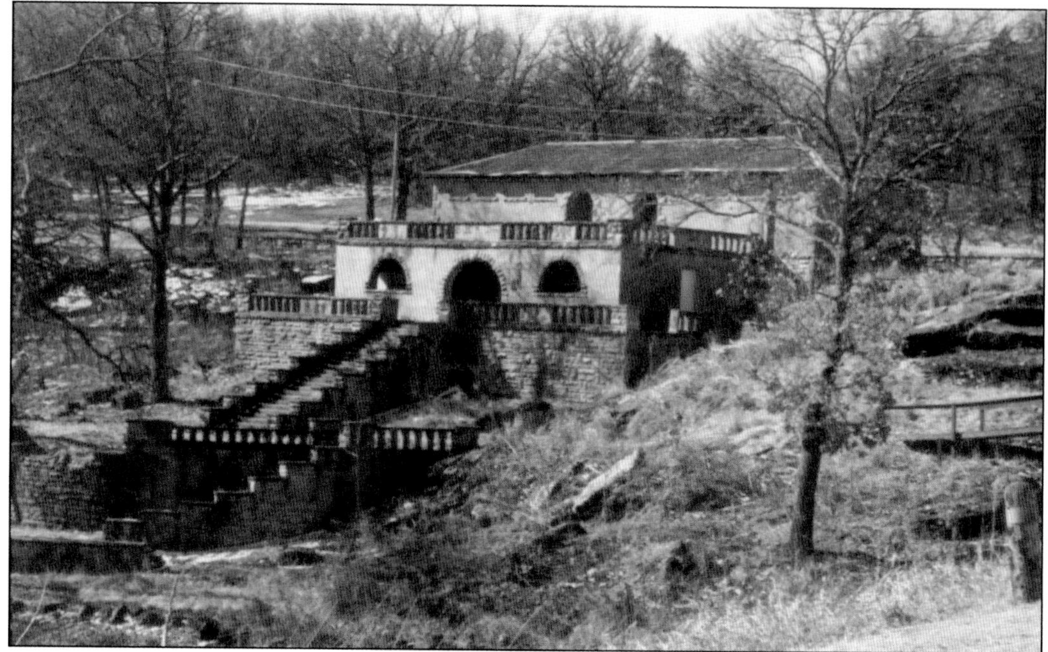

The Pawnee Lake bathhouse was built as a Works Progress Administration project in 1930s. The bathhouse, made of native cut stone, is on the shore of a 1940 freshwater swimming pool. The pool featured sand beaches and a diving platform. The bathhouse has been restored and is maintained by the City of Pawnee. (Author's collection.)

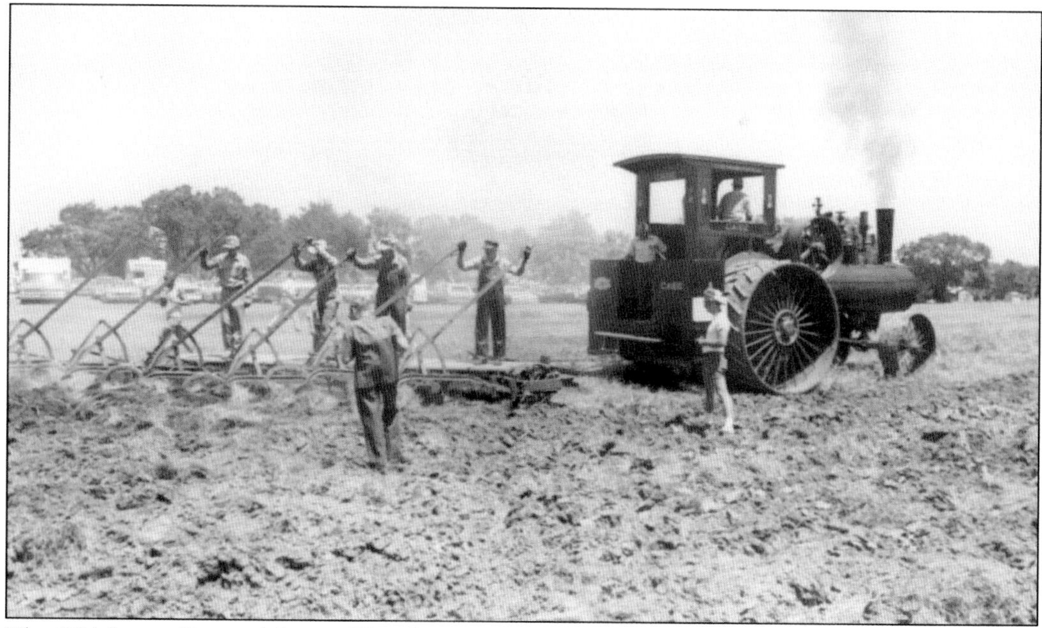

The Oklahoma Gas and Steam Threshers annual steam-engine show has been held annually at the Pawnee County Fairgrounds in Pawnee since 1974. It is a national event, attracting thousands to view some of the last remaining steam-powered farm implements still operable. This is a demonstration of an antique Case steam tractor pulling a gang of plows at the event. (Courtesy of the *Pawnee Chief.*)

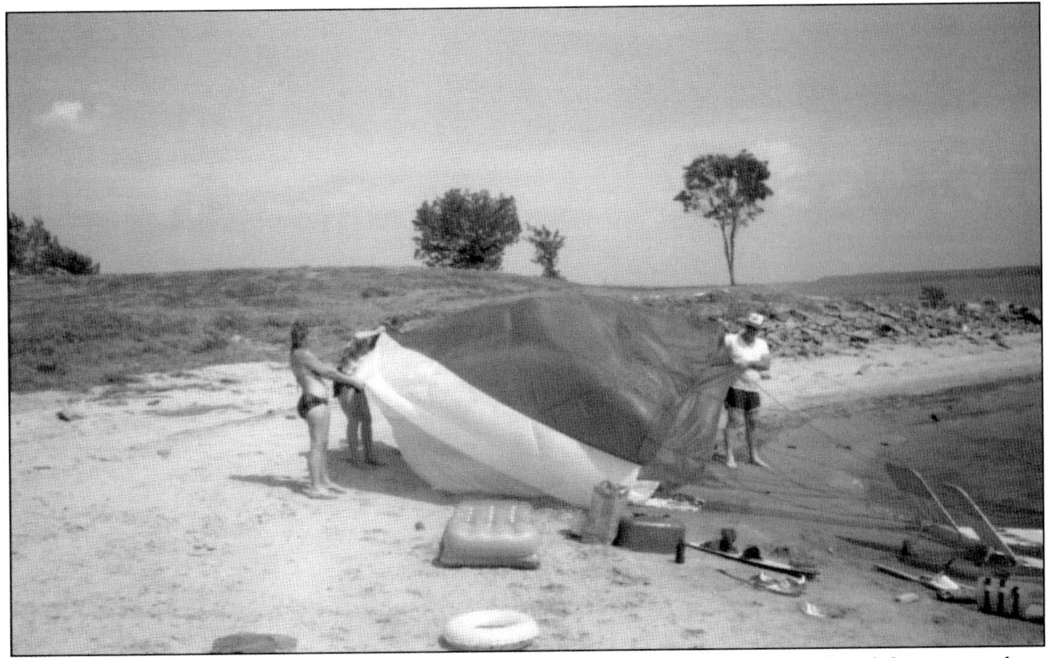

Visitors to Keystone Lake are shown preparing to launch a parachute used to lift a water-skier into the air. The lake's sandy beaches and warm water attract thousands of sun-seekers every year. Although not native to the area, one alligator was pulled from the lake in mid-1990 after being hooked by a fisherman. (Author's collection.)

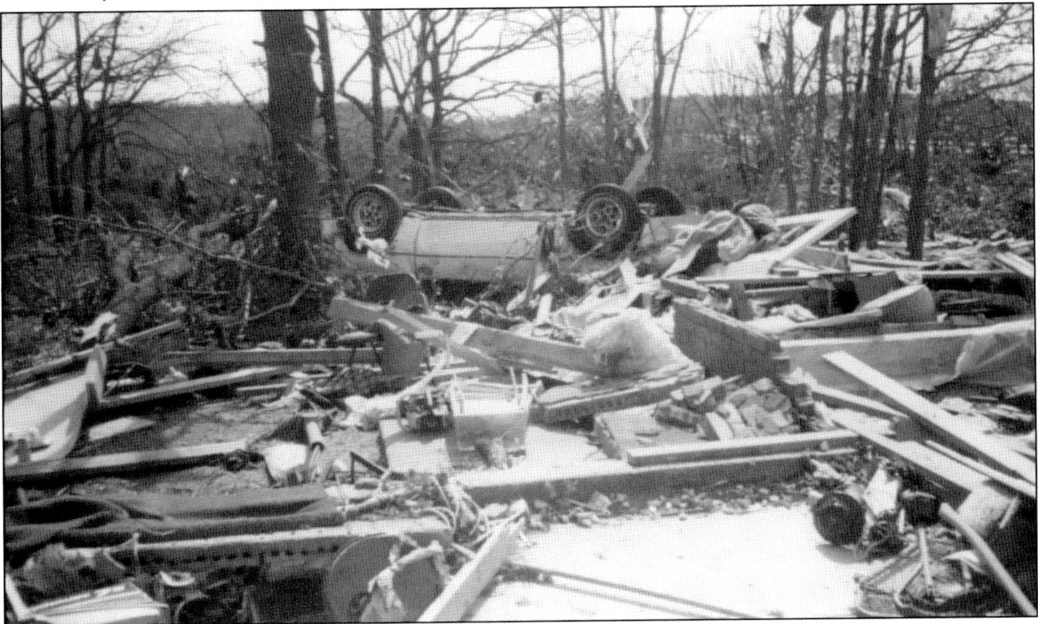

On March 26, 1991, a massive F5 tornado, the strongest possible, left a huge swath of destruction through eastern Pawnee County. The storm was so massive that it appeared as a huge black cloud that blotted out the horizon. This is part of the remains of the town of Westport, on Keystone Lake, southeast of Cleveland on US 412. At least 80 homes were destroyed in the community. (Author's collection.)

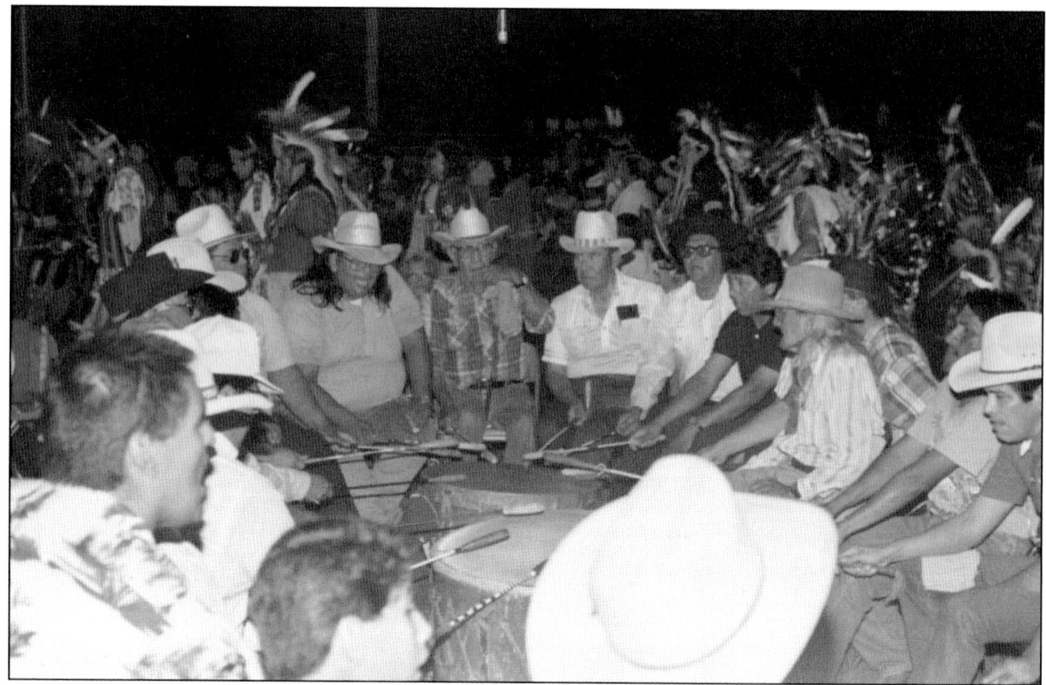

A circle of drummers performs at a Pawnee Powwow. Known as the "Keepers of the Drum," one of the most important positions in Pawnee culture, the drummers beat out the rhythm music of the dance. Notice the dancers in tribal dress in the dance circle dancing counterclockwise around the drummers. (Courtesy of the Pawnee County Historical Society.)

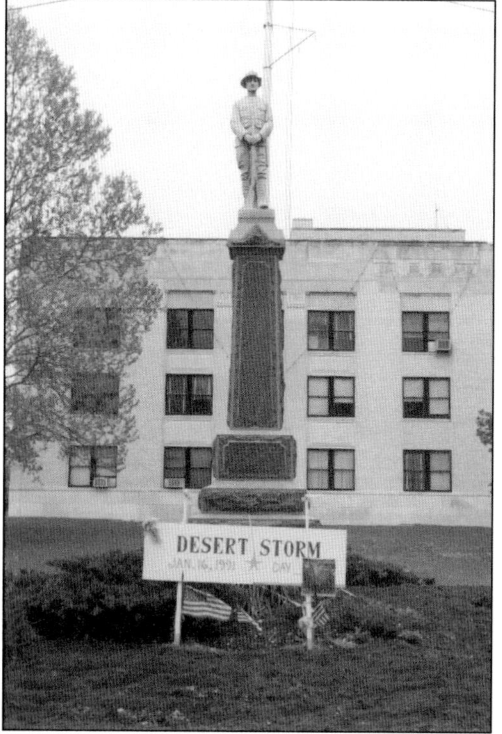

Pawnee has long had a tradition of honoring its military veterans. The yellow ribbons represent those residents from Pawnee County who served in Operation Desert Storm in the Southwest Asian campaign in January 1991. The statue in the photograph is the memorial to those Pawnee County citizens who served in the World War I. (Courtesy of the Pawnee County Historical Society.)

US Marine Corps captain Craig Berryman is being welcomed to Cleveland after returning from Operation Desert Storm. Berryman's Harrier-8B fighter bomber was shot down on January 18, 1991, behind enemy lines. He was held as a prisoner of war for 37 days before being released. (Author's collection.)

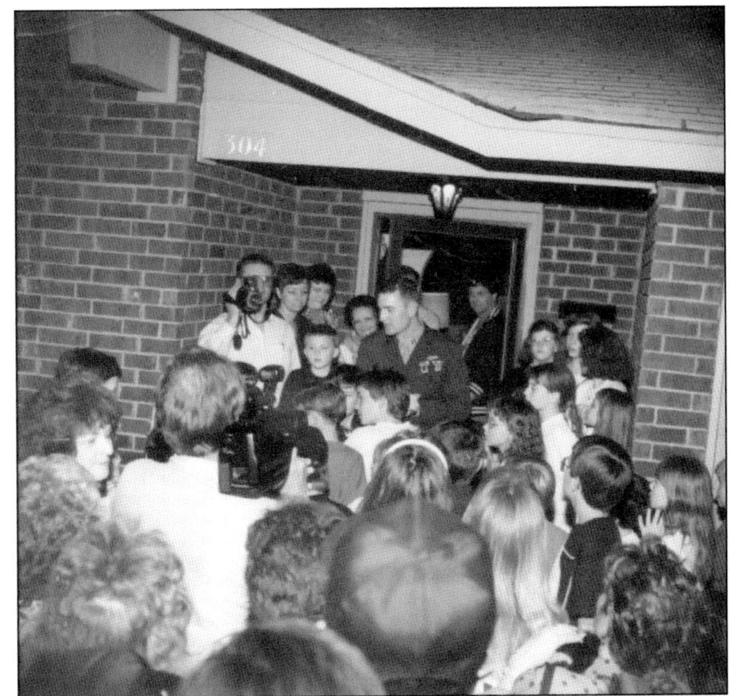

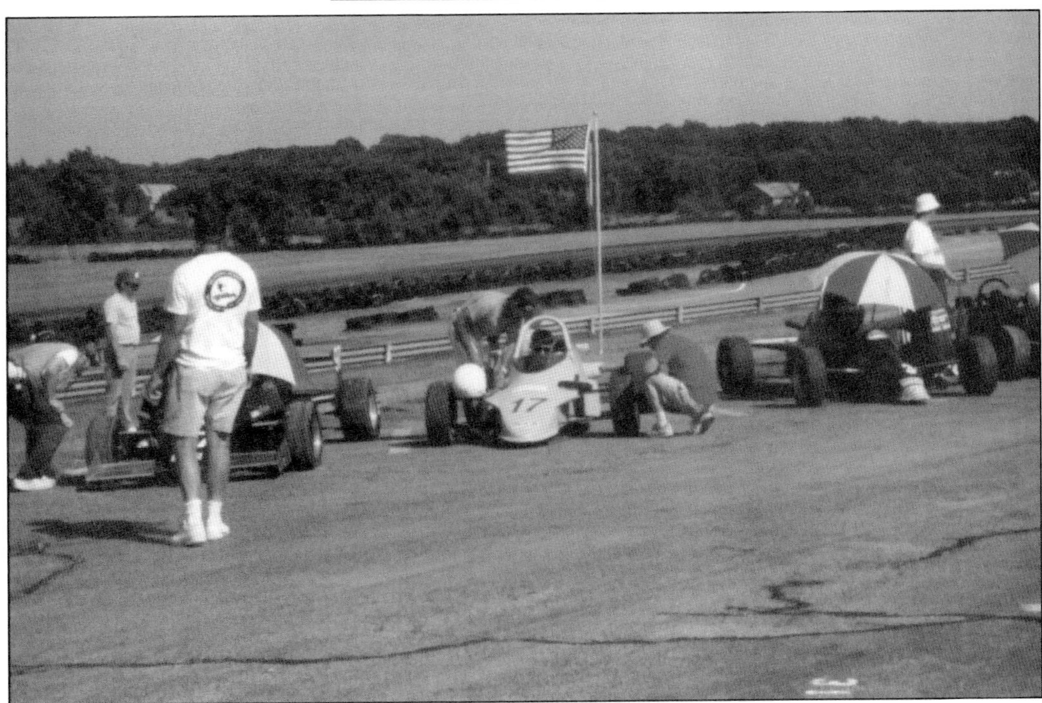

Hallett had a long history of automobile and horse racing dating from a dirt track built for the Pawnee County Fair in the early years of the 20th century. This legacy was revived in the 1990s, with the opening of the Hallett Motor Speedway, which attracts racing enthusiasts nationwide during its racing season. Both modern and antique cars compete on the track. This is a Formula Ford Class race just getting ready to start. (Courtesy of the Pawnee County Historical Society.)

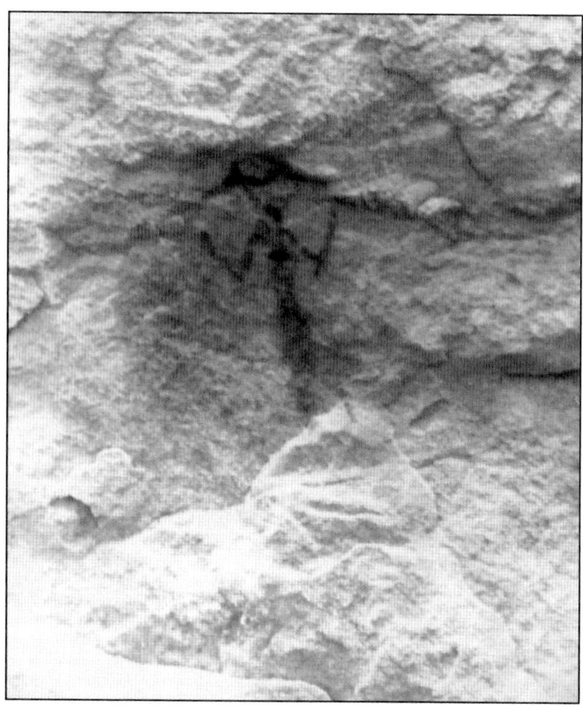

These 1,200-to-1,500-year-old Native American pictographs were found inside a stone overhang on the shore of Keystone Lake in Pawnee County. These pictographs are some of the earliest indication of prehistoric inhabitants of Pawnee County. One figure is red and the other is black. (Author's collection.)

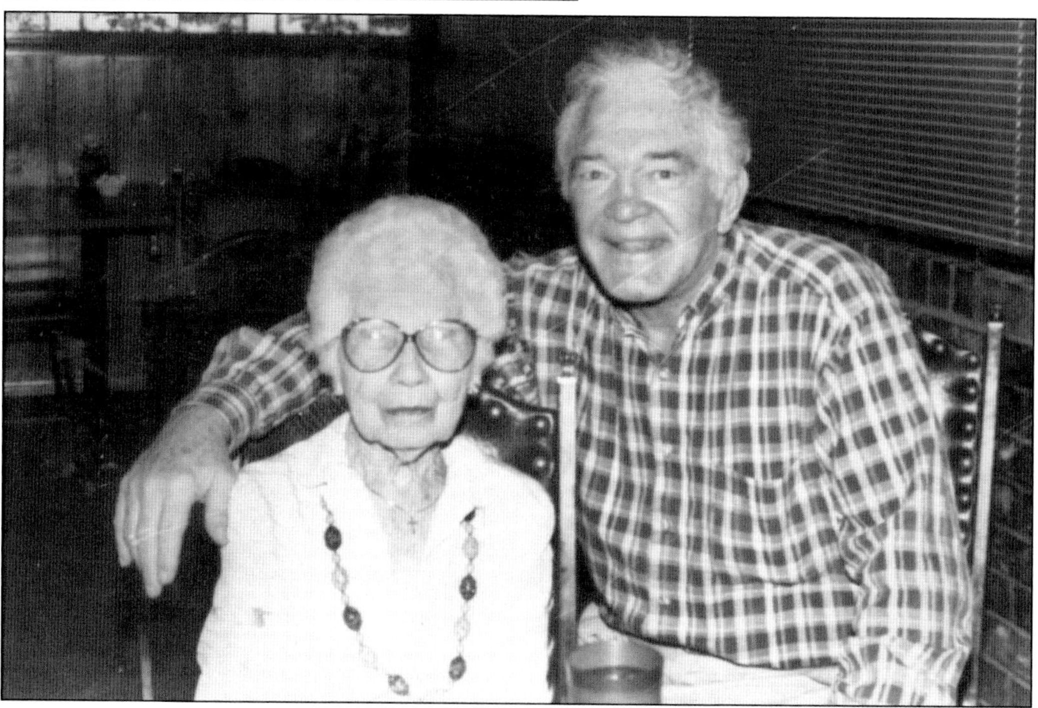

Billy Vessels, the 1952 Heisman Trophy winner for the outstanding college football player of the year, visits Cleveland on Pioneer Day. After graduating from Cleveland High School, Vessels played for legendary University of Oklahoma football coach Bud Wilkinson. A statue of Vessels stands in front of the Cleveland Events Center. On Vessels's right is Irene Jordan, his high school algebra teacher. (Author's collection.)

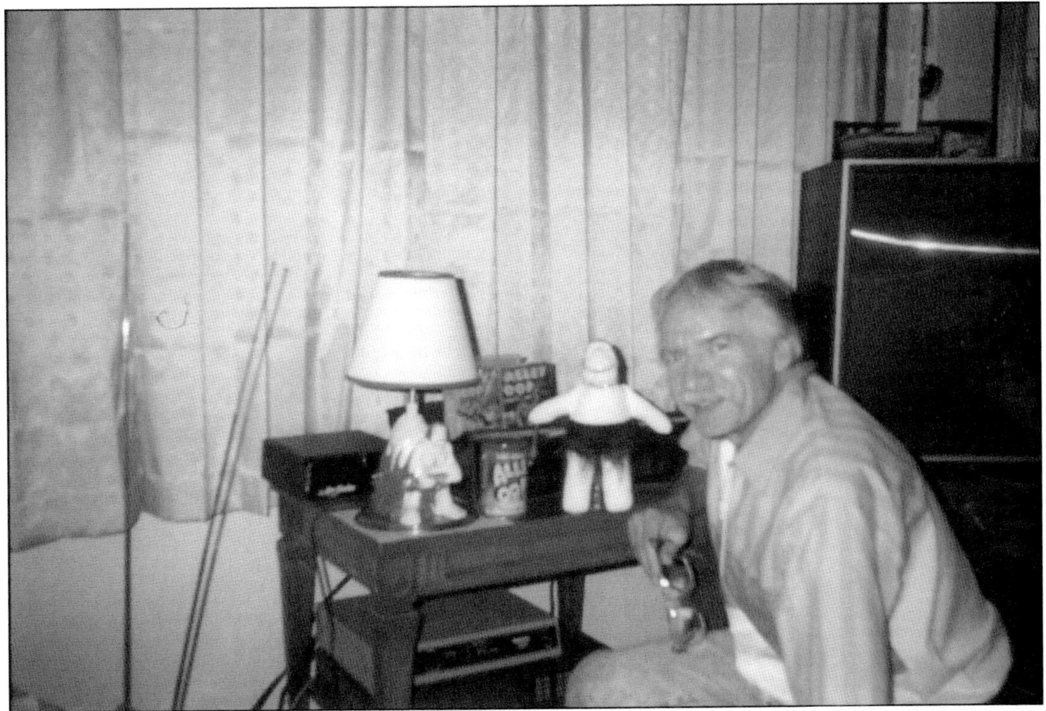

Jack Bender, creator of the *Alley Oop* syndicated comic strip, poses with some of his *Alley Oop* memorabilia at his home near Terlton. (Author's collection.)

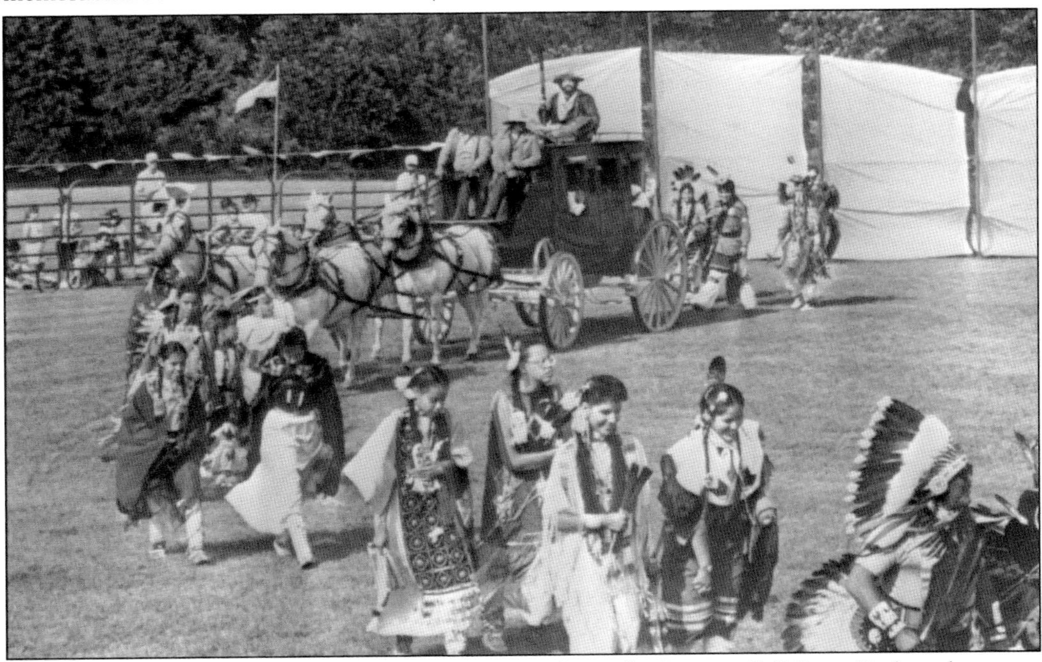

Pawnee Bill's Wild West Show is performed annually at the Pawnee Bill State Park and attracts large audiences. Shown here is the Indian and cowboy parade at the start of the show. Most of the performers and reenactors come from Pawnee County. (Courtesy of the Pawnee County Historical Society.)

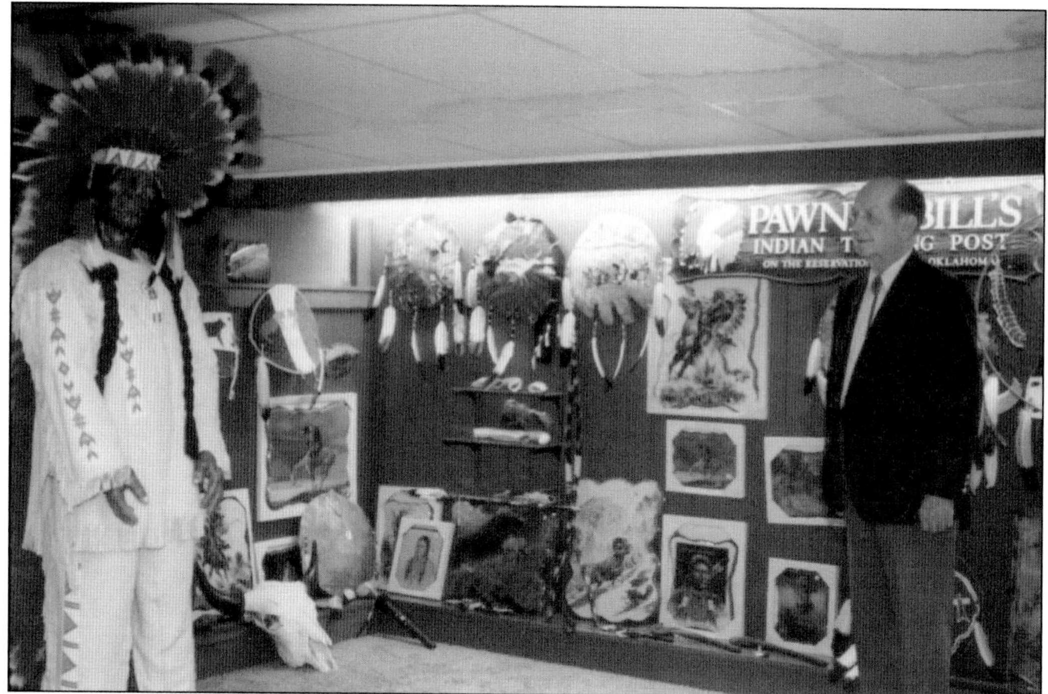

Pawnee Bill's Indian Trading Post is the world's premier supplier of authentic Native American dress and artifacts. It was started by Ray O. Lyon at Old Town and later managed by Glen Lyon, shown here on the right. Lyon contracted with local Indians to manufacture his merchandise. At one time, Lyon was the largest dealer in eagle feathers in America. Because the ownership of eagle feathers is closely regulated by the federal government, once a year federal officials visit the facility and count the eagle feathers on hand. (Courtesy of the Pawnee County Historical Society.)

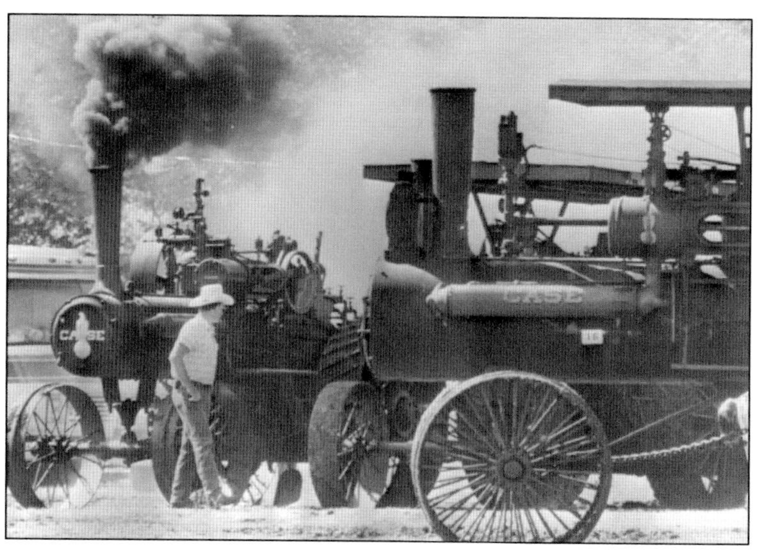

Belching smoke, this Case steam-powered tractor is part of the exhibition line at a Pawnee Oklahoma Gas and Steam Threshers Show. Prior to 1904, when the Hart-Parr Engine Manufacturing Company introduced the first gasoline-powered tractors, the huge steam tractors and horses or mules dominated Pawnee County agriculture. (Author's collection.)

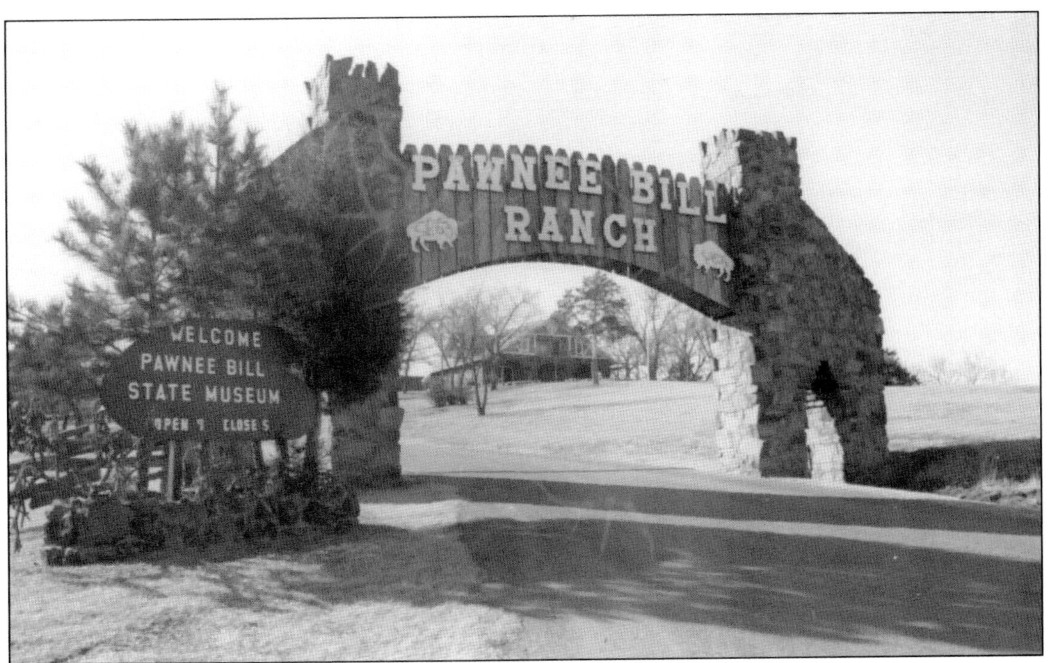

The Pawnee Bill Ranch State Park occupies the original homesite of Gordon and May Lillie. A 5,000-foot Pawnee Bill Museum was built on the property to house the memorabilia of Pawnee Bill's and May's life. In addition, a Pawnee Bill Memorial Rodeo is held annually. The park is west of Pawnee on US 64. (Courtesy of the Pawnee County Historical Society.)

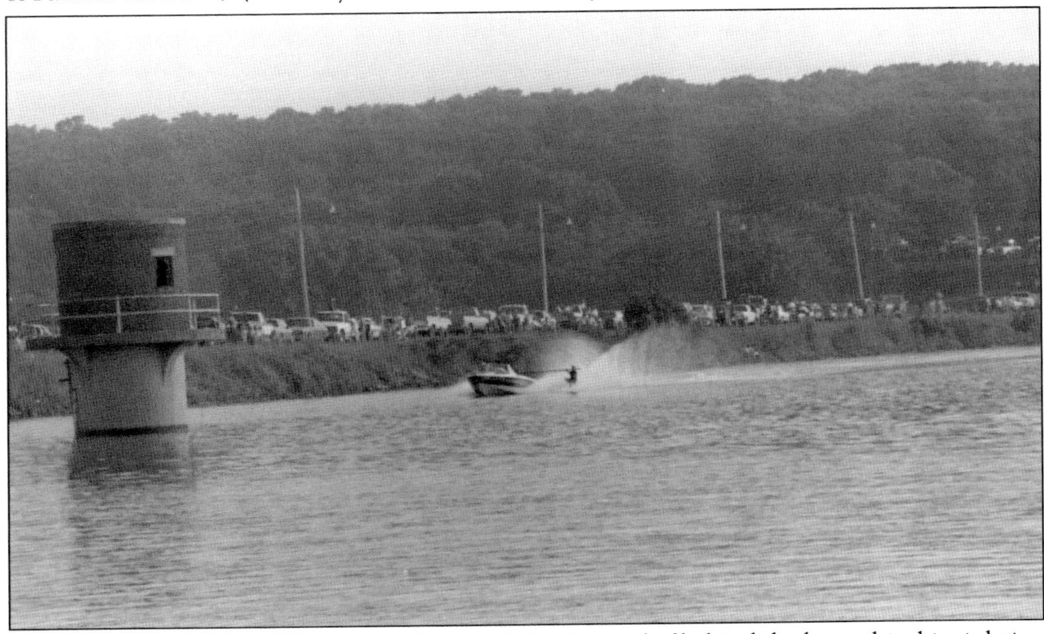

Water-skiing was a popular activity at Pawnee Lake. Instead of behind the boat, this skier is being pulled by a pole alongside the craft. Work was started on the 300-acre lake as a Works Progress Administration project in 1932 and finished in 1933. In 1940, a swimming pool and recreational center was completed on the lakeshore. Admission was 20¢ for adults and 10¢ for children. (Courtesy of the *Pawnee Chief*.)

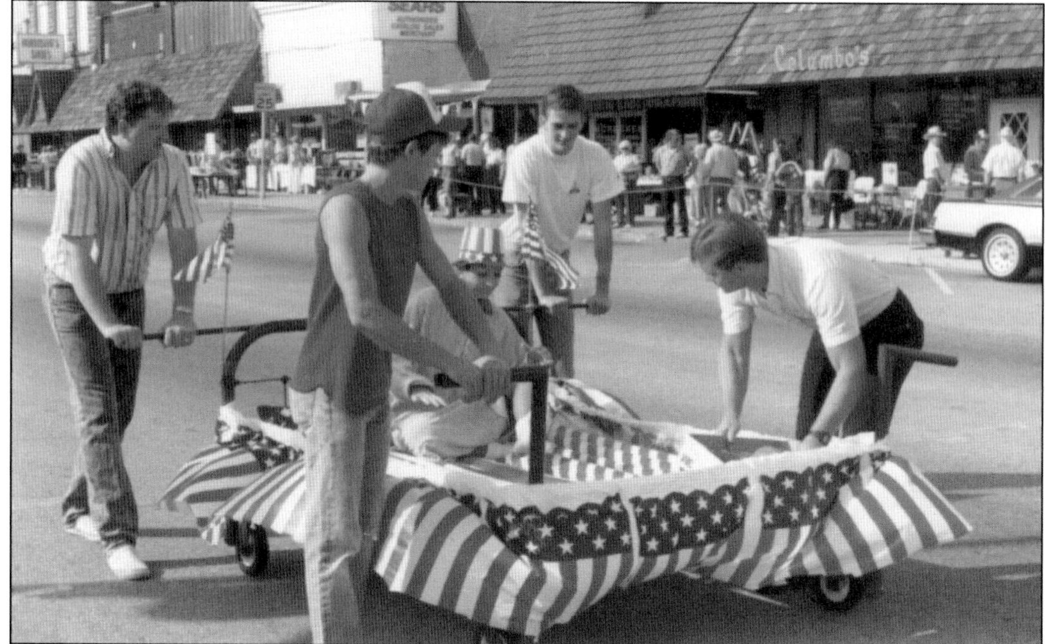

Founded on the day of the opening of the Cherokee Strip, Cleveland's annual Pioneer Day Parade and Celebration honors Cleveland's pioneering families. Many of the town's old-time residents take advantage of the event to hold reunions and enjoy the parade, food, and street dance. A variety of games and contests are held on that day, including bed races down Broadway Street. (Author's collection.)

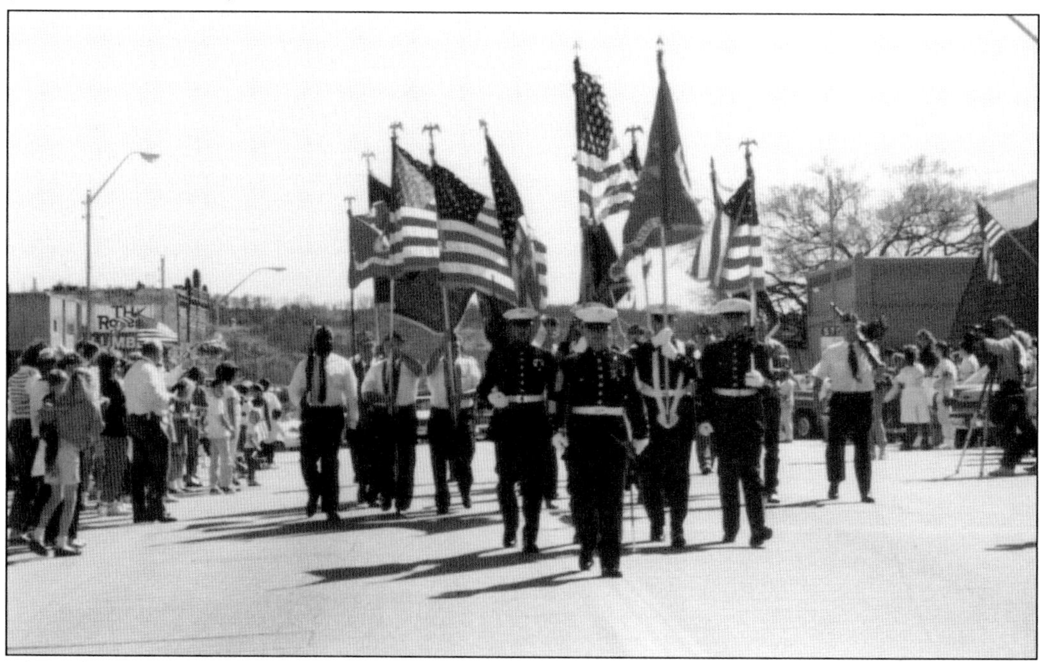

The color guard leads the welcome home parade on March 21, 1991, in downtown Cleveland that was held for Operation Desert Storm hero and prisoner of war Craig Berryman and his wife, Leigh, upon his release. Berryman graduated from Cleveland High School in 1980. (Author's collection.)

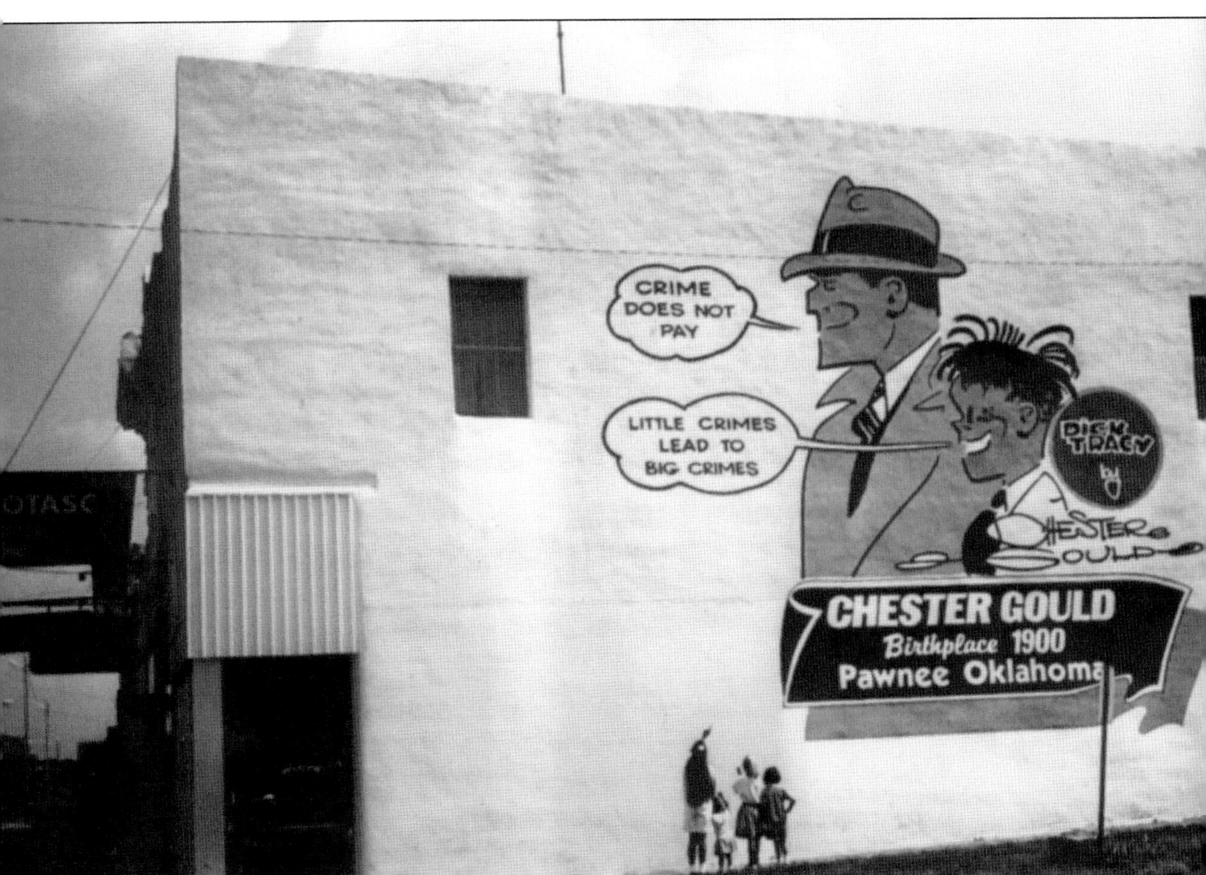

The *Dick Tracy* mural on the side of the Hale Building at the corner of Sixth and Harrison in Pawnee honors its most famous citizen, Chester Gould. Gould relied on his childhood memories of local residents on which to base the *Dick Tracy* characters. The comic strip was picked up by Republic Motion Pictures to run as a weekly serial distributed to theaters throughout the country. (Courtesy of the Pawnee County Historical Society.)

Discover Thousands of Local History Books Featuring Millions of Vintage Images

Arcadia Publishing, the leading local history publisher in the United States, is committed to making history accessible and meaningful through publishing books that celebrate and preserve the heritage of America's people and places.

Find more books like this at
www.arcadiapublishing.com

Search for your hometown history, your old stomping grounds, and even your favorite sports team.

Consistent with our mission to preserve history on a local level, this book was printed in South Carolina on American-made paper and manufactured entirely in the United States. Products carrying the accredited Forest Stewardship Council (FSC) label are printed on 100 percent FSC-certified paper.

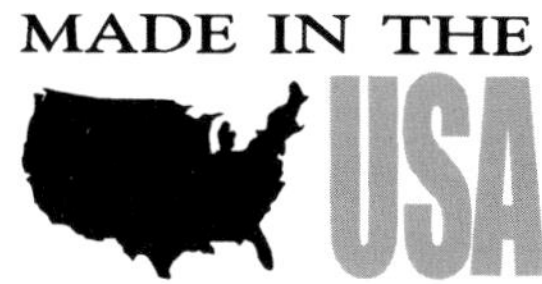